Honour Consciousness, Religion and Gender

International Comparative Social Studies

VOLUME 60

The titles published in this series are listed at *brill.com/icss*

Honour Consciousness, Religion and Gender

Brazilian and Pakistani Lived Experiences in Australia

By

Flavia Bellieni Zimmermann

BRILL

LEIDEN | BOSTON

Originally published in hardback in 2024.

This project has been funded by the Australian Government Research Training Program Stipend Scholarship and supported by the University of Western Australia.

Cover illustration: Brazilians and Pakistanis in Australia, 2024. © Elizabeth Zimmermann.

The Library of Congress has cataloged the hardcover edition as follows:

Names: Bellieni Zimmermann, Flavia, author.
Title: Honour consciousness, religion and gender : Brazilian and Pakistani lived experiences in Australia / by Flavia Bellieni Zimmermann.
Description: Leiden : Brill, [2025] | Series: International comparative social studies, 1568-4474 ; volume 60 | Includes bibliographical references and index.
Identifiers: LCCN 2024033568 (print) | LCCN 2024033569 (ebook) | ISBN 9789004711235 (hardback) | ISBN 9789004711242 (ebook)
Subjects: LCSH: Women and religion–Brazil. | Gender identity–Religious aspects–Catholic Church. | Women and religion–Pakistan. | Gender identity–Religious aspects–Islam. | Brazilians–Australia–Social conditions. | Pakistani–Australia–Social conditions. | Women immigrants–Australia–Social conditions. | Hegel, Georg Wilhelm Friedrich, 1770-1831. | Foucault, Michel, 1926-1984.
Classification: LCC BL458 .B45 2025 (print) | LCC BL458 (ebook) | DDC 200.82095491–dc23/eng/20240911
LC record available at https://lccn.loc.gov/2024033568
LC ebook record available at https://lccn.loc.gov/2024033569

Typeface for the Latin, Greek, and Cyrillic scripts: "Brill". See and download: brill.com/brill-typeface.

ISSN 1568-4474
ISBN 978-90-04-75676-2 (paperback, 2025)
ISBN 978-90-04-71123-5 (hardback)
ISBN 978-90-04-71124-2 (e-book)
DOI 10.1163/9789004711242

This book is printed on acid-free paper and produced in a sustainable manner.

Contents

Preface

This book is the result of several years of research to develop an understanding towards women's experiences of honour in the East and the West. Exploring unchatterd waters led to this comparative study which examines Brazilian and Pakistani migrant women's lived experiences of honour consciousness, and how its gendered dimensions are manifested among these women in Australia.

The first part of this book explores the concept of honour in Brazil and Pakistan, and how it is manifested in migrant women's lives in the Australian cultural context. The book looks at the stories of migrant Brazilians and Pakistanis in Sydney and Perth and how honour, religion and gender shapes their identities, although calibrating their views to Australian culture.

In the last part of this book I contrast and compare Brazilian and Pakistani women's lived experiences of honour consciousness and religion, and how it continues to impact notions of womanhood in Australia.

The key contributions from this book is o bring forward original data discussing the intersections of honour, religion and gender, looking at these stories through new epistemological lenses.

In this book I discuss how Foucault's episteme of "regimes of truth" and "power" provides an explanation to Brazilian and Pakistani women's lived experiences of honour consciousness, and how it impacts their livelihoods in Australia. Through this perspective, the book moves away from Foucault's approach to "docile bodies," by applying his power-knowledge episteme to lived experiences of migrant women. This new perspective provides a "way out" from the "power dilemma," suggesting policy-based solutions to de-construct "strategies of power." I propose a fresh approach to the use of Foucualt within gender studies. My perspective uses Foucault's rationale to explain the dynamics of power, how it reproduces gendered systems of oppression. However, its acknowledgement should not be an end in itself, but rather a means to highlight how these interactions consolidate gendered roles at the level of human consciousness.

Through epistemic disobedience lenses, I propose new approaches to the framing of violence towards Brazilian and Pakistani women and fresh epistemological perspectives to Foucault and gender. The book understands the significant underrepresentation of the literature discussing the intersections between honour, religion and gender, and women and migration, leading to a policies lacking eficacy. I discuss in this book honour at the level of human consciousness, challenging previous approaches to gender and gender policy aimed for migrant women, and violence towards women. I truly hope that this book can initiate a conversation towards new emerging policy approaches on gender mainstreaming (and "side streaming"), and the articulation of "Feminisms," and new Feminist discourses in the Global North's diaspora with Global South scholarship.

Acknowledgments

I am grateful for the opportunity to discuss issues and ideas which have for many years been of my research interest. This research is the result of a lifetime passion for political science, lived experiences of migrants, and women's issues. This project has a broad interdisciplinary scope, discussing honour within the boundaries of political science, gender studies, international comparative studies, philosophy and policy.

First and foremost, I acknowledge the several personal challenges I had in the first year of this project, starting this project on a part-time capacity and without a scholarship. From the second year onwards, however, this research was supported by the Australian Government Research Training Program (RTP) Scholarship. I am grateful for this research grant. Thanks to the support of this scholarship, I have been able to complete this research in the equivalent of four and a half years of full-time research at the University of Western Australia. I also received additional support for my field work in Sydney through the Graduate Research School Travel Awards.

I would like to thank the University of Western Australia for the opportunities and resources it provides and all those who helped me to use them – Reid library staff, the Graduate Research School staff as well as our colleagues and staff from the School of Social Sciences. I would like to thank my supervisors Professor Samina Yasmeen and Dr Renae Barker for their support and for working around the clock to meet research deadlines. After I was appointed to a lecturing position at UWA it was additionally challenging to bring this ambitious project to completion. I thank them for their patience. I also thank all academics and students from our school and other disciplines, who played an important role in my academic development and throughout these years of research: Seth Appiah-Mensah, Raisa Akifyeva, Ridwan Ridwan, Giulia Marchetti, Atbin Mahabbati, Isaac Frimpong, Isaac Mensah, Apriwan Apriwan, Amjed Al-Masaoodi, Sheryl Makara, Ella Prihatini, Azim Zahir, Leila Ben Mchareck, Ke Zhu, Ratih Kabinawa, Sahar Kiarashi, Duong Thuy Hang, Valentina Utari, Shevaun Drislane, Jacob Broom, Troy Lee-Brown, Joshua McDonnell, Mona Chettri, Dominic Dagbanja, Yu Tao, Greg Acciaioli, Richard Vokes, Jeannette Taylor, Jie Chen, Katie Atwell, Ky Gentry, Kelly Gerard, Amin Saikal, Thritty Bhanja and Kirsten Martinus. I also would like to thank our head of school Professor Amanda Davies for her understanding, and for alleviating my workload in the semester prior to the submission of this work.

I would also like to acknowledge and thank Professor Cristina Rocha from Western Sydney University for her generosity and for supporting me as Visiting Fellow at Western Sydney University during my field work in Sydney in 2019.

Her assistance was indispensable for the completion of my fieldwork in New South Wales and data collection. Thank you for your kindness and hospitality.

The support of many other friends has been indispensable for the completion of this project. I would like to thank Colonel Michael Brennan for his friendship and support throughout the years, Dr. Anita Williams for reading an early draft of chapter 1 and for our invaluable discussions about Foucault's episteme within gender studies.

In conclusion, I thank all my participants and community leaders who found time to share their views with me, and sit down and talk, at times over of a cup of hot drink. I am grateful for all kinds of help received by them and for their generosity with their time. The privacy terms of this research do not allow me to name them, but I remember them, and their invaluable input, and I am grateful to them. With this book I accomplish a promise made to participants: that their voices will break free, and their stories will be heard across the globe. I truly hope that this book is the first step towards raising social awareness, and shifting academic discussions on women in the Global South, which will lead to policy change.

Figures and Tables

Figures

Tables

Abbreviations

HBV	Honour Based Violence
UK	United Kingdom
US	United States of America
RA	Research Approval
PCF	Participant Consent Form
PIF	Participant Information Form
RPM	Risk Management Plan
DMP	De-identification Management Plan
DV	Domestic Violence
GBV	Gender Based Violence
UN	United Nations
CEDAW	Convention on the Elimination of all Discrimination Against Women
VAWG	Violence Against Women and Girls
IBGE	Brazil's Bureau of Statistics
PAWA	Pakistani Association of Western Australia
FGV	Fundação Getúlio Vargas
COVID-19	Coronavirus
LGBTIQ+	Lesbian, gay, bisexual, transgender, and the intersex
TGEU	European Report on Transgender
NAWSA	National American Woman's Suffrage Association
PCB	Brazil's Communist Party
CUT	Central Única dos Trabalhadores
CNTE	Confederação Nacional dos Trabalhadores em Educação
STF	Brazil's High Court
APWA	All Pakistani Women's Association
PPP	Pakistani People's Party
WAF	Women's Action Forum
NGOS	Non-Government Organisations
UNDP	United Nations Development Programme
CALD	Culturally and Linguistically Diverse

Introduction

The main aim of this book is to explore the intersections between honour and religion and how they shape gender in Brazil and Pakistan, and how these are transmitted to Australia. This study illuminates the relationship between honour consciousness, religion, and gender through the lived experiences of Brazilian (Christian) and Pakistani (Muslim) women living in Australia. Through grounded theory – an inductive research method – I explore the connections between honour consciousness and religion in their lived experiences and the factors that shape these views.

In a globalized world, with the fluidity of national borders and increasing migration, there is a need to develop a greater understanding of multicultural communities worldwide. Societies are becoming more diverse in their ethnic, racial, and religious composition. This book explains the lived experiences of Brazilian Christian and Pakistani Muslim women in Australia, a multicultural society. Although coming from different faith groups, the lived experiences of these women converge in what is deemed "honour-based cultures." This book explores the hybridity of their lived experiences and how they shift, change, and adapt in Australia.

This book fills a void within international comparative studies, by contributing with a detailed examination of lived experiences of honour consciousness and religion of both Brazilian (Christian) and Pakistani (Muslim) migrant women, examining the gender impact of honour in Australia.

The first part of this book explains how honour consciousness shapes the lives of Brazilian and Pakistani women in their countries of origin, and the relationship between honour, religion and gender highlighting the question: is honour consciousness experienced differently by men and women? I explore in this book how lived experiences of honour consciousness and religion in Brazil and Pakistan are hybridised and operate on a spectrum. These are manifested through gender power relations and demonstrated through "moderate" and "extreme" notions of honour consciousness. This is explained through an intersectional perspective (Collins, 2012, 2015; Crenshaw, 1989). The hybridised and heterogenous lived experiences of honour consciousness are predominantly influenced by race, class, and region, with multi-axes of inequality shaping gender politics.

Participants from both sample groups explained how their views have been shaped by the parent's values and familial upbringing, creating "different notions" of honour. Based on their stories, honour consciousness and religion oscillate between 1) "Extreme" notions of honour consciousness, manifested

via female suppression, violence towards women and honour killings, and 2)"
Moderate"notions, manifested via traditional notions of womanhood within
the family, reconciled with women's agency, political activism, and the fight
against violence towards women.

Then the book discusses data results from qualitative interviews with
Brazilian and Pakistani women in Australia. Using semi-structured interviews I
explain how honour consciousness and gender power relations are transmitted
into the Australian social context. The flexibility of these semi-structured interviews, and the use of grounded theory, gave greater freedom for participants
to share their lived experiences of honour both overseas and in Australia. This
study's framework brings to the fore a new perspective on experiences of honour consciousness, and how these impact gender power relations. The book
gives voice to the interviewed Brazilian and Pakistani migrant women through
their stories of honour about how their understandings have shaped their identity and their views on religion and gender, both overseas and in Australia.

In the final part of the book, I move on to compare Brazilian and Pakistani
women's lived experiences through Hegel's and Foucault's epistemes. Drawing from interview results, the book explains how "honour consciousness"
as "regimes of truth" is transmitted to Brazilian and Pakistani women's lived
experiences in Australia. Gendered power and social reproduction, however,
continue, adapting, shifting, and negotiating with Australian culture and
Australian multiculturalism.

In this section, I conflate epistemological principles from Hegel's human
consciousness with Foucault's "regimes of truth" and "power," explaining
Brazilian and Pakistani lived experiences of honour, religion, and gender in
Australia. The last section of this book brings a new perspective to the use
of Hegel and Foucault's epistemology within feminist studies, applying their
episteme to explain migrant women's lived experiences of honour in Australia. This combination of Hegel's and Foucault's episteme has not been previously used by scholars and hence constitutes an original contribution. With
this new episteme, I conflate the Hegelian framing of honour consciousness
with Foucault's power-knowledge's episteme of "regimes of truth" and "power"
to explain (Brazilian and Pakistani) women's lived experiences of honour in
Australia.

The book aims to address the following questions:

1. How is honour consciousness experienced by women in Brazil and Paki-
    stan? Are there different lived experiences of honour consciousness
    (depending on background)?
2. What is the relationship between honour consciousness and religion in
    Brazil and Pakistan?

3. How does honour consciousness shape lived experiences of gender in Brazil and Pakistan? Is honour consciousness experienced differently by men and women? How and why?
4. Could honour consciousness be transmitted to the Australian diaspora? How and why?
5. Does honour consciousness continue to shape women's lived experiences of religion and gender in the Australian diaspora? How and why?

By studying Brazilian and Pakistani migrant women's experiences in Australia, and what I classify as "honour consciousness," I illustrate the hybridised experiences of migrant women and how these shape their views towards religion and gender.

The book highlights the heterogeneity of lived experiences of migrant women in the West, following the work of Werbner (2002) with migrant Pakistani women in the UK, exploring their lived experiences in the Australian social context. By developing a comparative analysis, I break down essentializing academic perspectives towards honour killings (and honour-based violence, HBV) as an issue originating from South Asian and Muslim countries. In the 30 interviews conducted with migrant Brazilian Christian women and migrant Pakistani Muslim women in Australia, results demonstrated that both cohorts experienced honour as a key element of "who they are" and of "their values system" and "notions of right from wrong."

Global migration is a highly complex phenomenon, having an impact on individual's cultural, religious, and ethnic perceptions of gender-related norms and social expectations. Arguably, when relocating to a new country, the views of migrants are influenced by their culture, religion and understanding of gender norms. These perceptions are their cultural lenses, which continue to provide meaning about the world around them, as well as influencing societal views on the role of men and women. Indeed, with the new technologies, such as emails, mobile phones and video calls, there are increasing transnational connections between migrants and "their homes." This can lead to a growing ambivalence about their way of life, with the norms and values of the home country still influencing the diaspora's ways of living and thinking (Werbner, 2004). These dynamics change, however, for the second and third generations of migrant families, from inter-personal transnational networks to inter-communal and inter-organisational connections (Werbner, 2004).

Nonetheless, this book moves away from predominant perspectives on migrants within a transnational context (Werbner, 2004, 2002), transnationalism and integration processes (Erdal, 2014; Slany, Kontos & Liapi, 2010; Baubock, 2003), and patterns of mobility (Brettell & Hollifield, 2014). I focus on the lived experiences of migrants and the study of "honour" and "the culture of honour," addressing it at the level of the individual and of human consciousness. I acknowledge, however, that participants' views on honour consciousness are shaped not only by their interactions in Australia, but also by their interactions with their country of origin, with family members living overseas, and social media platforms such as WhatsApp and Facebook. Through Hegel's human consciousness episteme, the book regards Brazilian and Pakistani lived experiences of honour as "honour consciousness." In this book, I delve deep into women's consciousness by listening to their lived experiences of honour in Australia.

The book explores the lived experiences of honour, religion, and gender holistically, and how it impacts gender politics. Violence towards women (and honour killings) is not a central preoccupation of this research. Although Brazilian and Pakistani women taking part in this survey did not report suffering any form of violence in Australia, the themes of honour and violence were discussed during interviews. This is an issue shaping "extreme notions" of honour consciousness, manifested through female subjugation and violence towards women. Arguably, violence suffered by Pakistani women is honour-based violence. Data results demonstrate that Brazilian women hold "honour consciousness." Thus, through epistemic disobedience lenses, violence towards Brazilian women should be re-classified as honour-based violence.

This research introduces primary data on Brazilian and Pakistani lived experiences of honour, religion, and gender. I follow the work of Sonia E. Alvarez (2009), and her articulation of Latin American and African Brazilian women's voices in "side streaming" their lived experiences, by spreading feminist knowledge horizontally into a wider array of class and racial-ethnic communities and socio-cultural spaces, including parallel social movements. Raising awareness of lived experiences of honour consciousness and religion of migrant Brazilian and Pakistani women, through their perspectives, and its gendered dimensions in Australia is a central contribution of this study.

The book builds upon Burke's (2012) views on women's agency in their religious practices when dealing with gender-traditional religions such as Catholicism and Islam. It examines how honour shapes Catholicism and Islam and the gender identity of Brazilian and Pakistani women in Australia, an issue not previously addressed by the literature. I acknowledge that women from gender-traditional religions might develop their understanding of religion and gender, and exert agency when interpreting religious texts. Through this perspective, they can reconcile their faith with gender equality. In addition to Burke's views on how traditional religious views can be reconciled with religious women's agency, the book draws from Stirling (2013), unpacking the layered experience of religious, cultural, and ethnic identities in Australia, and how Muslim women's identities shift and are negotiated with Australian culture.

I acknowledge the broader scholarship discussing migration studies, gender, and religion. The work of Fiddian-Qasmiyeh (2014) looks at refugees, gender and the Sarawi politics of survival; Selby (2018) examines lived experiences of Muslim Canadians; Saunders, et al. (2016) explores the intersections of migration and religion through interdisciplinary lenses; and Hagan & Ebaugh (2003) examines migration and transnationalism. However, this is not the main objective of this research.

For the purposes of this book, I will then provide a brief overview of the literature on Brazilian and Pakistani migrants and their lived experiences in three Anglo-Saxon Western nations: United States, United Kingdom, and Australia.

There are several studies exploring Brazilian migration experiences to the US, and their experiences in the diaspora (Assis, 2014; Belsito, 2016; Debiaggi, 2002; Marcus, 2009; Martes & Fazito 2010; Martes, 2001; Martes & Rodriguez, 2003). Migration is a complex and nuanced experience, fraught with psychological and socio-cultural implications. It is a process going beyond an individual's geographical dislocation. When discussing the condition of Brazilian women in the US diaspora, there are studies examining gender, migration and women's agency in the US social context (Assis, 2014). For instance, Debiaggi (2002) conducted research exploring changing gender roles. Debiaggi contends that migration can involve the loss of what a country of origin represents, including language, habits, rules and societal norms, and including how individuals understood gender roles. In her work, she contends that Brazilians moving to the United States face a different socio-cultural environment, particularly when dealing with gender roles, focusing on acculturation practices and how Brazilian gender roles are experienced in the US.

Brazilians in London are increasingly an important migration group, but still under-represented in the literature and in the national consciousness (Sheringham, 2013). There is literature on Brazilian migration to the UK which discusses the impact of Brazil's economic and social changes and migration waves to the UK (Dias & Júnior, 2018). When dealing with Brazilian migration experiences in the UK, I draw on literature dealing with Brazilian experiences in the diaspora in London (Martins, 2020). In this work, Martins explains the lived experiences of Brazilians in London, and how their societal views on social class, race and gender translate to the UK societal environment. In this ethnographic study, with in-depth interviews, Martins describes how classist views of Brazilian upper-class members continued to be experienced in the UK diaspora in London. This work highlights the ways in which these classist upper-middle class views in Brazil are intrinsically connected to issues of race. When discussing the re-framing of class difference in London, Martins eluci- dates (via participants interviews) the othering of lower-class and uneducated (and usually of colour) Brazilians in London. These lower-socio economic and racialized Brazilians are seen as "disgusting" and their behavior is seen as being related to their African roots.

When examining Brazilians and their lived experiences of migration and religion in London, there is literature discussing Brazilian churches and trans- national identities. Sheringham (2013) contends that the lack of visibility in the public discourse disregards complex networks of social interconnectivity. The paper explains how churches play a notable role in providing emotional support and a sense of belonging to Brazilians in London. In this context, Sher- ingham argues that the transnationality of Brazilian migrant religious institu- tions goes beyond categorizations of the "local" and the "global," and it is rather religious transnational institutions which are carving a place "in the middle."

In the Australian social context, due to geographical barriers and additional travelling costs, Brazilian migrants are usually upper middle-class students or individuals moving to Australia on skilled visas (Rocha, 2014). Nonetheless, the Australian community is fragmented between the first and second wave of migrants, since the first migration wave was predominantly of lower-socio economic status.

Rocha (2019) discusses in "God in is control: middle-class Pentecostalism and international student migration" how church connections operate "like a family" for Brazilian students in Australia. For these students, coming from a cultural background which emphasizes family ties, migration can be an iso- lating and challenging experience. Brazilian Pentecostal churches in Australia operate as a "big family," helping Brazilian students who may be living under precarious visa conditions, and with a temporary migration status, to find a sense of belonging in Australia and even to pray for their visa extensions. This work provides an insight into the Brazilian views on family and religion, and their deep familial roots.

Werbner (2007) explains the complexity of lived experiences of South Asian Muslim women in the West (France and the UK). She focuses on the French "headscarf affair," and the UK's debate over Muslim women's *niqab*, and how it encourages negative public perceptions of Muslim women's purity and veiling practices. The *hijab* "ban" in France, Werbner (2007) argues, can potentially be seen as a human rights violation. There is extensive literature discussing hon- our in the light of honour violence in the South Asian and Muslim communi- ties in the migration setting (Aujla & Gill, 2014; Khan & Saleem, 2018; Mucina,

2018; Tonsing & Barn, 2017). This literature classifies honour violence as form of honour killing.

Literature exploring Pakistani migrant experiences in the Western diaspora has a strong focus on the UK experience. The literature delves into the hybridized (and "chaordic") transnational experience of Pakistanis in the UK, and how this experience impacts lived experiences of citizenship, religion and gender (Werbner, 2002), on transnationalism and living abroad and marrying within Pakistani ethnicity and religion (Charsley, 2013), on masculinity and Pakistani transnational marriages in the UK (Charsley, 2005), on transnationalism and gender (Sanghera & Thapar-Björkert, 2017), as well as on mobility and migrant imaginaries of Pakistani descent living in the Norway and UK (Bolognani & Erdal, 2017).

Werbner (2002) explores the organizational and moral dimensions within the Pakistani diaspora in the UK, laying out their political leverage through social mobilization. Werbner explains the organizational flaws of diasporas, but also how they have still managed to diffuse structures of shared moral responsibility within the community, within an organized chaos ("chaorder"). This work highlights the lack of a clear organizational cohesion within the Pakistani diaspora, with regard to setting up community goals, organizing political protests, philanthropic drives, and cultural ceremonies. Werbner discusses the hybridity of the diaspora in the UK, since on one hand they are spontaneously organized, but at the same time they exhibit predictability in the way they reproduce their lived experiences in the country. Her work sheds light on the layered experiences within this diaspora through the dissemination of Sufi cults, as well as women's movements. It also contextualizes the lived experiences of migrants from post-colonial countries in the West. Pakistani migrants, although inherently heterogenous in their composition, share a commitment in the fight for enhanced citizenship rights in the UK.

Khuwaja et al. (2013) discuss the post-migration experiences of migrant Pakistani Muslim adolescent women living in the United States. Khuwaja et al. argue that there are several challenges faced by young Pakistani Muslim women settling in America, and how American culture demands adaptation to the host country. The main factors affecting young Pakistani Muslim women's adaptation to American culture include positive motivation for migration, family bonding, social support networks, positive family attitudes and good communication with their teens, willingness of Pakistani Muslim adolescents to learn other cultures, availability of English-as-second-language programs, and a broad range of community activities developing a sense of belonging and creating a positive meaning to their migration experience. Khuwaja et al. provide background information about the leading factors dealing with migrant adaptation of adolescent Pakistani Muslim women in the United States, highlighting how Pakistani Muslim migrant's identities adapt, shift and change in relation to the host country and its culture.

Begum (2019) discusses the resistance from within of Pakistani women living in the US diaspora. She examines the experience of Pakistani women in the US with regard to all facets of their identity, including Pakistani migrants as well as Pakistani citizens. She focuses on violence towards Pakistani women and on those systems which facilitate the perpetration of violence, such as a lack of institutional and state intervention, as well as insufficient intervention by religious leaders. Taking a multidimensional approach in how to examine the condition of women in Pakistan, Begum's work also makes a valuable contribution to academic discussion about Pakistani women's identities in the Western diaspora. She maps out the challenges faced by Pakistani women as migrants in the US, and how their identities as Pakistani, women, migrant and South Asian can adapt and change in the US socio-environment.

Fijac and Sonn (2004) discuss the condition of Pakistani-Muslim immigrant women in Western Australia and how their identities interact with the broader Pakistani community in the diaspora, and how they negotiate and adapt to Australian culture. They explore the perceptions and the impacts of Pakistani women's lived experiences and views in shaping their identities in Australia, as well as the views of the broader Pakistani community. Fijac and Sonn contend that being a Muslim, and the role of religion, is a core part of their identities in the Australian diaspora, as it is for the broader Pakistani community, throughout their resettlement process in the country. They argue that the key challenges faced by Pakistanis in Australia were structural racism and exclusion, although at the same time, social support structures and gender roles provided a continuum to Pakistani identity, and a sense of belonging within the Pakistani community.

The book builts upon literature discussing the lived experience of Muslims in Australia, which illuminates key issues for this research's discussion. Yasmeen (2010, 2008) explores Muslim identities in Australia and the implications for inclusion and exclusion, as well as delving deep into the lived experience of Muslims and how they experience inclusion and exclusion. She argues that in the post-September 11 War on Terror, Muslims worldwide are becoming the "other," seen as a potential threat to the Western way of life. The "securitization" of Muslims in the West leads to stereotypical views of Islam and Islamophobia, compromising their sense of belonging and sense of social inclusion. Yasmeen explores Muslim identities in the Australian context, and the dynamics of diversity, the historical roots of Islam in Australia (with a focus on Western

Australian Muslims), the role played by Muslim schools, what it means to be a Muslim, and the role of religion in shaping Muslim identity in Australia.

Furthermore, Stirling et al. (2014) discuss the concept of lived religion and how it is used to describe the way religion is lived among Muslim women in Brisbane, Australia. They provide a new perspective on the concept of lived religion, previously used for Christian groups, and expand it to apply to diasporic Muslim women in the Western world. Stirling et al. conducted a longitudinal study discussing the experiences of migrant Muslim Turkish and Iranian women, the ways in which they have adapted to a secular Australian culture, and how their religious views and practices have been shaped. This work contends some women have adjusted to Australian society by becoming more religious, attending the local mosque, and contributing to religious and cultural events. Other women, however, filtered their religious beliefs through shaping their religious practices in Australia to suit their personal lives, changing, or blending their religious beliefs with Australian culture and other religious beliefs. For instance: some women became more secular, some more spiritual, with others blending Islamic practices and beliefs with Christianity or New Age beliefs, in a process of "shifting, negotiating and remaking" their religious identities in Australia.

In this book I explore the nuances of honour consciousness, and how it is hybridised, shifting from "moderate" to "extreme" notions of honour consciousness and religion, and how they impact gender power relations. Migrant women taking part in this survey predominantly hold "moderate" notions of honour consciousness, impacting gender reproduction in Australia. According to interview results, however, "extreme" notions of honour consciousness and religion can also translate to the Brazilian and Pakistani communities in Australia. Although the women taking part in the interviews did not report suffering violence, there were reports of women's suppression and violence in these communities. The book points out how Brazilian women's and Pakistani women's lived experiences of honour consciousness "change," and how these are negotiated with Australian culture and Australian multiculturalism. However, honour continues to impact social reproduction and gender politics among migrants in Australia.

It gives an explanation on how migrant Brazilian women hold notions of honour consciousness in the light of traditional views of the family (in this case as interpreted by Catholicism). Although most participants were nominal Catholic Christians, the respondents also included practising Evangelicals and Roman Catholics, Spiritism Kardecists, and Spiritualists. All 15 Brazilian women interviewed held what I classify as "honour consciousness," as well as being influenced by what is referred to as "cultural Christianity" (Cogell,

2001; Inserra, 2019). In interviews with Pakistani Muslim women, however, they explicitly conflated their lived experiences of honour consciousness with Islam and the "values of Islam."

The research contributes to the scholarly debate by highlighting the similarities and differences between Brazilian Christian (through cultural Christianity) and Pakistani Muslim notions of honour consciousness, religion and lived experiences of gender in Australia. This comparative study breaks down essentialist perspectives towards South Asian communities, Muslims, and honour. Another key contribution of this book is to demonstrate the interplay of history, religion, and culture in shaping the differences between Brazilian and Pakistani notions of honour consciousness and religion, and their lived experiences of gender in Australia. The book addresses honour at the consciousness level, paving the way to new emerging policy on gender mainstreaming (and "side streaming"), as well as the articulation of "feminisms," and new "feminist discourses" in the Global North's diaspora with Global South scholarship. The book is organised in six chapters, as follows:

Lastly, the author needs to acknowledge her background and the reasons inspiring several years of research which resulted in this substantive body of work. The researcher's origins which are Brazilian and female, from an upper-middle-class background, white, having lived in a major Brazilian city until her early 20s. The author grew up listening to narratives of honour, shaping her consciousness as a Brazilian migrant woman after moving to Australia in the early 2000s, and then settling in Perth, Western Australia. My lived experiences, which diverge significantly from Brazilian stereotypes of free sex, Carnival, and women in feathered scad clothes, instigated a curiosity towards women's stories of honour consciousness and the impact of honour in their lived experiences of gender. It is worth noting that Brazilian stereotypes of "free and easy sex" are a by-product of the coloniser's whitening hegemonic practices, with the systemic sexual exploitation and objectification of women of Indigenous and African descent (the social "other"). Thus, the researcher acknowledges the roots of honour in Brazil as Eurocentric and as a whitening discourse, which looks down on "other" women's behaviour when it does not uphold those standards of honour and purity introduced in Brazil with the Portuguese, which were widely disseminated through intersections of honour and religion in Catholicism.

I carried out interviews with Brazilian women in Sydney, New South Wales, in the capacity of a social researcher, political scientist, and Brazilian political analyst with a commitment to objectivity. Nonetheless, my Brazilian and Latino background needs to be acknowledged, as my Brazilian and migrant background makes me an insider researcher. I acknowledge the limitations presented by insider research, but also its benefits. Having Brazilian heritage and speaking the Portuguese language was an advantage, as cultural and language barriers were not an issue. This provided me with greater insight into women's narratives of honour, gender power relations in Brazilian society, as well as Brazilian women's experiences in the Australian diaspora.

When dealing with the Pakistani samples and data analysis, who were interviewed in Perth, Western Australia, I was an outside researcher, mitigating any research biases, and views which could be influenced or affected by the researcher's own story, roots, race, class, and overall background. This closes the gap in insider research limitations, with the comparative study bringing forward insight into the honour consciousness of both sample groups.

The overrepresentation of Muslim, South Asian, and Pakistani women in the literature discussing honour-based violence and its intersections with gender contributed to this comparative study. The study endeavours to break down essentiallizing views towards Pakistani Muslims in the West. Connections with Pakistani leaders facilitated access to gatekeepers in Perth, Western Australia. I am grateful for their support and for all participants who shared their stories in this book. This research would be impossible without their generosity and trust.

The broader aim of this book is to challenge stereotypical views towards Pakistani and Brazilian women living in the West, by listening to women's stories and empowering them through their voices, and to explore overtones in their lived experiences of honour, religion and gender in Australia.

Chapter 1 – Brazil's Honour Consciousness and Women's Lived Experiences of Gender

This chapter discusses honour consciousness in Brazil and lived experiences of women, and how this is manifested through gender power relations in Brazilian society. I begin this chapter by exploring Brazil's state formation, geography, and its ethnic and religious diversity. Then I provide an overview on religious views in Brazil, explaining the role played by "cultural Christianity" in honour consciousness and lived experiences of gender. The last part of this chapter explains the effects of class and race in Brazilian women's lived experiences.

In this chapter I explain the evolution of honour consciousness, the interplay between honour and religion through "cultural Christianity," and how race, class and region have shaped Brazil's intersectional experience of honour and gender. I also explain the role played by "coloniality of power" in shaping Brazil's intersectional lived experiences of honour and gender. I argue that honour consciousness is key in understanding Brazil's gender power relations. Honour consciousness and traditional views of the family (within religion) are pivotal drivers behind "extreme" and "moderate" notions of honour and the way in which they are externalised. I explain how Brazilian women's "extreme" and "moderate" notions of honour consciousness consolidate gender power relations in Brazil. In "extreme" notions of honour consciousness women resist "less" to gendered power and male hegemony. However, in "moderate" notions of honour consciousness women resist "more" to gendered power, having greater societal agency.

Chapter 2 – Brazilian Women's Honour Consciousness and Lived Experiences of Gender in Australia

In this chapter I discuss data results from 15 in-depth interviews with Brazilian Christian women living in Sydney, New South Wales.[1] Drawing from these interviews, I explain how Brazilian Christian women's lived experiences of honour consciousness, and traditional views of the family (within religion), are manifested in gender power relations in Australia. Gender power relations are demonstrated through women's predominantly "moderate" notions of honour consciousness, and how it is manifested through gender relations.

Firstly, I demonstrate through the interviews Brazilian Christian women's perceptions of honour consciousness and traditional views of the family (within religion) in Brazil. I argue that the Brazilian Christian women interviewed for this study hold predominantly "moderate" views of honour consciousness. They are critical of Brazilian Christian women (and Brazilian Christian men) who hold what are deemed "extreme" notions of honour. Next, I discuss how women's perceptions of honour consciousness is trasmitted to Australia. In the last part of this chapter, I explain how honour consciousness and traditional views of the family (within religion) continue to shape gender relations in Australia.

Chapter 3 – Pakistan's Honour Consciousness and Women's Lived Experiences of Gender

This chapter discusses honour consciousness in Pakistan and lived experiences of women, and how this is manifested through gender power relations

---

1 Interviews with Brazilian (Christian) women in Sydney, New South Wales, were conducted during my tenure as visiting fellow at Western Sydney University, June–July 2019.

in Pakistani society. I begin this chapter by exploring Pakistan's state formation, geography, and its ethnic and religious diversity. Next it provides an overview of Islam in Pakistan and *izzat*, explaining the role played by honour consciousness and religious consciousness in lived experiences of gender. The last part of the chapter explains the effects of class, caste and region in Pakistani women's lived experiences of honour consciousness and gender.

I argue that honour consciousness and religious consciousness are key to understand Pakistan's gender power relations. Honour consciousness and religious consciousness are key drivers of "extreme" and "moderate" notions of honour and the way in which they are externalised. I discuss how Pakistani women's "extreme" and "moderate" notions of honour consciousness and religious consciousness consolidate gender power relations in Pakistan. In "extreme" notions women resist "less" to gendered power and male hegemony. However, in "moderate" notions women resist "more" to gendered power, having greater societal agency.

Chapter 4 – Pakistani Women's Honour Consciousness and Lived Experiences of Gender in Australia

In this chapter I discuss data results from 15 in-depth interviews with Pakistani Muslim women living in Perth, Western Australia. Drawing from these interviews, I explain how Pakistani Muslim women's lived experiences of honour consciousness and religious consciousness are manifested in gender power relations in Australia. Pakistani Muslim women interviewed in this study predominantly hold "moderate" views of honour consciousness and religious consciousness. They are critical of Pakistani Muslim women (and Pakistani Muslim men) who hold "extreme" notions of honour. Gender power relations are demonstrated through women's predominantly "moderate" notions of honour consciousness and religious consciousness, and how they are manifested through gender relations.

In the first part of the chapter, I explore through the interviews, Pakistani Muslim women's perceptions of honour consciousness and religious consciousness in Pakistan. Next, I discuss how women's perceptions of honour consciousness and religious consciousness translate to Australia. The final section of this chapter explores what changes in Pakistani Muslim women's lived experiences of honour consciousness and religious consciousness, and how honour consciousness continues to shape gender relations in Australia.

Chapter 5 – A New Perspective to Hegel, Foucault, and Gender

Based on interview results, this chapter explains how migrant women's lived experiences of honour consciousness are consistent with Hegel's epistemological perspective of human consciousness, and its self-reflective character. The chapter also outlines how Foucault's theory is manifested in gender power relations.

In this chapter I provide the epistemological perspective underpinning this book. This epistemological approach to Hegel and Foucault within gender studies is used to understand Brazilian and Pakistani women's lived experiences of honour consciousness and gender, and how these are manifested in Australia. This combination of Hegel's and Foucault's episteme has not been used by gender scholars in the past, and hence constitutes an original contribution.

Through this new episteme, honour consciousness is conflated with Foucault's "regime of truth," reproducing gender power relations. These consolidate men's hegemony in Australia. Honour consciousness is manifested through gender power relations. This is demonstrated through women's "moderate" and "extreme" notions of honour consciousness, and women's challenges to break away from gender power structures. Power makes "more" concessions in "moderate" notions of honour consciousness but is manifested with "less" power resistance in "extreme" notions of honour consciousness.

Chapter 6 – A New Perspective to Hegel's and Foucault's Episteme and Migrant Women's Stories

In this final chapter I compare data findings from interviews conducted with Brazilian Christian women in Sydney and Pakistani Muslim women in Western Australia. This chapter compares the similarities and differences in their lived experiences of honour consciousness, and how it is manifested through gender power relations in Australia. The chapter explains how their lived experiences are consistent with Hegel's epistemological perspectives on phenomenology and human consciousness, as well as Foucault's power-knowledge episteme.

In this chapter I explore how the interplay of history, religion and cultures shapes their different lived experiences of honour consciousness and gender. In their lived experiences, honour consciousness has a self-reflexive character when they distance themselves from "other" notions of honour, regarded as "extreme." "Other notions" provide meaning to their lived experiences of honour consciousness, which are predominantly "moderate." In such case, women resist "more" to gendered power. I highlight key differences when investigating

Brazilian and Pakistani lived experiences of honour. For instance, Brazilian Christian women discuss honour consciousness when considering traditional views of the family (within religion). In the Brazilian case study, this is the result of "coloniality of power" and Brazil's whitening practices shaping "cultural Christianity," whereas Pakistani Muslim women explicitly conflate honour consciousness with religious consciousness (Islam).

The chapter then compares the similarities and differences between Brazilian and Pakistani notions of honour consciousness, and how these impact gender power reproduction in Australia. I explore what predominantly remains "the same" and "what changes" in their lived experiences of honour, religion, and gender in Australia. This section explains how the interplay of history, religion and culture shapes their different lived experiences of honour and gender. I then explain how the data results, and their lived experiences of gender, are consistent with Foucault's power-knowledge episteme. They are manifested similarly to "regimes of truth," giving a continuum to male hegemony. Gender power reproduction, however, shifts and adapts, and is negotiated with Australian culture and multiculturalism.

CHAPTER 1

Brazil's Honour Consciousness and Women's Lived Experiences of Gender

I discuss in this chapter how Brazil's honour consciousness sets out double standards when dealing with male and female roles: there are strict codes of conduct, purity, and control for white European women, whereas there is complete sexual freedom for men in their interactions with non-white, non-European women. As contended in previous sections, honour consciousness, which is the colonisers consciousness, are ideals incorporated throughout Brazilian society.

Brazil has been discovered by Portuguese Pedro Álvares Cabral in 1500, and until 1815 this has been regarded as Brazil's colonial period. In 1815 the Portuguese Royal family relocated the metropolis' centre of power to Rio de Janeiro during Europe's Napoleonic Wars, elevating Brazil to a kingdom in union with Portugal and Algarves (Holanda, 2007). Brazil's independence from the Portuguese Crown was declared on 7 September 1822 by Don João VI's son, Prince Don Pedro I. The 1822–1889 period is known as Brazil's Empire, with the Portuguese heirs remaining as heads of state under a Constitutional Monarchy (Holanda, 2007). Brazil's first Republican period started with the Republic's declaration in 1889, and this lasted until 1964 (Holanda, 2007). In 1964, Brazil's military staged a coup d'état, and this period of government ended in 1985. Since then, Brazil has been going through a "re-democratisation period." Brazil is a country with great ethnic diversity, but has been marred by the mis-treatment of its Indigenous peoples during the times of colonisation, as well as the ill-treatment of African slaves. From colonial times until the end of Brazil's Empire, there was no separation between church and state, with Catholicism being Brazil's official religion (Holanda, 2007). Brazil's colonisation and history goes some way towards an explanation of the current and acute social divides and different lived experiences based on class, social status, race, and region (in both urban and rural areas).

In the 19th century, Catholicism became the official religion of Brazil and was formally institutionalised into the country's political and social systems. Whilst this formality has eased greatly, Brazil still has one of the largest Christian populations in the world. According to the World Bank Data (2020), *Brazil* has a population of over 212 million people. Data from the Pew Research Centre indicates Brazil as being the second largest Christian nation in the world with 175,770,00 believers, behind only the US (Pew Research Centre, 2011). Statistical data shows Brazil's religious composition with 54.2 per cent of Catholics, 20.5 per cent of Evangelicals (unspecified), 3.7 per cent of Pentecostal evangelists, 2.0 per cent of Afro-American cults (Umbanda), 0.8 per cent of Protestants, 0.7 Jehovah's witnesses, 0.6 per cent of Adventists, 0.3 Believers without formal affiliation to any religion, 0.1 per cent of Mormons, 2.8 per cent of Other religions, 12.1 per cent No religion, 0.4 per cent Agnostics, and Unsure about affiliation at 0.9 per cent. A 2019 Datafolha Survey indicates that over 80 per cent of the Brazilian population follows Christian beliefs, with 50 per cent of Catholics, 31 per cent of Evangelicals and only 10 per cent "without religion" (Datafolha, 2016).

Although predominantly Christian, Brazil is characterised as diverse in its religious and racial composition. The main racial and ethnic groups in Brazil are composed of whites of Portuguese and other European descent such as Italians, Germans and Polish, mixed-race individual regarded as "pardos," and blacks from African descent, as well as "yellow"[1] from Indigenous or Asian descent. This racial composition is distributed throughout all regions of Brazil (North, Northeast, Central-West, South, and Southeast). Brazil's South is predominantly white European, and the North and Northeast regions are predominantly of mixed race and "pardos."

According to Brazil's Bureau of Statistics (IBGE, 2013), Brazil's racial composition in some states is as follows:

TABLE 1.1   Brazil's racial distribution (in some major states)

Region	Pardos	Black	"Yellow"	White (racial percentage)
Amazonas	72.4	5.3	1.6	5.3
Paraiba	56.6	5.0	0.8	31.9
São Paulo	16.6	10.2	1.9	51.4
Rio Grande do Sul	16.2	6.6	0.4	63.5
Mato Grosso	54.1	11.7	1.0	30.4
Federal District	50.6	11.6	1.0	29.5

SOURCE: BRAZIL'S BUREAU OF STATISTICS (IBGE, 2013)

---

1 Brazil's Bureau of Statistics (IBGE) and other governmental official documents classify Brazilian individuals of Indigenous or Asian descent's race as "yellow."

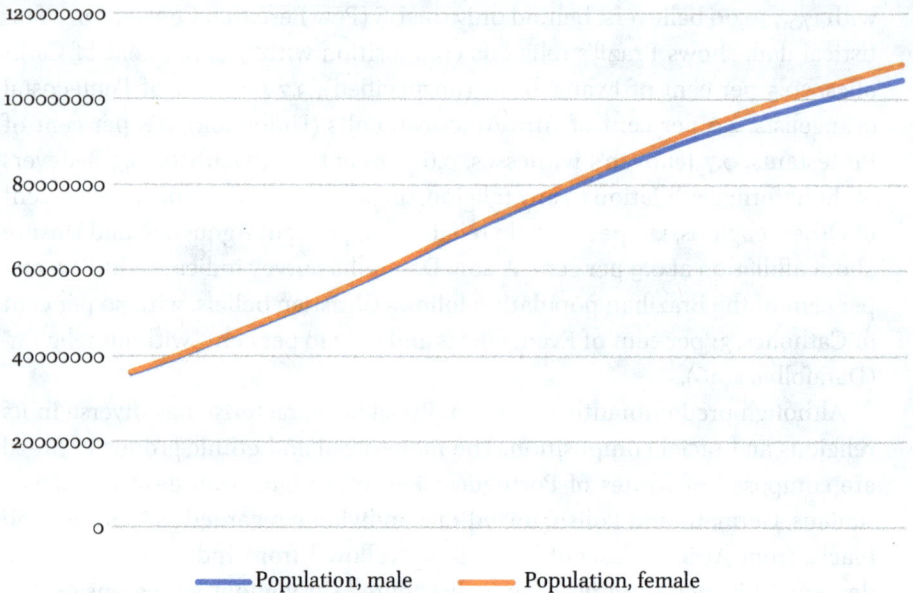

FIGURE 1.1   Brazil's gender distribution
SOURCE: THE WORLD BANK, BRAZIL (2020)

Brazil's Bureau of Statistics highlights that racial miscegenation can dilute an individual's self-identification with their racial group (IBGE, 2013). Another issue in Brazil is related to a reluctance amongst individuals of darker skin tone to accept their racial group. This is the result of past whitening colonial practices, the structural stigmatisation of individuals of colour (predominantly of African descent), and social privileges given to individuals from white European background.

Figure 1.1 above shows the numbers of females 107, 521, 000 and males, 100, 333,000 in Brazil. In 2020, Brazil's Bureau of Statistics (IBGE) shows Brazilian women living until 80,1 years, with men living until 73,1 years. Less Brazilian males than females reflecting Brazilian females' higher life expectancy (World Bank, 2020).

Figures from Brazil's Bureau of Statistics indicate the demographic density throughout the states, with those states in the Central-West, South, and Southeast having high population numbers, concentrated in highly industrialised cosmopolitan city centres called "megalopolis" (*megalópoles*). Examples of "megalopolis" are the cities of São Paulo and Rio de Janeiro. Other industrial centres are found in Brazil's regions of the Central-West, South, and Southeast. There are huge social contrasts between the living standards of Brazilians living in big industrial hubs and the major city centres in the Central-West,

TABLE 1.2   Populational distribution by region (2014)

Regional Population Distribution in Brazil States	Population (estimated)
São Paulo	44,035,304
Minas Gerais	20,734,097
Rio de Janeiro	16,461,173
Bahia	15,126,371
Rio Grande do Sul	11,207,274
Parana	11,081,692
Pernambuco	9,277,727
Ceara	8,842,791
Para	8,073,924
Maranhão	6,850,884
Santa Catarina	6,727,148
Goias	6,523,222
Paraiba	3,943,885
Espirito Santo	3,885,049
Amazonas	3,873,743
Rio Grandedo Norte	3,408,510
Alagoas	3,321,730
Mato Grosso	3,224,357
Piaui	3,194,178
Distrito Federal	2,852,372
Mato Grosso do Sul	2,619,657
Sergipe	2,219,514
Rondonia	1,748,531
Tocantins	1,496,880
Acre	790,101
Amapa	750,912
Roraima	496,936

Note: Estimated numbers

SOURCE: BRAZIL BUREAU OF STATISTICS (IBGE) 2018

and the less developed areas in North and Northeastern Brazil. According to Fundação Getúlio Vargas (FGV) figures in Brazil's report "Where are the Rich in Brazil," Florianópolis has the highest income per capita, followed by Porto Alegre and Vitória. São Paulo is the fourth wealthiest Brazilian state, followed by Brazil's capital city Brasília and Rio de Janeiro (FGV, 2019).

Brazil's regions North, Northeast, Central-West, South, and Southeast are also divided into three geo-economics regions measuring the country's industrial levels: Amazon, Northern and Centre-South (Geiger, 1967 cited in Alves, 2016). The Amazon region is composed of the Amazon Forest region, and is a region of low demography. The economy in this region is based on agrobusiness, and mining with a free tax hub in the city of Manaus. The Centre-South region is one third of Brazil's territory, and has the highest number of inhabitants; it is the most developed region in the country and is the economic centre of Brazil. Brazil's Northern region is 30 per cent of the country's territory (Alves, 2016). This region had the first settlements during the colonial era, and there are high socio-economic contrasts between the inhabitants of the wealthy coastal areas and those living in rural areas (*sertão*), which are predominantly agricultural (Alves, 2016).

Table 1.3 indicates the main socio-economic differences between the Centre-South and Northern regions of Brazil. The former is highly industrialised, and the major financial centres, universities and Brazil's cosmopolitan city centres are located in this region (Alvez, 2016). By contrast, Brazil Northeast region is predominantly agricultural, and historically less industrialised and developed than the country's Centre-South. The Northern rural areas, called *sertão,* is an area with high levels of illiteracy, with many living below the poverty line (Alvez, 2016). Brazil's elite groups live predominantly in the Northern coastal line, whereas impoverished communities are located inland. These inland

TABLE 1.3   Brazil's Centre-South (urban) and Northern (rural) distribution

Brazil urbanisation: Urban population (Centre-South)	Rural population (Northern)
– Highly urbanised and developed socially, economically, industrially, with higher life expectancy – Areas of higher population density in the country – Migration flow from rural areas since the 1970s increasing urban population in states such as Rio de Janeiro and São Paulo	– This region experiences severe social contrasts with rural areas highly affected by severe droughts. Less industrialised, agriculture and tourism are the main economic activities. – Areas of lower population density if compared to industrial centres – Migration flow from rural areas to big industrial centres, decreasing the rural population since the 20th century

Note: The Amazon region was not included due to its low population density.
SOURCES: IBGE (2017) AND ALVES C.G. (2016)

areas experience severe droughts, and have low levels of life expectancy, with an economy which is predominantly agricultural.

The Human Development Report (2020) shows Brazil's Gender Inequality Index of 0.408, ranking 95 out of 162 countries. This index measures the country's level of inequality in achieving three main development goals: 1) health, 2) education and 3) access to economic resources. Brazilian women persistently experience high levels of inequality in these three key areas. Brazil's Human Development Index value for females is 0.760 in comparison to 0.765 for males, with a Gender Development Index of 0.993.

According to the Global Gender Gap Index (2021), Brazil was rated 94 out of 156 indicating high levels of gender inequality between men and women in the areas such as political empowerment, economic participation and opportunity, educational attainment and health, with COVID-19 aggravating the gender gap. In 2021 Brazil's overall gender gap index increased to 0.695, with women having 30 per cent less opportunities than men. According to the "A Snapshot of Gender in Brazil Today: Institutions, Outcomes, and a Closer Look at Racial and Geographic Differences" (Gukovas et al., 2016), race and geography still play a significant role in women's empowerment and access to education in Brazil, with women of African and Indigenous descent continuing to be at a disadvantage. The report stated: "Tackling racial and geographic inequalities is critical for reaching gender equality, as it is certainly harder – and in some cases impossible – to raise aggregates of female progress if large sub-groups of women lag behind." The report concluded: "It would be a disservice to large swaths of the population to only set targets for women on average when non-white women and those living in the northern parts of the country are systemically below the average."

The World Bank (2017) highlights that race and geography increases Brazilian women's likelihood of a violent death. In 2017 the World Bank ranked Brazil as the fifth highest in number of femicides in Latin America. The South of Brazil had the lowest rates of femicides in the country, and the only region recording a decline in the killings of women between 2003 and 2013. Conversely, in the North and Northeast of Brazil, femicides increased 70 per cent during the same period. The increase was amongst Afro-Brazilian women and women of indigenous descent (World Bank, 2017). In the Northeast region, femicides have increased among Afro-descendent women at a rate of 103 per cent in the last decade. In Brazil, Indigenous women are highly vulnerable to violence, with 4.6 per 100,000 registered homicides, and with suicide rates of 5.8 per 100,000 – more than twice the national average of 2.2 females per 100,00 (World Bank, 2017).

Factors such as race, geography, and socio-economic standing, impact women's level of education and access to better living conditions. These factors are key in shaping "different notions" of honour consciousness and lived experiences of gender throughout the country.

The Northeast huge social contrasts and arid conditions found in the Northeast aggravate women's living conditions, since they have less access to education, information, and protection from violence. Brazilian women from the Northeast's inland rural areas predominantly experience "extreme" notions of honour consciousness. However, these co-exist with "moderate" notions of honour consciousness in the coastal cities. With honour consciousness suffering intra-cultural variation, "moderate" and "extreme" notions of honour are manifested throughout Brazil's regions.

Cultural notions of honour consciousness have evolved throughout Brazil's history, being consolidated during colonial times and until Brazil's independence. The bedrock of Brazil's core cultural values and institutions were laid down during this period. Brazilian society lived under colonial Portuguese rule from the time of the first expedition in 1532 until 1822 with Brazil's Independence. During colonial times, the Portuguese Crown implemented its institutional and legal framework for all those living on Brazilian soil (Ramos, 2012). Thus, Portuguese cultural norms, legal, political, economic framework and religion were incorporated into the emerging Brazilian society (Ramos, 2012). White Portuguese who migrated to Brazil received financial incentives from the Portuguese Crown, such as overseeing land and slaves, and thus formed elite groups within the emerging country (Ramos, 2012). The Crown's financial benefits and gains were substantive, but the greatest benefit for Portuguese early settlers was to consolidate their political power and prestige in colonial Brazil.

The emerging Brazilian colonial elite brought with them Portuguese traditions and customs – including the *bloodline* tradition together with honour consciousness. This was an important tradition associated with family prestige and social respectability, as blood is transmitted from generation to generation (Ramos, 2012). The concepts of family honour, prestige and social respect should also be transmitted down through the generations. Honour is acquired through a family's *bloodline,* then retained through family traditions (Ramos, 2012). And since women are the bearers of children and responsible for giving birth, it was of fundamental importance to ensure that the family line was not "contaminated." From the viewpoint of honour consciousness, women ought to be pure, chaste or simply "vessels of honour." Following the honour code, female marital unfaithfulness is thus seen as an unforgivable crime (Ortner,

1978). Both family and masculine honour depends upon female sexual purity, chastity and social respectability.

In 1643 Brazil received the 1603 Portuguese Philippine Ordinances into its legal system. (Doria, 1994). The Philippine Ordinances was embedded in Medieval concepts of the Holy Inquisition. The principles enshrined in this legal document placed women in a position of submission and inferiority, and women's rights were represented by their fathers or husbands (Doria, 1994). Moreover, the Ordinances gave husbands the prerogative to murder their wives if caught in the act of adultery (Ordenações Filipinas, 1603/2022). The philosophy behind it saw women as the property of their husbands (Doria, 1994).

Under the Philippine Ordinances, a man could lawfully kill his wife (Ordenações Filipinas, 1603/2022). It required the testimony of a witness that the murderer was married to the victim (Ordenações Filipinas, 1603/2022). The Ordinances allowed the murder of an adulterous wife by both wealthy and poor men alike. This legislation intended to punish adulterous women, as the adulterous woman's sin ought to be "washed with her own blood."

With Brazil's Independence from Portugal in 1822, Brazil enacted its first Criminal Code. The 1830 Brazilian Criminal Code did not erase the vestiges of Medieval morality from Brazil's legal framework (Caulfield, 2000). In the 1830 Brazilian Criminal Code, husbands were no longer allowed to kill their wives in the case of adultery. However, the 1830 Criminal Code deemed all acts of adultery a crime against civil society, domesticity and the state, with the prerogative of incarcerating an adulterous spouse for up to three years (Hermann & Barsted, 1995). According to the 1830 Criminal Code, to incarcerate an adulterous spouse, husband accusers had to prove that the extramarital *liaison* was a regular and stable one, not a casual sexual encounter. Male casual sexual encounters were not seen as a crime under Brazilian law, as in Brazilian society a male's extramarital affairs are seen as "an inherent part of their nature" (Hermann & Barsted, 1995). Conversely, only the presumption of adultery would be sufficient to incarcerate a woman (Hermann & Barsted, 1995). Brazilian women's offences against sexual honour had to be harsher, since they had broader implications: They jeopardises "the moral authority of the church and state, the inviolability and public reputation of a household, private paternal authority, individual integrity, and family patrimony" (Almeida, cited by Caulfield, 2000, page 23).

During Brazil's Republic, the 1890 Criminal Code continued the differentiation between male and female adultery. However, the new criminal legislation designed individual's self-defence in such a way that a husband who killed his wife under the "honour defence" could still be acquitted (Hermann

& Barsted, 1995). According to the Brazilian legislation this type of crime falls under Brazil's Civil Code's framing of "crimes of passion"[2] (Eluf, 2021). Following the "honour defence" argument, a husband who killed his wife "in defence of his honour" would be protecting a right (his honour) that had been violated by his adulterous wife.

Brazil's conservative views on marriage are reflected throughout its legal system. For instance, in 1891 the Republican Constitutional Charter contained no provisions regarding the rights and duties of men and women under marriage. Chapter 4, session 72 stated that "The Republic will recognise the civil marriage, free of public charges" (Constituição Brasileira, 1891). Thus, the 1916 Civil Code regulated extensively "civil marriage and its formalities, requirements and effects, including nullity and annulment and the simple dissolutions by the *desquite* (divorce)," (Código Civil Brasileiro, 1916). According to the 1916 Brazilian Civil Code *desquite* includes the couple's separation only, as divorce was illegal under Brazilian law until 1977 (Lei do Divórcio, 1977). With Brazil's new 2002 Civil Code, the marriage legislation was updated. Marriage continued to be predominantly a heterosexual institution, with stable unions reserved to homosexual civil unions – *união estável homoafetiva* (Código Civil Brasileiro, 2002).

Only in 2013 through a High Court and National Justice Council ruling, was homosexual marriage allowed in Brazil. Nonetheless, the stigma towards lesbian, gay, bisexual, transgender, and the intersex community (LGBTIQ+) continues throughout the country. This is due to traditional views on family and marriage, as well as traditional attitudes with regard to both masculinity and femininity. According to the 2018 European Report on Transgender (TGEU, 2018), Brazil leads the global ranking on killings of LGBTIQ+ individuals. This reflects Brazil's honour consciousness, and these traditional views on the family, gender and masculinity. Therefore, honour consciousness and Catholic traditional framing of the family, and notions of womanhood is manifested in the early days of Brazil's legal system: the "honour defence" jurisprudence reflects such views.

---

2 The application of the "honour defence" argument has been recently deemed unconstitutional in 2021 by Brazilian High Court Justice Dias Toffoli (Jus Brazil, 2021). Previously, this jurisprudence acquitted husbands who killed their wives in the "name of honour" – a legal argument excluding their punishment. These crimes were classified under Brazil's Civil Codes of 1916 and 2002 as "crimes of passion" (Eluf, 2021).

1   Catholicism in Brazil, "Cultural Christianity" and Honour
     Consciousness

The Catholic Church is the leading faith in Latin America, with the church being an instrument of governmental power as well as the existing order to save the infidel's souls (Baldwin & De Souza, 2001). For centuries, Brazil's Catholicism has shaped collective and individual consciousness, consolidating Catholic interpretations of the Bible where men should be "in charge," constructing strict roles for men and women. According to traditional views of Catholicism, women should submit to their husbands, nurture them and their children. In such Catholic traditional views, women are the homemakers, the bearers of children, and exist within the domestic sphere. For Baldwin & De Souza (2001), the cult of the Virgen Mary known as *Marianismo,* has shaped ideals of female purity, self-sacrifice, and virginity throughout the continent. *Marianismo* is a leading variable in the formation of gender and women's consciousness in Brazilian society. Baldwin and De Souza (2001) argue that another variable influencing gender relations in Brazil is Latin American *Machismo.* Dengah et al. (2024) explain that machismo is characterised by male dominance and women's submission, and men's control of the decision-making power, family finances, and bearing the responsibility to defend the family honour.

     When dealing with individuals from the Christian faith and Catholics more specifically, *Marianismo* is an important variable in Brazil's gender relations. For Baldwin and De Souza (2001), *Marianismo* has a crucial impact in the social construction of gender. Brazilian women shape their identities based on purity and chastity, endorsing the Greek model of male supremacy. I argue that gendered perspectives based on honour consciousness are magnified by Brazil's Catholic approaches to gender and *Marianismo.* According to these, women's and men's behaviour can be contradictory and antagonising. For instance: women are expected to be pure, immaculate and virgin. On the other hand, men are supposed to be the Latino *stallions,* who should have his wife and children under his full control, as well as having as many extramarital affairs as he wishes. This in Brazil is something to be praised. These views are inherently part of Brazilian society, shaping Brazilian's lived experiences of gender amongst Christians, non-practicing Christians, and non-Christians.

     Brazil's gender construction leads us into a fascinating social landscape. As explained by Baldwin and De Souza (2001) there is a dichotomy and tension between traditionalism and modernity. There are different social expectations between individuals from the white middle and upper-middle classes, and the underprivileged, as well as mixed races. However, honour consciousness impacts all Brazilians. Honour consciousness and Christian views on female sexual purity are key elements shaping Brazil's gender power relations. These, however, suffer intra-cultural variation in a pluralist and diverse country such as Brazil. Honour consciousness, religion, traditional views of the family (within religion) and notions of womanhood are manifested along a spectrum. Religiosity in Brazil is drawn from notions of purity and modesty which are derived from Portuguese Catholic Christian culture. These views impact lived experiences of honour consciousness and gender throughout Brazilian society.

Brazil's Catholic views are key to understand the interplay between honour consciousness, traditional views of the family (within religion) and Brazil's notions of womanhood. In Brazil, Christianity generally plays a vital role in shaping institutions, honour consciousness and notions of womanhood, but Catholicism, is the Christian denomination with the greatest socio-cultural influence in Brazil's honour consciousness. Catholic views on notions of womanhood have shaped Brazil's socio-constructions on the role of men and women within family life.

Drawing from the Catechism of the Catholic Church, women and men are both endowed with fundamental rights. Women have the right to hold paid employment outside the home; however, their primary role is to work inside the family home and to ensure the functionality of domestic affairs (Catechism, 2022). The Catholic Church openly advocates for the equal protection of human rights of women and men, but at the same time it stresses that it is more important that women should work in the domestic sphere, with their focus on the greater good: their husbands and children.

In the words of John Paul II in the Encyclical *Familiaris Consortio* (1981, *The Situation of the Family in the World Today*):

> There is no doubt that the equal dignity and responsibility of men and women fully justify women's access to public tasks. On the other hand, the true advancement of women also requires that the values of their maternal and family role be clearly recognised in comparison with all other public tasks and with all other professions. Moreover, such tasks and professions must be integrated with each other if social and cultural evolution is to be truly and fully human (...). This will be more easily achieved if (...) a renewed "theology of work" clarifies and deepens the meaning of work in the Christian life (...) the original and irreplaceable meaning of housework and raising children. (...) Therefore, the Church can and must help today's society, insistently asking that the work of women in the home be recognised by all and honoured in its irreplaceable value.

Brazil's socio-historic Catholic framing of notions of womanhood and family life permeates every single aspect of Brazilian society. This influences all Christians denominations, as well as non-Christian groups. Brazil's laicity in the first Republic is hotly contested in the literature, as in practical terms, the Catholic church's influence and power continued mostly unquestioned (Leite, 2011). And even in contemporary times, religious teachings in Brazil's public schools consolidate Christian Catholic values and white European privileges amongst future generations (Da Silva Gonçalves, 2019)

The overwhelming socio-historical influence of Catholicism and Christianity in Brazil creates what is referred to as Brazil's "cultural Christianity" (Cogell, 200; Inserra, 2019). I draw from the definition of "cultural religion" from Demerath III (2000, p. 127), as a common syndrome "in which religion affords a sense of personal identity and continuity with the past even after participation in ritual and belief have lapsed." In Brazil's "cultural Christianity," traditional notions of womanhood and family life are seen as "honourable." These are strongly manifested in all Christian denominations in Brazil as well as in non-Christian groups.

In recent years, however, Brazil has been experiencing an Evangelical surge. According to a 2016 Datafolha survey, 44 per cent of Evangelicals are former Catholics. Data from Brazil IBGE (2012) indicates 86,8 per cent Brazilians identify as Christians, with 64,6 per cent of Catholics and 22,2 of Evangelicals. However, Catholicism is still the predominant Christian denomination in the country, with Brazil's ultra-conservative Evangelical movement the second largest Christian group.

Evangelicals (Pentecostals and Neo-Pentecostals) views of honour consciousness and traditional views of the family have been framed through traditional Catholic views on notions of womanhood and family. Nonetheless, their interpretation of the Gospels is taken literally (religious fundamentalism). Evangelicals' interpretation of religious texts is predominantly focused on the individual, rather than drawing from institutional tradition. This results in stricter codes of conduct for women, predominantly supporting views of female submission to male "headship" (Dos Santos & Petrus, 2021; Steigenga & Smilde, 1999). Such a perspective may increase the likelihood of domestic violence and femicides of Pentecostal women in Brazil (De Souza & Oshiro, 2018).

In Brazil, lived experiences of honour consciousness and religion intersects with the Catholic framing of traditional views of the family (within religion) and notions of womanhood. These are manifested through gender power relations throughout the country. Thus, although women may have a voice and have their fundamental rights protected, they are still seen as the "home makers," and the ones who should look after their husbands and children thus securing "family harmony." Brazil's honour consciousness and its interplay with religion is more visibly manifested within Evangelical Christian groups. Their literal interpretation of the Gospel has a strong focus on women's submission to men. Nonetheless, Catholics and Evangelicals can hold "moderate notions" of honour consciousness. These are manifested through women's empowerment, women's political participation and in the workforce, women having a voice in the public arena, and in the fight for women's rights. These are reconciled with traditional notions of womanhood and the role played by women within family life. Catholic and Evangelicals can also hold "extreme notions" of honour consciousness. In these notions, women lack agency, women are suppressed, and are unable to participate in political life, resulting in violence against women and *femicides*.

2   The Effects of Class, Race in Lived Experiences of Honour Consciousness and Gender

Brazil is inherently a multiracial society. And in the words of anthropologist Darcy Ribeiro, the country is a great ethnic and racial melting pot (Ribeiro, 1995). Indeed, Brazil is shaped from the mixing of Portuguese invader's blood with that of indigenous peoples and of Africans, both of whom were submitted, (although in different historical moments), to the scourge of slavery. Interracial relationships between the white Portuguese colonisers, Brazil's Indigenous peoples and the African population produced a nation of disparate racial origins and a unique culture, giving birth to a new people (Ribeiro, 1995). Brazil's uniqueness is a result of great racial miscegenation between white Portuguese with other races. Nevertheless, racial dilution did not erase the social divides between the still predominantly white elite groups and individuals of dark skin, and mixed races.

Brazil can be seen as part of both the "new" and the "old," since the Portuguese colonizer's culture was transplanted to the tropics. With the colonisation process, Portugal's honour consciousness has been incorporated into Brazilian society. Brazil's ethnic diversity provides the Portuguese coloniser's culture and honour consciousness a new framing, and a country of mixed-race people or *mestiços* (Ribeiro, 1995). Despite Brazil's racial and ethnic diversity, mixed-race and dark skin individuals continue to experience substantive exclusion. They are seen as the social "other." Brazilian elites' privileges and hegemonic power continues mostly unchallenged. Brazil's racial and economic inequalities have been shaped from colonial times, impacting class, race, as well as gender power relations.

Lélia Gonzalez (1988) contends that Brazil's so-called "racial democracy" is a myth consolidating racial domination. In her perspective, in Brazil there is both open and hidden racism. Open racism is a type of racism seen in the Anglo world, with hidden racism belonging to Latin America. The latter form of racism is pervasive and subtle and thrives with miscegenation theories, assimilation and the myth of Brazil's "racial democracy." This impedes an objective conscience against racism, hiding its daily cruelty since the myth of "racial democracy" waters down Brazil's racist practices and white hegemony.

The white coloniser's power has significantly shaped Brazil's gender relations. Ribeiro (1995) argues that during Brazil's colonisation period, Indigenous women were pursued and had sexual relations with white Portuguese colonisers. Most men were sent to Brazilian shores in order to populate and dominate the land. Indigenous and African women have never been seen on the same social standing as white Portuguese white women (Ribeiro, 1995). The offspring of these relationships were *bastardos,* children born out of wedlock who did not enjoy any legal rights under Portuguese or Brazilian law. Sadly, as argued by the sociologist Gilberto Freyre, it is widely believed among Brazilian elite groups that white women are for marriage, black women for labour and *mulatas* (mixed-race women) for sex (Freyre, 1946/1956). With Portuguese and Spanish religious morality being strict and repressive, these men engaged in sexual practices forbidden to commoners in their European homelands. The colonisers engaged in exploitative sexual practices with the indigenous and African women but were excused of any degree of accountability.

The social expectation for white "elite" women, however, was different from female street vendors, maids, or African slave women. Women from upper class families from a white European background had to be confined to the domestic sphere. A "good marriage" was essential to preserve family alliances and guarantee a financially secure future, not only for their daughters, but also for their wives in the case of family misfortune.

As argued by June Habner (2012, p. 44):

> Elite women would be far less exposed to masculine observers since they would be reserved to their homes most of the time. Therefore, such stories are based upon occasional conversations between visitors with unmarried women and married ladies (senhoras) from wealthy Brazilian families. According to such stories, these families were patriarchal ones, the father and husband playing an authoritarian role, exerting dominion over his sons and daughters with his wife being submissive to his power, whereas the "head of the household" would surround himself with concubines or would have extramarital relationships with African slaves. His

wife, conversely, was indolent and passive in nature, who would rarely leave the family home, would give birth to countless children and usually would punish rashly their African slaves. (Translated from Portuguese)

As argued by Freyre (1946/1956) in "Masters and Slaves," Brazilian society has been shaped by the relationship between the white Portuguese landowner, his relationship with the Indigenous people (particularly indigenous women), and African slaves. Consequently, I argue, Brazilian society is inherently influenced by a "masters" and "slaves" consciousness, with the sadism of the "master" white European Portuguese towards their Indigenous slaves and, later, to their African slaves, shaping gender power relations (gender politics) in the country. Following Freyre' (1946/1956) perspective, Brazil's "masters" and "slaves" mentality shapes not only economic production and trade relations, but Brazilian society in broader terms. The role of the feudal lord ("the master") in exerting power over all those under his dominion (his wife, children, slaves, and his slaves' children) affects the entirety of Brazilian society (Freyre, 1946/1956). The domineering role played by the white Portuguese patriarch rendered women in a position of inferiority, submission and social hopelessness. This situated women as being sexually and socially submissive, and simply as projections of their fathers or husbands.

From the early stages of Portuguese settlements, sexual relations between the white Portuguese conquerors and Indigenous women were an everyday practice. However, the relaxed sexual practices and morals of the white colonisers came at a high price: the widespread infestation of syphilis (Freyre, 1946/1956). The infestation of syphilis *per excellence* was a social phenomenon attributed to the white European landowner's house, the "big house" ("casa grande") relationship with the "senzala" (African slaves hut). The plantation owner's son's sexual initiation would take place with one of their female African slaves, with him giving preference to the mulatto mixed-race ones. These were regarded as highly attractive and segregated for sexual pleasure only (Freyre, 1946/1956).

As soon as the landowner's son had gone through his rite of passage he would be contaminated with syphilis (Freyre, 1946/1956). In colonial Brazilian society there was immense social pressure for the precocious sexual initiation of boys.[3] A boy from the age of twelve on wards who was not sexually active would be mocked by his counterparts, male family members and acquaintances. One of

---

3   Brazilian boys from white wealthy families would start their sexual lives the tender age of 13 years old, and they would be sexually initiated with an African black female slave or a mixed-race girl ("mulata"), in Freyre (1946/1956).

the signals of syphilis infection would be the scars, which young boys would show to other males as a sign of male pride and virility.

The sexual permissiveness and abuse of power from white conquerors initially took place between them and Indigenous women, but then has moved into the relationship between white masters and African female slaves (Prado Junior, 1963/1967). In the words of Freyre (1946/1956) this form of "sadism" and "masochism" has evolved between the sexual encounters of the white master and female Indigenous women and female African slaves. The relationship between the European male conqueror and Indigenous and African women was characterised by his abuse of power as master of the land. The Portuguese, driven by their lust and passion, would vent it against their victims, who were the indigenous women and the female slaves under their power and authority (Freyre, 1946/1956). In this sense, the landowner's sexual advances towards women of colour were an acts of power, meant to submit those women to his will. In the words of Freyre, the "sadistic" nature of the relationship between the master and the women under his power would go beyond this. For Freyre, the active and "sadistic" nature of the white conqueror would be encouraged by the "masochistic" and passive role played by all African slaves, both male and female. What I deem as the "plantation field power politics" has broadly shaped and influenced Brazilian society broadly and is a leading factor behind the history of authoritarian rule, nepotism, corruption, and the abuse of power by members of ruling groups. These social relations invariably shape Brazil's honour consciousness, and the ways in which class and race influence "different notions" of honour and lived experiences of gender.

As argued by Freyre (1946/1956), in Brazilian society, the "sadism" perpetrated, encouraged, and stimulated by the relationship between the white master towards the coloured slaves impacted not only the power relations between the white European male and his wife but also power relations between the white "lady of the house" and their African female slaves. This highlights the intersectional experience of Brazilian women of colour. The feminine expressions of sadism could be even more ferocious and vile. White females would inflict incredible punishments upon female slaves and *mulato girls* if it was suspected that they had attracted their husbands' favour and attention (Habner, 2012). What is deemed as the "slave field power politics" sadistic and masochistic practices go beyond the immediate sphere of Brazilian sexuality and domestic life, and has greatly influenced broader Brazilian history and political relations, as well as gender power relations.

Following this line of thought, the scourge of slavery, first of Brazil's first peoples then of Africans, has shaped Brazilian history, society and culture. Arguably, to this day, African slavery feeds into Brazilian consciousness, and into the elite groups' sense of entitlement and their lack of empathy shown towards those of lower socio-economic classes, who are usually of mixed race or African descent. Consequently, Brazil has deep moral scars from colonial practices and the enslavement of Indigenous and African peoples. From the birth of the nation, Brazilians experienced substantive social divides and was accustomed to human exploitation. These social cleavages have had a fundamental impact on the intersections of class, race, and gender shaping Brazil's lived experiences of gender. As it is argued by Caio Prado Júnior (1963/1967, p. 4):

> I refer not only to traditions and to certain glaring anachronisms that exist at any time or in any place, but to fundamental characteristics to the economic and social structure. In the economic sphere, for instance, it could be said that free labour has not yet been organised throughout the country. In many parts of the country, there is an active process of adjustment, a successful effort in this direction, but strong traces of the slave regime are still present.

With the social effects of Brazilian slavery still subsiding, ethnicity and race are key variables determining social mobility, social ascendance and influence. The social effects of the Brazilian culture of honour, in part means that having good social ties and relationships are essential to acquire good jobs and ascend socially. In a society with deep class and racial divides, white women were traditionally seen as "women to get married with," and who should then be confined to the realm of domesticity, living under control by the "man of the house." In Brazil's ideals of masculinity, men ought to be strong, pro-active, the breadwinner and virile. Women's chastity in Brazilian society is seen as a fundamental component of family honour, but man's sexual experiences before and after marriage make them popular amongst their peers. Traditionally, in Brazilian society, there would be women for "marriage" and women "for fun." In colonial times, white males had casual sexual encounters with mixed-race women and African slave women. Obviously, there were no social expectations that the "breadwinner" and "head of the household" ought to be faithful to his white European wife. The white woman, in her turn, would punish harshly her slaves and the female African slaves for having affairs with her husband.

3 Coloniality of Power

I argue that what is referred to as "coloniality of power" is a key episteme to understand the different axes of power permeating Brazilian society, and the impact of social class, race, and gender in Brazil's experience of honour. This epistemological approach provides greater depth to historical accounts of class, race, and gender differentiation in Brazilian society, as well as the differentiation in the lived experience of honour – what is deemed "different notions of honour." The terminologies "coloniality of power" and "coloniality of being" coined by Peruvian sociologist Anibal Quijano are key epistemological approaches in decolonial theory and critical studies. According to Quijano, coloniality is "the most general form of domination in the world today, once colonialism as an explicit political order was destroyed" (Quijano, 2000, p. 541). In Quijano's view, coloniality is not an experience expressed in one set period, rather it is an overarching experience that continues to influence and shape Latin American livelihoods to this day. The values of the colonisers and class systems introduced during colonial times continue, reproducing the colonial's power systems and European colonial hegemony.

In the light of this episteme, although Eurocentrism has a socio-economic impact, it goes beyond it: it has an all-encompassing impact on Latin American culture, and the way in which social structures, and society itself emerge. With the systematic genocide of Indigenous peoples throughout the continent, their subjection was enforced through a colonial sponsored system of cultural repression (Quijano, 2000). Through his perspective, race differentiations are central to the colonial order, as well as colonial hegemonic power, with European white supremacy, and their values, ruling overall and supressing racialized non-white "others." The "coloniality of power" has effects on societal values, system of production, the distribution of labour, and generates the "coloniality of being" – where the European ideals, values (and even beauty paradigms) are seen as "superior," "more advanced," and of greater "sophistication." Quijano's coloniality of power generates the "coloniality of being" and of "the imagination" – with the latter suppressing Indigenous values, forging new Latin American identities which are Eurocentric and based in white superiority (Quijano, 2000).

Drawing upon the epistemological contribution of Argentinian theorist and philosopher Maria Lugones, Quijano's "coloniality of power" and "coloniality of being" can be seen through a gender perspective. Lugones argues Quijano's "coloniality of power" is not sufficiently gender aware. In Lugone's perspective, Quijano's approach to "coloniality of power" and "coloniality of being" is overtly heteronormative and disregards the intersectional experience of women of colour and subaltern groups (Lugones, 2008). For Lugones, colonialism creates the "colonial modern gender system," where colonialism not only creates systems of racial classification, but also introduces European gendered norms to the new world (Lugones, 2008). Accordingly, there are two faces to the modern colonial gender system: The "light side" associated with the white bourgeois family promoting heteronormativity, and the "dark side" repressing alternative expressions of sex, gender and sexuality. Arguably, alternative experiences to sex and gender flourished in pre-colonial America (Lugones, 2008).

Brazilian scholar Lélia Gonzalez contextualises the impact of "coloniality of power" in African Brazilian women's lived experiences of class, race and gender. Influenced by Frantz Fanon's view of the colonized inferiority, Gonzalez (1988) contends that once defeated and subdued, colonised bodies end up internalising racialized ideals of society and self. According to Gonzalez, Latin American racism leads to a racial alienation sustained through a whitening ideology, where "the desire to whiten ("cleanse the blood," like it is said in Brazil) is internalised, with the simultaneous negation of your own race, your own culture" (Gonzalez, 1988, translated from Portuguese, p. 27). According to this view, the colonizer's culture, race and standards of beauty are something to strive for, and seen as "civilised," "sophisticated" and "evolved."

Arguably, these power systems are inexorably connected with white values, with honour being a component in the coloniser's hegemonic forces in the continent. Although Quijano and Lugones allude to the Latino experience more broadly, Brazil's societal distribution of power, and lived experiences of class, race and gender is fundamentally shaped by the "coloniality of power" and the "coloniality of being" (and imagination). These factors are essential to grasp Brazil's layered society and the power tensions in the lived experience of honour consciousness.

Through this epistemological perspective, honour consciousness can be seen as an integral part of Portuguese European colonialism, shaping Brazil's nuanced lived experience of honour consciousness. This is intrinsically related to the colonisers and the colonised unequal lived experience of class, race, gender and sexuality. By implementing colonial hegemony, white culture, social structures and heteronormativity become an integral part of Brazilian society, and social ideals that individuals from all classes, races and gender strive for – since it is seen as "superior" and "civilised" and "beautiful." Moreover, colonial hegemony and heteronormativity consolidated through honour consciousness shape Brazil's masculinities and femininities. These gendered approaches exist throughout Brazilian social structures, giving a continuum to social reproduction. Brazil's white elite groups, following the coloniser's white traditions and culture, are the coloniser's "deputies in the land." They provide continuum to colonial hegemony and social whitening practices implemented from Brazil colony to contemporary times. The white colonizer's views on honour and gender give rise to "extreme" notions of honour consciousness, manifested through female suppression and women's lack of agency. A nuanced appraisal of lived experiences of honour consciousness, however, is key to unpack the spectrum between "extreme," "moderate" and "other experiences of honour" by the social "other."

Brazil's cultural divides between the Southeast and rural areas, and the Northeast affects an individual's education and access to information, and women's lived experiences of honour consciousness throughout the country. There are huge socio-economic divides between Brazil's more urbanised areas, predominantly in the Southeast region, from those less industrialised, particularly in rural areas of the Northeast, called the *sertão*. In this region, women predominantly experience "extreme" notions of honour consciousness and gender.

Brazil's Northeast region, the *sertão* is Brazil's hinterland. This region's geography and drylands are called *caatinga* and is economically backward when compared to other parts of Brazil, because of the dry terrain, constant droughts, and the low density of population. This is an area of Brazil dominated by *coronéis*, landlords of Portuguese European descent who exert dominion over the impoverished mixed-race local population. Brazil's *sertão* is a region of huge social divides marred by low levels of education. The *coronéis* influence (*coronelism*) exploits the local population's lack of education, economic disadvantage and religious beliefs for electoral gains, consolidating the power of their families throughout generations (Souza Júnior, 2015). Although an impoverished region, Brazil's Northeast is rich in folklore and traditions, immortalised in the Brazilian literature by Euclydes da Cunha em *Os Sertões* (Da Cunha, 1902). There is extensive literature discussing honour culture, and the value of honour (Santos, 2011), and the influence of *coronéis* in Brazil's backlands (Souza Júnior, 2015).

Literature suggests that Brazil's Northeast's leading cultural trait is the culture of honour (Tomas, 2016). Marta Santos (2011) explains that the climate, severe droughts, and creeping poverty are constant issues in this region, well-known for their social contrasts, and for the local figure of the *sertanejo* (the man from the backlands). The *sertanejo* is impoverished, but he is "honoured" (*honrado*) and "respected" (*respeitado*). Following this line of thought, the daily challenges faced by the Brazilian backland's *sertanejo* exacerbated by the difficulty in cultivating an unfertile and dry soil and in providing for his family, may well aggravate his need to reaffirm his masculinity (Santos, 2011). In the *sertanejo*'s view, any acts that jeopardise either his role as the "head of the household" and the "breadwinner," or his strength, courage, and leadership, needs to be dealt with – usually through the use of violence. By being an honoured man (*homem honrado*), even though the *sertanejo* is financially impoverished, he would still be "a real man," a man of honour. Arguably, aggression and violence could be the means by which he was able to reaffirm his masculine honour to the wider society, since a man (even if deprived of material possessions) "naturally" possess the attributes to protect his masculine pride (Santos, 2011).

To understand the social relevance of masculine pride it is important to reflect on the condition of women who challenged traditional masculine roles and Brazilian patriarchy. As an illustration, in 19th century Brazil any single or widowed Northeastern woman living independently from a man would be vulnerable to gender-based violence. They would be financially independent, holding jobs such as maids or servants, or would sew clothes in exchange of cash. Nevertheless, there are several reports of single, financially independent women being assaulted on the streets, raped and even suffering public floggings. They were "punished" by the men within their communities for talking to other males "disrespectfully" (Santos, 2011). Others suffered physical violence followed by rape for rejecting the sexual advances of a particular man (Santos, 2011). These acts of violence were the ultimate social instrument to reaffirm masculine honour and patriarchy in Northeastern Brazilian society (Santos, 2011). As can be seen, in an honour-based society such as Brazil, women should fit the social stereotype of being passive, submissive and financially dependent on men. A woman without a man by their side to "protect them" from other males would be vulnerable to gendered violence and sexual abuse.

The Brazilian character of the Northeastern man, the man of the backlands (the *sertanejo*), and his narratives to enforce masculine honour is a predominant cultural trait of the region. However, there is a distinction between experiences of honour in Brazil's *backlands* from that of Brazil's major cities due to the *sertão*'s rural setting. In this environment, family ties and systems of kinship are key parts of social organisation – intrinsically related to the honour consciousness. The Brazilian *sertanejo* is an individual who would be willing to resort to violence and killings if his honour is undermined: he would claim to "lavar a honra com sangue" (cleanse one's reputation with blood). As argued by Johnson and Lipsett-Rivera (1988) Latino young man would be encouraged from an early age to "act like a man." In other words: to take physical risks or to resort to physical violence or aggression would be socially accepted, as an instrument to establish masculine authority and power. Masculine honour and honour consciousness manifest themselves throughout Brazil. But there are different experiences of honour depending on each region. Drawing from Tomas' concept of intra-cultural variation of honour in Brazil (Tomas, 2016), honour consciousness is present throughout Brazilian society, though suffering intracultural variations based on the regional demography and urbanisation levels.

In Northeastern Brazilian communities, for instance, it would be a common narrative in case of female adultery that the man would lose his connection with the children. When a woman "goes astray" and a man must walk out of his house, this would also mean that he leaves his children behind (Mayblin, 2011). In Brazilian society, the main attachment between the children is with their mothers. Thus, in the case of a relationship breakdown the children traditionally favour the mother, the one who bore them and cared for them, instead of their fathers. This might be due to the fact that in traditional Brazilian society women are associated with the private realm of the family, home and domesticity (Habner, 2012). In a society built upon masculine pride and honour, female infidelity would be seen as an "unforgivable" crime. Since a man who is betrayed by his wife is a "cuckold", his life would be "disgraced" (Mayblin, 2011). In such case, masculine honour would be tarnished beyond repair. That man's life had been put to shame, and social demise would follow (Brandes, 1987; cited in Mayblin, 2011).

Addressing marital unfaithfulness in Northeastern rural Brazil, Maya Mayblin (2011, p. 138) describes the recurrent discourse, and the sentiment of locals when a man becomes a "cuckold:"

> Your life is as good as over. M(m)y host father affirmed when I once raised the subject. Pressing the men, I knew on this issue, I found they were only too keen to explain. The cuckold becomes, in the words of another man, like a pig: an object of ridicule and disgust. Others said that the betrayed man loses his appetite for sex and withdraws from the world. The masculine realm of bars, markets, and snooker rooms becomes an unbearable place to be, and this affects his ability to drink and "negociar" (do business) with other men. Both these activities are essential means by which men build social relations and broaden social networks.

Lived experiences of men and women are different, with greater social acceptance with regard to male unfaithfulness. Female sexual purity is essential to preserve family life and reputation. And the effects of female marital unfaithfulness are far-reaching, impacting a man's virility, his reputation before his peers and society, as well as his relationship with his children. Honour consciousness attributes women's spaces within the domestic sphere, looking after her family and children. In case of female marital unfaithfulness, the man would lose his nourishment within the safety of the family as well as his relationship with his children (as is it a woman's responsibility to nurture and raise children). Through men's perspective, the consequences of female lack of chastity and sexual control can be seen as "disastrous" (Mayblin, 2011).

Brazilian feminist waves have challenged honour consciousness' and traditional views of the family (within religion) to a certain extent. Brazil's feminism and the awareness on the condition of women has its roots in Brazil's 19th century social movements, and the fight against the country's socio-economic divides as well as the end of African slavery. African women suffered multi-axed inequality, based on being African, a woman as well as a slave, whereas white women were oppressed for being restricted to the private sphere and looking after their families.

Brazil first wave of feminism, the fight for citizen's rights, starts in the 19th century with Nisia Floresta. During Brazil's Empire women gained the right of being formally educated, and Floresta is regarded as one of Brazil's first feminists (Duarte, 1997). She was an educator and founded the first girl's school in Brazil and was the first woman to have her work published (Duarte, 1997), breaking away from women's constraints in the private sphere.

However, only in the Republican era were Brazilian women able to consolidate participation and activism in Brazil's public sphere (Soihet, 2013). Women from lower socio-economic backgrounds already worked to support themselves and their families (in the care sector, and industries), but women from middle-class and upper social class had to fight for their rights to join the workforce.

Women's aspiration to access education, the right to vote and to run for office suffered great opposition during Brazil's Republican Constitution in 1891, with many regarding such rights "unconstitutional." Leolinda Daltro, the first Brazilian woman to graduate as a lawyer and join Brazil's Bar Association, founded Brazil's Feminist Republican Party in 1910 to pressure the government to reconsider women's right to vote (Karawejczyk, 2014). In November 1917 Daltro organise a protest with 84 women, propelling congressperson Mauricio Lacerda to propose a bill giving women's rights to vote. However, this bill was not even heard in parliament (Karawejczyk, 2014). Again, in 1919 a similar bill was proposed by congressperson Justo Chermont before Brazil's Senate, but with no success.

Brazilian society, politicians and state authorities strongly opposed the rights of women outside the home. In support of such views were "scientific" perspectives, which regarded women as physically fragile, intellectually inferior to men and unsuited for public life (Soihet, 2013). Brazilian society emphasised that women's "natural habitat" was within the family, looking after her children and her husband as her primary occupation. Brazil's society was highly critical of the feminist movement and women's demands for the rights to vote, which were present in theatre plays, chronicles, caricatures, in Brazil's press, with the national discourse ridiculing the movement (Soihet, 2013).

In 1922 Bertha Lutz joined the first Interamerican Women's Conference in Baltimore, establishing connections between Brazilian feminists with the National American Woman's Suffrage Association (NAWSA) – a branch which shaped North American feminism. Inspired and supported by NAWSA president Carrie Chapman Catt, Lutz founded Brazil's Federation for the Feminine Progress (Soihet, 2000). This branch of Brazil's feminism and the fight for women's rights draws from North American feminist ideals.

Only on 24 February 1932 did Brazil established the universal secret vote, including women. Brazil is the second country in Latin America to give women the right to vote. Voting rights, however, were suspended during the Getúlio Vargas dictatorship, which lasted from 1937 to 1945, suppressing women's movements until the end of the regime (Soihet, 2013). With the end of the war women's movements re-articulated, appealing to both middle class women and to those living in shanty towns (*favelas*). Brazil's women's movements fought for the end of discrimination based on sex, and were also concerned with other issues affecting the interests of Brazilian women, such as health, children, and even land rights (Soihet, 2013). In 1946, the Feminine Institute for Constructive Service was founded – the "embryo" of The Women's Federation of Brazil. This consolidated the Brazil's women's movement with left leaning political actors such as Brazil's Communist Party (PCB) (Soihet, 2013). Their main cause was to fight for women's rights in a classless society, with the de-construction of other systems of oppression. This highly politicised faction of Brazil's women's movements did not appeal to all sectors of Brazil's society, and suffered political repression for its association with communism. The communist party was deemed illegal, until after Brazil re-democratisation in 1985 (Biblioteca Nacional), thus stigmatising feminists aligned with the communist movement.

In 1946 there was also a branch of the Brazil's women's movement, comprised of those who joined the First Feminine Convention of the Federal District, which had the motto: "We will not give up of our femininity and this is why we want our place in society" (Soihet, 2013, p. 97). These women advocated high levels of female agency and political participation but stated "they didn't want to subvert the sexual roles within the family" (Soihet, 2013, p. 98). This part of the women's movement reconciled women's voices and political activism with traditional notions of womanhood and Catholic traditional views of the family. Following traditional views on womanhood and the family, women's primary role is to nurture their husbands, their children, and to look after their homes. In this movement, women declared their commitment to defend their homes, domestic economy and the rights of the children (Soihet, 2013). One of their greater causes was the fight for "world peace" (Soihet, 2013). This conservative section of Brazil's women's movements distances itself from

French style feminism, and the label of "feminists," since they do not challenge gender roles, or demand greater parity with men in all levels of society.

Brazil's second feminist wave engages with the 1960's fight for sexual and reproductive rights. In this feminist wave, with the anti-conception pill, women start to question notions of womanhood and their role as mothers and home makers (Rodrigues & Freitas, 2021). Birth control and abortion are issues of global discussion. However, Brazilian Catholic views on tradition, family life and notions of womanhood prevented the legalisation of abortion, which is still a crime in Brazil (unless in cases of rape and of health risks to the mother).

The third feminist wave ("resistance feminism") raises awareness to intersectional axes of inequality, and the condition of women of African descent and lower socio-economic backgrounds in Brazil (Duarte, 2019). During Brazil's military dictatorship (1964–1985) women's movements articulated against oppression and censorship, in the fight for re-democratisation and amnesty laws. Therezinha Zerbinie, a lawyer, founded the Feminine Movement for Amnesty, uniting mothers and wives whose children or husbands had been exiled or arrested by the regime (Duarte, 2019).

During the "years of lead" there is the emergence of Brazil's Black Movement, with Gonzalez, breaking down Brazil's myth of "racial democracy" (Gonzalez, 1984). She brings to the fore of Brazil's feminism the symbolic violence towards women of colour, and the layers of inequality suffered for her "Africaness" and blackness, and for being a woman.

In the 1970s Brazil's social resistance feminist movement joined forces with other liberation movements, such as the rights of African Brazilians and homosexuals (Costa, 2005). The social resistance feminism thus spread out throughout Brazilian society, raising awareness to issues associated with childcare, housework, reproduction, sexuality and violence towards women (Costa, 2005).

Brazil's most recent feminist wave is technological feminism, regarded as a fourth wave of feminism.[4] In this new feminist movement social networks

---

4 Brazilian women's from the margins political and social expression through *Funk* music is seen in the literature are a potential avenue for women's empowerment in Brazil (Mazer, 2019). There are Brazilian women MCs using *Funk* as a platform in the fight for social justice and to denounce Brazilian women of colour' lived experiences of exclusion, and the daily challenges of women living in Brazil favelas (*shanty towns*). However, what is classified as *Funk Putaria* (*Funk of Whores*) is increasingly becoming popular. Coutinho (2021) view's it as a potential pathway for women's empowerment in Brazil. These women advocate the right of sexual promiscuity, and "my body my rules, and can do what I please," emerging as a response to Brazilian women of colour's institutional oppression, marginalisation and sexism. *Funk Putaria,* nonetheless, is a movement from the margins and highly criticised by most women

and digital activism play a central role in the fight against sexual harassment, violence against women and femicide, freedom of choice and the female body (Rodriguez, 2022). Digital networks create platforms for dialogue and awareness raising, as well as organising political protests. For example, digital platforms helped in 2018 millions of women to take streets in Brazil with the hashtag "NotHim" (Ele*Não*). This hashtag emerged as a response to then presidential hopeful Jair Messias Bolsonaro running for office – a former army officer well-known for his misogynist remarks and support of torture (O'Doherty, 2018).

Women throughout Brazil joined the ForaBolsonaro movement supporting the Impeachment of President Bolsonaro after 2020's anti-democratic demonstrations, with presidential attacks against Brazil's institutions and the Supreme Court (Bellieni Zimmermann, 2020). In 2021 on the Nacional Day for Women's Mobilisation, Brazilian women organised national protests under the hashtag "BolsonaroNeverAgain" (Ohana, 2022). These protests had the support of CUT (Central Única dos Trabalhadores) and CNTE (Confederação Nacional dos Trabalhadores em Educação), protesting high costs of living, Brazil's economic crisis, and opposing President Bolsonaro's 2022 re-election bid.

Although there are several feminist waves and movements supporting women's empowerment, in Brazil there is strong social resistance towards radical feminism. There is strong stigmatisation attached to the word "feminist," with Brazilians associating it with women who lack femininity (Rago, 2001). For instance, in Brazil, feminists such as Betty Friedan have been characterised (and systemically ridiculed) as individuals lacking sexuality and as "embittered women," in stark contrast to their lived experiences (Rago, 2001). Stereotypical views disseminated by Oswaldo Cruz, which regarded suffragettes as being "scary," as well as the left leaning *Pasquim* tabloid in the 1970's labelling of feminists as "ugly, unhappy, and sexually rejected," are predominant in Brazilian society (Rago, 2001, p.59). Men and women alike continue reproducing these pejorative views of feminists in Brazil today. The feminist cause "betrays" cultural values associated with tradition, family life and

---

in Brazil. According to field work notes, most Brazilian women taking part in this survey were highly critical of *Funk Putaria* as an expression of women's empowerment in Brazil. They regard *Funk Putaria* as doing "what men want" and "actually compromising women's rights," as well as something "shameful." Although a movement within Brazil's marginalised communities and within women of colour living in the outskirts of Brazil's city centres, some white middle-class women are joining this movement. This demonstrates how hybridised, lawyered, and diverse are women's lived experiences of gender in Brazil, and a manifestation of "power resistance" against structural gender power relations consolidated through the honour code.

women's domesticity. Brazil's "well-behaved" women's movement reconciles honour consciousness with traditional views of the family. These notions of womanhood are reconciled with women's agency, the fight to end violence against women, women's rights, political participation, and equal access to paid employment.

Although there is women's empowerment in Brazil as demonstrated through women's movements, honour consciousness continues to reproduce gender power relations. And even within those movements, women still make compromises with regard to those institutional and social norms privileging men. Gender power relations can be demonstrated through Brazilian women's "extreme" and "moderate" notions of honour consciousness. In "extreme" notions of honour consciousness women resist "less" to gendered power and male hegemony. However, in "moderate" notions of honour consciousness women resist "more" to gendered power, having greater societal agency, and promoting social change.

A manifestation of Brazilian's "extreme" views of honour consciousness and traditional views of the family (within religion) is demonstrated by the high levels of violence towards women and femicides. Through epistemic disobedience lenses, the crime of femicide should be seen as form of "honour killings." "Extreme" views of honour consciousness and traditional views of the family (within religion) are predominant in rural and less industrialised areas of the country, and amongst women from a lower-socio economic background, who did not access education and who consequently have fewer opportunities in life. Such women, as well as those of African descent, are being predominantly victimised.

Since 2019, in Brazil crimes of femicide, the murder of women because they are women, have been on the rise (Forum de *Segurança Pública*, 2019). These have surpassed the total annual numbers of murders in the country, already one of the highest globally. The condition of women and girls has deteriorated further during the COVID-19 crisis, with many girls over the age of sixteen experiencing some form of violence during the pandemic (Forum de *Segurança Pública*, 2020). Through epistemic disobedience lenses, this chapter explains that the elevated numbers of femicides and cases of violence against women in Brazil should be seen as a manifestation of "extreme" notions of honour. Femicides and violence towards women in Brazil should be dealt with as honour-based violence (HBV).

Figures from the United Nations' "The Violence Map: Homicides Against Women in Brazil" (Waiselfisz, 2015) are staggering. In 2013 alone 4,762 female murders were reported to Brazilian police authorities. Of those 4,762 reported female murders, 2,394 were perpetrated by a family member or partner, comprising 50,3 per cent of all female murders reported in that year (Waiselfisz, 2015). This would translate into seven women being murdered every day by the hands of a family member or a partner. Additionally, the "Violence Map" indicates that from those 2,394 female murders, 1,583 women were killed by their partners or ex-partners, comprising 33,3 per cent of all reported female murders (Waiselfisz, 2015).

"The Violence Map" shows that the homicide rate of white females in Brazil is on the decline since 2003 (2003–2013), from 3,6 per cent to 3,2 per cent for each 100 thousand female murders, whereas the rates of black women and girls have increased from 4,5 per cent to 5,4 per cent for each 100 thousand female murders, comprising a 19,5 per cent increase in the victimisation of black women and girls (Waiselfisz, 2015). Proportionally to the Brazilian population in 2013, there were 66,7 per cent more black women and girls' murders if compared with the rates of white women's murders (Waiselfisz, 2015). Between 2003 and 2013 there was a 190,9 per cent increase in the victimisation of black women and girls. This report demonstrates how Brazilian women of African descent are hugely disadvantaged in Brazil, due to limited access to education, opportunities, and more broadly to the justice system and crime impunity more broadly, as well as to the socio-historical inequalities suffered by Brazil's African descendants (Waiselfisz, 2015).

However, when dealing with "extreme" notions of honour consciousness as manifested through female oppression, violence towards women and the killings of women are not restricted to less developed areas, or to women who did not access education, or just to those of African and coloured descent. Brazil has one of the highest rates of violence towards women in the world. According to the Wilson Centre's Brazil Institute (2021), Brazil is one of the most dangerous countries for women in the world, with the highest levels of gender-based-violence and femicides in Latin America.

Until 2021, the "honour defence" argument was invoked by defence lawyers throughout Brazil to acquit husbands who killed their wives in the name of honour. Brazil's "extreme" notions of honour consciousness and this form of "honour killings" can be traced down through this legal institute.

Between 1990 to 2016 period approximately 58 cases have argued the honour defence to acquit husbands who killed their wives (Ramos, 2012; Pimentel et al., 2006). In most cases, the popular Jury has acquitted husbands who killed their wives "in the name of honour" (Ramos, 2012; Pimentel et al., 2006), with courts of appeal reforming lower courts decisions (Ramos, 2012; Pimentel et al., 2006). Nonetheless, there were at least three cases where the court of appeal confirmed the popular Jury decision, acquitting husbands who killed their allegedly unfaithful wives (Ramos, 2012; Pimentel et al., 2006). Decisions from the state court of appeal confirming the popular Jury decision were made by the São Paulo Justice Tribunal, Acre and from the Superior Justice Tribunal (Pimentel et al., 2006), with a decision acquitting a husband for inflicting "punches" to his partner for her marital infidelity. Only in 2021 did Brazil's Supremo Tribunal Federal (STF), the High Court which deals with constitutional matters in a unanimous decision, rule the "honour defence" jurisprudence unconstitutional. Justice Dias Toffoli (cited in Jus Brazil, 2021) sustained in his decision:

> (The honour defence) is a practice that cannot be sustained in the light of the 1988 Constitution, as it protects the dignity of the human person, the prohibition of discrimination and the right to equality and life injured should not be transmitted in the course of the criminal proceedings in the pre-litigation and procedural phase under penalty of the nullity of the respective postulation act and the judgment, even if this is practised before the jury. (Translated from Portuguese)

Brazil's STF decision is welcomed, but confirm fears this jurisprudence unless deemed unconstitutional, would continue in the Brazilian legal system. In his decision, Justice Toffoli acknowledged the endemic levels of violence towards women and *femicides* in Brazil (Jus Brazil, 2021). Given the honour-violence nexus indicated by the literature, I argue that acts of gender violence towards women in Brazil are embedded in honour consciousness, and these should be re-classified as honour-based violence (HBV) for policy purposes, crime prevention and for victim support.

But why the "honour defence" argument, as well as jurisprudence, are not classified as HBV? In Brazil, these crimes are classified as crimes of "passion" (Eluf, 2021; Vargas, 2015), which I contend is a misrepresentation. Following Mignolo's (2011) epistemic disobedience perspective, Eurocentric knowledge and ways of knowing have dominated the international debate regarding honour-based violence (HBV), and have also taken into account stereotypical approaches attributing such crimes as prevalent in non-European and non-white countries in South Asia and the Muslim world.[5] Thus, Brazil's "honour

---

5 Violence against women in Latin America is classified by the United Nations as "crimes of passion," not as honour crimes (Welchman and Hossain, 2005). The UN's CEDAW General Recommendation No 19, Violence against Women (1992) and several other documents frame "traditional attitudes" to women leading to violence and oppression through Eurocentric lenses. Other UN's documents of relevance are Special Rapporteur on Extrajudicial, Summary and Arbitrary Executions (UN document E/CN 4/2000/3, 25 January 2000, paragraph 79), Mission to Afghanistan (UN document E/CN.4/2003/3/Add.4, 3 Feb. 2003, paragraph.

defence" argument, and jurisprudence gives leeway to acts of violence towards women embedded in Brazil's honour consciousness.

Violence, and the killings of women in Brazil "in the name of honour" should be regarded as HBV. In a Kafkaesque way the literature discussing honour cultures includes the Mediterranean and South American societies as honour-based cultures, and yet, is reluctant to classify crimes in the defence of honour in these regions as HBV. I argue that this is the by-product of European influence in the international system, as well as United Nations international guidelines of HBV, reproducing Eurocentric knowledge and ways of knowing. This can be seen as a misrepresentation, which then affects crime prevention plans and strategies to deal with victims or potential perpetrators of HBV in Brazil and Latin America. Honour consciousness and the effects of honour on lived experiences of gender should be seen as key variables contributing to the honour-violence nexus. And as such, understanding honour consciousness is the way forward to diminish Brazil's skyrocketing levels of gender-based violence, violence towards women and girls, and the killings of women (femicides).

On the other hand, "moderate" notions of honour consciousness and traditional views of the family (within religion) are predominantly manifested within Brazilian Christian women with "moderate" views of Christianity. These are usually women who profess to be "nominal" Christians, from middle and upper-class, living in highly industrialised areas, or in Brazilian "megalopolis," and who have had access to education. Brazilian women holding "moderate" notions of honour consciousness enjoy high levels of agency, political participation and activism. They predominantly reconcile Catholic views on the family and traditional notions of womanhood with women's rights, the right to have paid employment, and the fight against violence against women and Brazil's high levels of femicides.

In contemporary Brazil, there was a significant advancement in the legislation protecting the rights of women and girls. Since the 1970s women's transnational groups have been active in the international arena, advocating social change and equal rights for women and girls in Brazilian society (Matos & Simões, 2017). The Brazilian "lipstick lobby" was a strong influence before the United Nations raising awareness of the condition of women in Brazilian society. Consequently, the 1988 Constitution enshrines equality between men and women: and the universal protection of the rights of women

---

42), Report of the UN Special Rapporteur on violence against women, its causes and consequences (UN document E/CN.4/2002/83, 31 Jan. 2002, paragraph 21), cited in Welchman & Hossain, 2005.

(Constituição Brasileira, 1988). However, only in 2005 was adultery no longer a criminal offence under Brazilian Law (Lei no 11.106, 2005; Pimentel et al., 2006).

Other legislative achievements include the 2006 Maria da Penha Law, vanguard legislation protecting women from gender-based violence, and domestic violence. Yet, despite the advancement of formal rights of women, the "honour defence" Jurisprudence, until recently, was still a legal loophole used by defence teams in Brazil.

As explained by Alvarez (1990, p.54):

> The feminist movement, despite being part of the broader women's movement, stands out for defending women's gender interests, for questioning the cultural and political systems constructed from the gender roles historically assigned to women, by the definition of its autonomy in relation to other movements, organizations and the State, and by the organizational principle of horizontality, that is, the non-existence of hierarchical decision-making spheres.

In Brazil, the "broader" women's movement is manifested predominantly in a "well-behaved" feminism (Costa, 2005), reconciling Catholic tradition and family life with notions of womanhood with women's activism, political participation, and representation.

In 2022 approximately eight million women took the streets in the fight against violence towards women and in support of the "OutBolsonaro" (ForaBolsonaro) movement. As a counterpoint, conservative right leaning women launched the hashtag "WomenWhoSupportBolsonaro" (MulhersQueApoiamBolsonaro), manifested in ultra-conservative protests throughout the country. In 2018 the hashtag "WomenForBolsonaro," (*MulhersComBolsonaro*) had over 440 thousand followers (Época, 2018). As can be seen, Brazilian women's fight for rights and participation in the political arena, and political representation is hybridised, and is manifested within Brazil's left-leaning and ultra-conservative groups.

Ultra-conservative and right leaning women's movements in Brazil predominantly reconcile the fight for women's rights, and having a voice in the public arena, within the boundaries of traditional, family, and religion, and traditional notions of womanhood. However, they are not "new political actors" in Brazil's public arena. In March 1964 women joined the "March for Liberty and for the Family" (Bellieni Zimmermann, 2018). This ultra-conservative protest was organised by leaders of the Catholic Church who supported military intervention in order to prevent a communist uprising. In these protests they emphasised the following claims: 1) for women's traditional role as wife and mother within the family, 2) the practice of Christian life, 3) the democratic order and 4) the protection of the constitution.

Today Brazil's female representation in the lower house is composed pre-dominantly of Bolsonaro supporters aligned with ultra-conservative forces (Teofilo, 2021). These Brazilian female politicians reconcile women's rights of having a voice, agency, political participation and representation with the tra-ditional Catholic views of family life and traditional notions of womanhood.

As can be seen, Brazilian women can enjoy high levels of agency, have a voice, access to paid work, engage in political activism, political participation, as well as being represented in parliament, and join in the fight against vio-lence towards women, and the killings of women. However, women, predomi-nantly conservative Brazilian women, reconcile traditional views on the family and notions of womanhood with political activism and agency. Although they "resist" gendered oppression through political agency, they also consolidate male privileges through their support towards traditional gender roles.

Brazilian women's lived experiences of honour consciousness and tradi-tional views of the family (within religion) are hybridised and oscillate between "extreme" to "moderate." Evangelical women in Brazil, for instance, enjoy high levels of agency and political participation, but might uphold some notions of honour consciousness and traditional views of the family (within religion) which could be classified as "extreme." For instance, they support notions of womanhood which encompass female submission towards male "headship," and traditional gender roles within the family. In the subsequent chapter I explore how Brazilian women's honour consciousness and gender power rela-tions are transmitted to Australia.

Brazilian Women's Honour Consciousness and Lived Experiences of Gender in Australia

Historically, Brazil experienced several incoming migration flows, but over the last three decades the flow has been reversed. Rocha (2014) explains that the leading causes behind Brazil's migration trend were the socio-economic crisis of the 1980s and 1990s, pronounced social inequality, rising crime rates and widespread violence. These are the factors triggering a substantial Brazilian diaspora worldwide. It is claimed in the 2000 census of foreign consulates, conducted by the Brazilian Ministry of Foreign Affairs, that approximately 1.5 million Brazilians had left the country in the previous two decades (Rocha, 2014). However, as stated by Brazil's Foreign Ministry in the 2019 census, the number of Brazilians living overseas has dropped from 3 million in 2008 to approximately 2.5 million today. It is argued that since the global financial crisis there is an increasing trend towards Brazilian migrants returning to Brazil, as developed nations introduced tighter migration policies thus making it increasingly difficult for Brazilians to migrate permanently (Brazil's Foreign Ministry, cited in Rocha, 2014).

According to the 2010 Brazilian census, the majority of Brazilians living overseas are women, accounting for 53.8 percent of citizens living overseas, whereas men's rates are approximately 46.1 percent (Brazilian Census, 2010). The majority of Brazilians living overseas are between 15–59 years old (94,3 percent); with Brazilian's aged between 20–34 years old accounting for 60 percent of nationals living outside the country. Women are the highest rates in all age groups. Brazil's Institute of Statistics (IBGE) argues that an individual searches for employment (without an extended family) is the leading cause for Brazilian's dislocation overseas.

Following Brazil's 2010 Census numbers, the leading destinations of Brazilians residing overseas are: 1) The United States (23.8 percent); 2) Portugal (13.4 percent); 3) Spain (9.4 percent); 4) Japan (7.4 percent); 5) Italy and 6) England, representing 70 percent of the total number of Brazilian migrants abroad. These are countries with a socio-cultural bonds with Brazil, due to Brazil's past European migrant intakes. Thus, the ten leading European destinations for Brazilians residing abroad (Portugal, Spain, Italy, England, France, Germany, Switzerland, Ireland, Belgium, and Netherlands) account for

© FLAVIA BELLIENI ZIMMERMANN, 2025 | DOI:10.1163/9789004711242_004

49 percent of total numbers; more than half of all Brazilians are in the United States, a well-known and geographically convenient migrant destination for Brazilian nationals. Most Brazilian overseas migrants come from the Southeast region[1] (49 percent), with 21.6 percent of migrants originally from São Paulo, 16.8 percent from Minas Gerais and 7.1 percent originally from Rio de Janeiro. Other regions such as the South of Brazil account for 17.7 percent; Northeast 15 percent; Northwest 12 percent and Northern Brazil with approximately 6.9 percent respectively.

Brazilian migrant flow to Australia has been a constant phenomenon over the last 40 years. Arguably, there are two defining waves of Brazilian migration to Australia. The first wave of Brazil born individuals started arriving in Australia during the late 1960's and early 1970's, under the Australian Government's assisted migration program from 1960 to 1970 (Fraguas, 2014).

The figure below indicates a progressive increase in the numbers of Brazilians in Australia since the 1970's:

The exact number of these arrivals until the 1966 census were subsumed in the general category of individuals from South American ancestry with a total

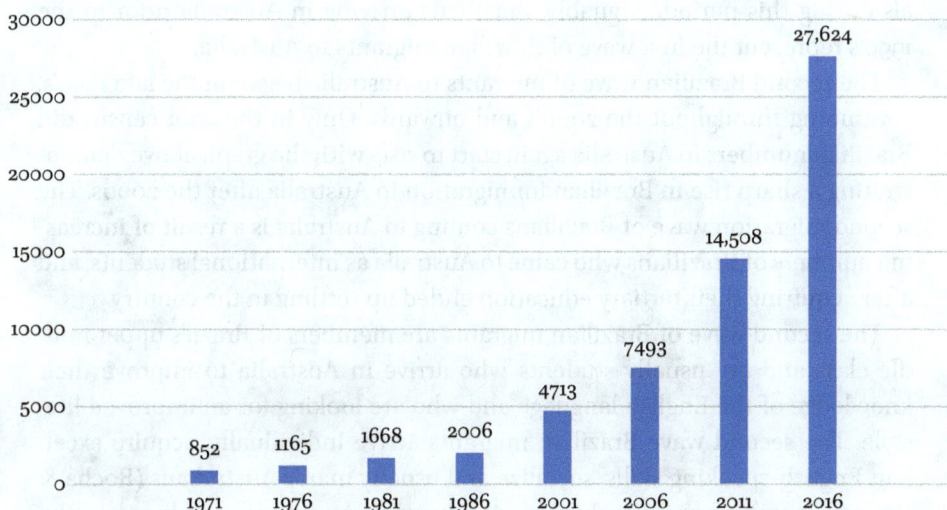

FIGURE 2.1 Number of Brazilians in Australia since 1970's

1 Southeast with high population numbers, in highly industrialised cosmopolitan city centres called "megalopolis." Examples of "megalopolis" are the city of São Paulo and Rio de Janeiro, see chapter 2 p. 36.

of approximately 1,049 individuals. Brazilian numbers were not mentioned as a specific category and no official numbers were recorded. Only in the 1971 census was Brazil mentioned as a specific overseas place of birth, with an estimate of 852 Brazilian born individuals living in Australia. Since the 1971 census, the number of Brazilians in Australia has progressively increased. Assis (1999) argued that Brazil's economic crisis and the hyperinflation of the 1980's had driven overseas immigration numbers, with Brazilians in search of greater job opportunities and better living conditions.

The first Brazilian wave of migrants to Australia (1970–1990) was predominantly from a lower socio-economic demographic, and they migrated to Australia in much lower numbers (Rocha, 2014). In Australia, Brazilians lost their "specific category" status between the 1991 and 1996 census, returning to the "other nationalities" category or South American place of birth. As stated in the 1996 census, there were approximately 28,530 South American born individuals living in Australia. According to the graph above, in 1986 there were approximately 2,006 Brazilian born individuals living in Australia. And only in the 2001 census did Brazilians regained their specific community status. Based on data census from 1986–2001, there were approximately 2,000 more Brazilians living in Australia, indicating a sluggish growth of Brazilian born individuals during this period. Arguably, Brazilians arriving in Australia prior to the 1990's represent the first wave of Brazilian migrants to Australia.

The second Brazilian wave of migrants to Australia began in the late 1990's, continuing throughout the 2000's and onwards. Only in the 2001 census did Brazilian numbers in Australia again start to rise, with the graph above demonstrating a sharp rise in Brazilian immigration to Australia after the 2000s. The second migration wave of Brazilians coming to Australia is a result of increasing numbers of Brazilians who came to Australia as international students, and after acquiring their tertiary education ended up settling in the country.

The second wave of Brazilian migrants are members of Brazil's upper middle class and are usually students who arrive in Australia to improve their knowledge of the English language and who are looking for an improved lifestyle. The second wave Brazilian migrants arrive individually, acquire excellent English-speaking skills, socialize and usually marry Australians (Rocha & Vasquez, 2013). Consequently, there is a huge socio-cultural gap between the first and second wave of Brazilian migrants to Australia, with the community being internally fragmented between these two groups (Rocha, 2006; Rocha & Vasquez, 2013; Wulfhorst, 2011).

As indicated by census data and in the graph above, the second wave of Brazilians arrived in Australia in the late 1990's, with numbers continuously growing until the 2016 census. According to the 2016 Australian census, Brazilian migrant numbers are not of great significance if compared to other diverse groups in Australia, such as the Indian and Chinese communities. Nevertheless, when dealing with overseas born individuals in Australia, Brazilians are the second fastest growing community in Australia, with a 13.9 per cent average population growth between the 2011–2016 period (Australian census, 2016). And some argue that current numbers are underestimated due to the high influx of Brazilian international students into Australia (Rocha, 2013).

The figure below shows numbers of Brazilians today in Australia based on geographical location and gender.

According to 2016 census numbers, there are approximately 27,624 Brazilians living in Australia today. Graph figures shows that most Brazilians settled in New South Wales, with women's migration rates being higher than men's migration rates in all major Australian states and territories (Australian census, 2016). Interestingly, higher numbers of women than men reflect a global trend in Brazilian overseas migration. As stated by the 2010 Brazilian census, a

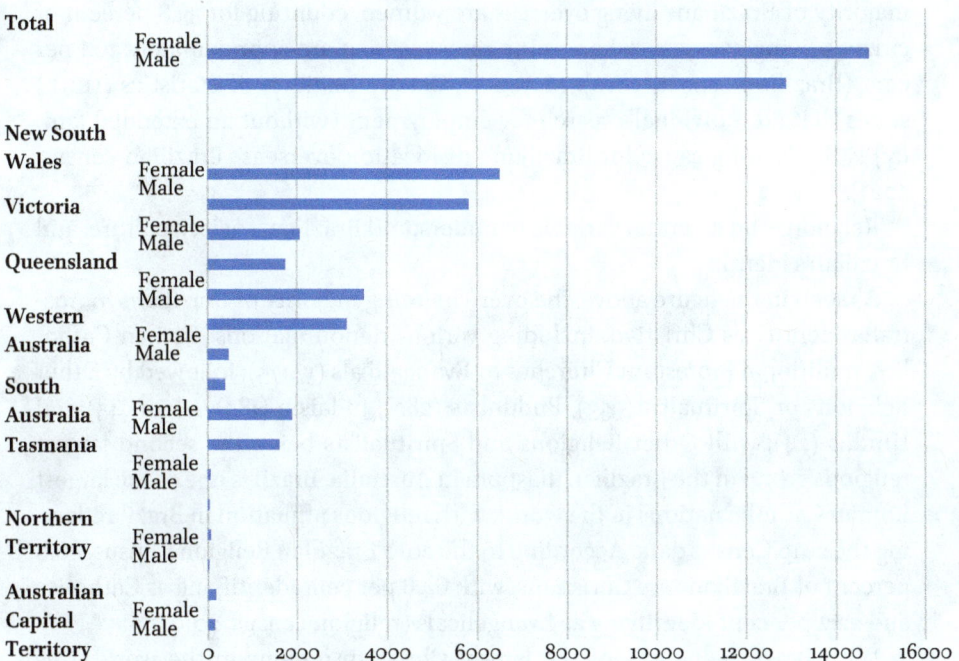

FIGURE 2.2   Brazilians in Australia by gender
SOURCE: AUSTRALIAN CENSUS, 2016

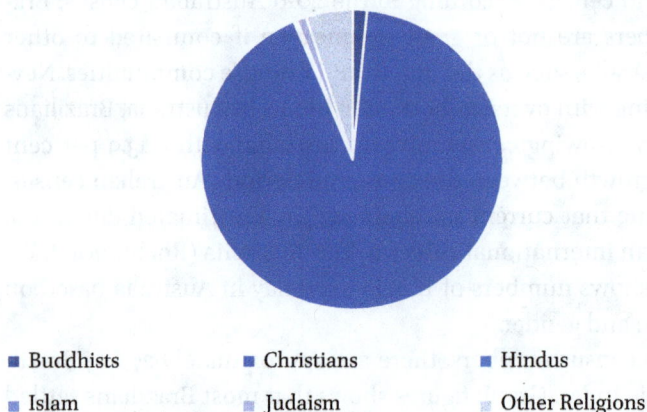

- ■ Buddhists   ■ Christians   ■ Hindus
- ■ Islam   ■ Judaism   ▫ Other Religions

FIGURE 2.3   Brazilians in Australia – religious affiliation
SOURCE: AUSTRALIAN BUREAU OF STATISTICS, CENSUS 2016

majority of Brazilians living overseas are women, counting for 53.8 percent of citizens living overseas, whereas the rates for men are approximately 46.1 per cent (Brazilian census, 2010). Moreover, Brazil's Institute of Statistics (IBGE) states that an individual's search for employment (without an extended family) is the leading cause for Brazilian's dislocation overseas (Brazilian census, 2010).

Religion is an essential variable to understand Brazilian society, culture, and Brazilian's identity.

As seen in the figure above, the overwhelming majority of Brazilians in Australia identify as Christian, including various denominations: Roman Catholics, traditional Protestant Churches or Evangelicals (17,175); followed by Other Religions or Spiritualist (933), Buddhists (282), Judaism (185), Islam (45) and Hindus (24); with Other Religions and Spiritualists being the second largest religious group in the Brazilian diaspora in Australia. Brazil is one of the largest Roman Catholic nations in the world, with religious affiliation in Brazil reflecting the 2016 Census data. According to the 2010 Brazilian Religion Census, 86.8 percent of Brazilians are Christians, with 64.6 per cent identifying as Catholics and 22.2 per cent identifying as Evangelicals (religion census, 2010).

With Brazil being one of the largest Christian nations in the world, this chapter contends that religion is an integral part of Brazilian identity. Consequently, Australian Brazilian faith demographics is an important variable for this study's sample validation.

1   Data Analysis

This section discusses the emerging themes from interviews with 15 Brazilian Christian[2] women living in Sydney, New South Wales.[3] I explain why honour consciousness and Brazil's traditional views of the family (within religion) are key variables to understand women's lived experiences of gender in Australia.

My Brazilian heritage, and being a member of the community in Perth, together with the assistance of colleagues at Western Sydney University, were instrumental to gain access to community leaders in Sydney, New South Wales. Community gate keepers established the first connection with members of the Brazilian community. After meeting each member of the community, I applied the snowballing method for participant recruitment, with samples reflecting a broad range of views within the community in Sydney. Spending time with community leaders and members of the community ("deep hanging out"[4]) gave me insight into community dynamics and leading views towards honour, religion and gender.

Participants are referred to by numbers and have been de-identified at the early stages of this research. In the figure below I include each participant's number with their culturally sensitive pseudonyms, and this is followed by charts with the participant's demographic composition:

Table 2.1 displays Brazilian participant's age and registered marital status. This figure demonstrates a wide age range of collected samples, with the majority of participants being married. Figure 2.3. shows the sample's religious affiliation in Australia. This figure shows that the overwhelming majority of samples profess the Christian faith, with most samples identifying as Catholic, followed by other Christian Protestant denominations and Evangelicals. Two samples declared to be of Other Faith or Spiritualists, reflecting contemporary

---

2   The Catholic Church's values are part of Brazilian culture and society, influencing the lives of practicing Christians, nominal Christians, and the lives of individuals involved with other faith groups such as individuals from a strong Catholic background who are spiritualists or follow Allan Kardec's "Spiritism." This religion follows the *Gospel According to Spiritism*, using some Christian concepts in the light of Kardecism (Kardec, 2010). Spiritism or Kardecism is followed by many former Catholics or even nominal Catholics in Brazil, a country well-known for its spiritual syncretism.

3   Interviews with Brazilian (Christian) women in Sydney were conducted during my visit to Western Sydney University, June–July 2019.

4   "Deep hanging out" is an ethnographic technique where you spend time with participants before or after the interviews. I explained to each interviewee that our conversations before or after the interviews would be incorporated into my field notes. For Browne & McBride (2015) this is regarded as a useful method to access politically sensitive information, and to break down any power imbalances between interviewer and interviewee

TABLE 2.1   Brazilian participant number and culturally sensitive pseudonym

Participant number	Pseudonym
Participant 1	Aurea
Participant 2	Clara
Participant 3	Alana
Participant 4	Maria Paula
Participant 5	Alice
Participant 6	Diolinda
Participant 7	Ana Gabriela
Participant 8	Marielle
Participant 9	Carina
Participant 10	Noemia
Participant 11	Viviana
Participant 12	Fiorela
Participant 13	Poliana
Participant 14	Laila
Participant 15	Olivia

Brazilian religious demographics in Brazil and Australia (census, 2016; religious census 2010).

Figure 2.6 includes the sample's level of education and occupation. This figure indicates that the majority of samples have university or tertiary education and are professional women, reflecting the second wave of Brazilian migrants to Australia (census, 2007; census 2011; census 2016). This figure demonstrates that samples represent Brazilian women from all socio-economic backgrounds and migration waves, since some respondents were students, labourers or working in community or personal services. Two respondents have family ties with the 1970's first wave of migration. Figure 2.7. lays out the sample's length of time living in Australia and their migration status. According to this graph, most participants have lived for more than 1.5 years in Australia, with the majority of samples holding Australian citizenship.

The wording used by the interviewees varied somewhat according to their generation and personal experiences. However, their lived experiences of honour and the meaning of honour is central to their sense of self, providing meaning to their interpersonal relations, familial relations and social relations in Australia. In all 15 interviews, Brazilian Christian women described honour as an essential part of their values, their sense of "what is right and wrong,"

TABLE 2.2   Brazilian participant race

Participant number	Race[a]
Participant 1	parda
Participant 2	parda
Participant 3	parda
Participant 4	white
Participant 5	white
Participant 6	white
Participant 7	white
Participant 8	parda
Participant 9	white
Participant 10	white
Participant 11	white
Participant 12	white
Participant 13	white
Participant 14	parda
Participant 15	parda

a   Participant' racial background follows Brazil's Bureau of Statistics (IBGE) classification of "pardos" (mixed race), "yellow" (Indigenous), "black" (African) and "white" (of European ancestry).

Participant Marital Status and Age

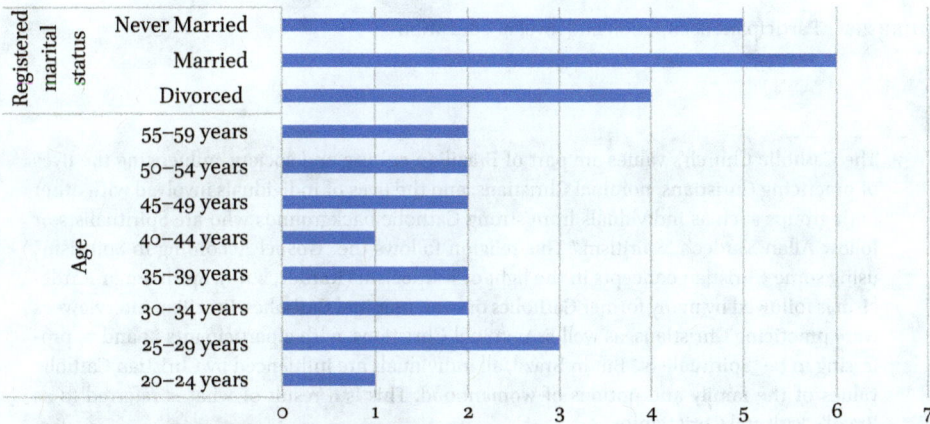

FIGURE 2.4   Participant marital status and age

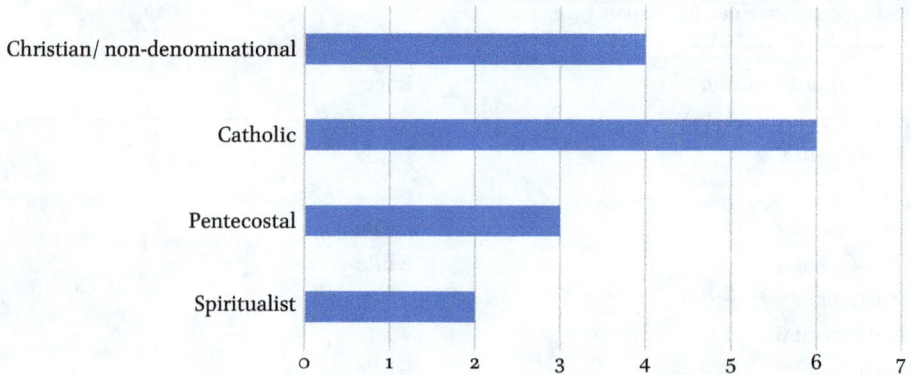

FIGURE 2.5   Participant religious affiliation[6]

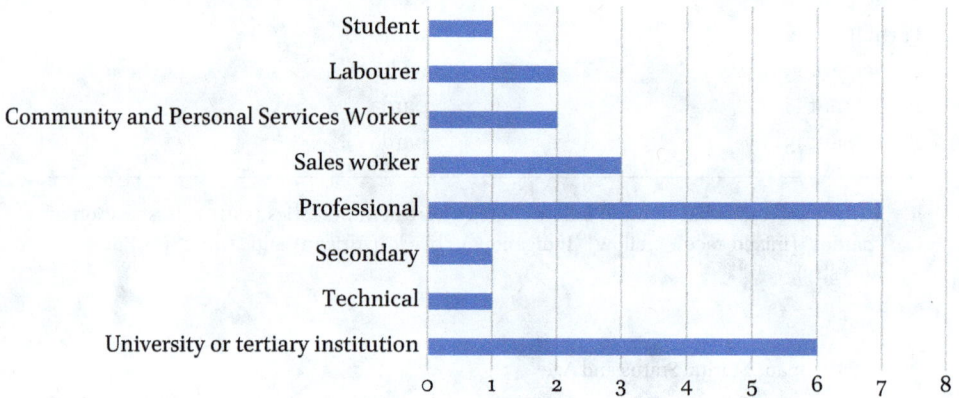

FIGURE 2.6   Participant occupation and level of education

---

5   The Catholic Church's values are part of Brazilian culture and society, influencing the lives
    of practicing Christians, nominal Christians, and the lives of individuals involved with other
    faith groups such as individuals from strong Catholic backgrounds who are Spiritualists or
    follow Allan Kardec's "Spiritism." This religion follows the "Gospel According to Spiritism",
    using some Christian concepts in the light of Kardecism (Kardec, 2010). Spiritism or Karde-
    cism is followed by many former Catholics or even nominal Catholics. Brazilian interviewees
    were practicing Christians, as well as nominal Christians, with 2 participants (4 and 7) pro-
    fessing to be "Spiritualists." But in Brazil, all individuals are influenced by Christian Catholic
    values of the family and notions of womanhood. This is a result of what is referred to as
    Brazil's "cultural Christianity."

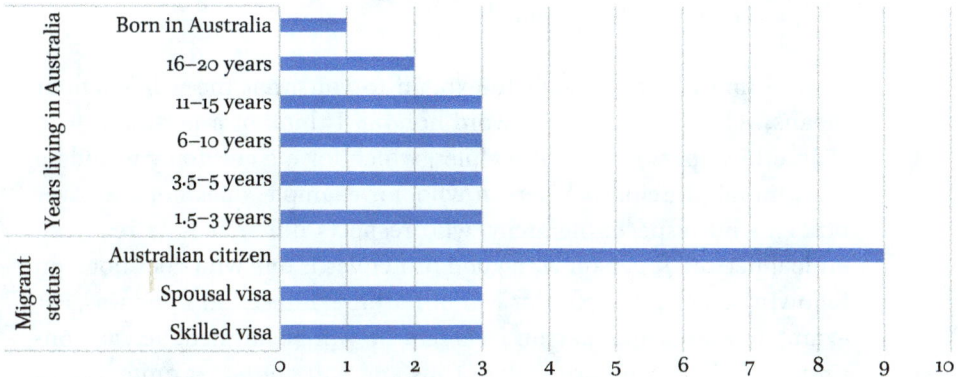

FIGURE 2.7   Participant years in Australia and migration status

with honour setting out moral standards of respect and pride within families. I explain in this chapter how the theme of honour as a "value," or a "moral value," consolidates traditional cultural views of the family (within religion, Catholicism), characterising Brazilian women's honour consciousness. This is a dominant theme in all of the interviews, providing meaning to Brazilian Christian women's lived experiences of honour.

The underlying themes in participant's conceptualisation of honour (as honour consciousness), participants may into more than one group, as follows:

Honour as a value and morality	Participants 1, 2, 4, 9, 5, 10, 11, 13, 14, 15
Honour as respect for family name, being respected in society, family pride	Participants 1, 5, 6, 7, 11, 12
Honour as respect and familial relations	Participants 3, 8, 10, 12
Honour as respect to family tradition and religion	Participants 9, 10, 11, 15

When providing a definition of honour, participants used these four sub-themes to explain the depth of honour in their lived experiences, with these sub-themes enmeshing and intersecting. These should not be seen in isolation but converging themes shaping honour as a "value" and honour consciousness in the Australian diaspora.

Participant 1 ("Aurea"), 25 years old

Look, I find it very difficult to explain to you what the word honour means. When I think of the word honour, I think of a person ... who is an ethical person, with principles, which for me culturally would be nice, moral principles. A person who, for example, does not step over others, who respects hierarchy, who respects differences, is really an ethical person. A person with good principles is one who does not stop following those principles for fear of harming himself in some way. For example: Even if that person feels that he will be harmed, he will continue to follow those principles of his and will not be corrupted, so to speak ... My mother raised me and my brothers, we were all raised to be honourable people, people who work with dignity, who work honestly to get the things they have, people who respect traffic laws, the laws of the country, people who think this is the best way for you to live. To live in a way that you don't step over others, in a way that you respect people, that you respect the laws.

Participant 2 ("Clara"), 28 years old

It depends on the context. Because for me, it is very personal. I think it depends very much on where you came from, what were the values that were given to you, then it will determine to whether it is an honour for me, or what it is not an honour for you.

Participant 3 ("Alana"), 20 years old

Honour has a lot of connotations for me, it means a lot of different things. But it's very closely tied with respect. And respect that it is due, most of the time. It is like respect that it is owed. But it also is similar to privilege. It's like it's an honour and privilege a very linked as well, in general, so when you say: Oh, it's an honour to do something for you, it's also very much a privilege to do something for you. But then they into some extent, have to be worthy of that honour, as well. So yeah, it's tied with respect and just decency and modesty of character and respect something like that... But for me, honour is like the biggest example and way of showing that you love someone is to honour them and to respect them. And it's such a big part of my family, because personally for me growing up in my family, all I ever wanted to do was to honour my parents and everything...

For me, it's not necessarily a cultural or a religious thing. It's just a personal thing for me, I've always found that I'm doing anything that my parents would approve of, and having people know about that would bring shame to my family.

Participant 4 ("Maria Paula"), 42 years old

The word honour means a concept of self-esteem, it's something of supreme importance that needs to be protected. In the sense of values, you know? It can be a moral value, then there are concepts of honour that I think are inserted in your mind while you're growing up, at school. But I believe that even if you haven't attended school, but even if no one told you that you should protect certain values. And that naturally we have protection instincts, instincts of self-preservation, things which are important for us, to maintain our integrity, your morals, your psyche, things that you cherish, so... I think this is a matter of honour. Protect the feelings, the values that are in essence important for you.

Participant 5 ("Alice"), 36 years old

For me it (honour) ... is very linked to values, honour and respect. In my opinion. And for examples, trying to have a life, trying to do things based precisely on these values. Its what I think honour is (...) Since I was a child, I was taught the values that my family has always passed unto us regarding being honest, you not harming others, respecting yourself and others. So, for us it was based on this vision.

Participant 6 ("Diolinda"), 52 years old

Look, I am from the Northeast.[6] The word honour for a Nordestino has a very strong meaning. The family thing, your name, your name your honour, right for us. So, honour for me is the meaning and you have

---

6 Brazil's Northern region is 30 per cent of the country's territory (Alves, 2016). This region had the first settlements during the colonial era, with high socio-economic contrasts between wealthy coastal areas from those living in rural areas (*sertão*), which is predominantly agricultural (Alves, 2016). Individuals born in the Northern region of Brazil are regarded as "Nordestinos," and it is a place well-known in the country for use of violence to protect individual honour ("to wash your honour with blood").

your name cleared, so to speak. People believe you; you are a credible person and have a respected name, right? People hear you. This to me is honour. The Northeast has a lot of that, the name, the family, the thing that for example: You can say everything but, your name is what you carry with you, and what you have most precious is your honour. So, you can't do anything that get in the way. For me honour is a very strong thing.

Participant 7 ("Ana Gabriela"), 50 years old

I think the first thing that comes to my mind would be pride. Yes, I think of pride. Not in the negative sense of the word but in the positive sense of the word. To be satisfied with your social position, with your status, with your identity, in short, many things... With your family, with your husband, with your children, in short, it would be a positive thing.

Participant 8 ("Marielle"), 32 years old

When I think of honour I think you're giving one as if it's prestige or respect. I will speak authority. Because for me it's more about authority. What I learned was more related to mom and dad, as a leader, or even at work. So, when I think about honouring someone, or what not, I'm a Christian, when I think about honouring someone I think about honouring God, which I believe. So, I always think, I always have this view a little bit of authority, but that's how it is in that sense.

Participant 9 ("Carina"), 35 years old

Honour for me is related to value. And I can't tell you. I think it's very personal to each one perhaps. Or according to the family, upbringing and education itself, because values are things that the agent inherits and learns. But for me it's completely linked to the values I have... It's like I still hear my parents saying. Honour is all you have. You know, like the most important thing you have to preserve, you know? And especially when we leave our house in our country and go live in another place, in my case, I came alone without a family without anyone, it was very strong, this thing is you wherever you are, preserve your honour. I think it's a strong thing culturally, I don't know if it's in my family, I don't know if it's in my city. But yes, and a strong thing.

Participant 10 ("Noemia"), 55 years old

Honour for me in relation, thinking about family, where I came from, what I learned, I see honour for me and when you deal with people, with family with people you transmit something to them, their behavior, the things you want to do, about your life or work. Something like that that relates to yourself. Like, you, as I said, with family, or involved with friends or with work. There are things you act that you don't want for yourself, you want a better relationship so you will act better. Regardless of the person not pleasing you. You have to say something about that relationship. In short: For me, honour is being good with yourself so you can achieve something with other people. [Honour] had a lot of influence on my parents, they were Catholic at the time and so I was raised within people gathering and praying in homes and that was very family oriented, a family thing at those meetings. And after a while I changed, my father became Evangelical and so is when I also got converted. That stuff filled me up more. So I think I improved more as a person, knowing more about religion, I saw that the honour between family, family and between people, is what makes you happier.

Participant 11 ("Viviana"),[7] 45 years old

Honour is a very subjective concept. But in my opinion, it would be something I'm proud of, something also somewhat related to my reputation. Quite this: a concept related to my reputation, and what others think of me, but also an intrinsic concept of mine. What I think of myself. What is important about me, what image do I want to convey and what is the concept that people have of me... Now with that question the following came to me. It is very much related to the concept of morality, the concept of honour. So, what my family told me, the word honour wasn't used a lot, I think, but the question of what you do is moral. So obviously

---

7   Although gender politics and migration are not the main focus of this research, Viviana explained that: "there is machismo and inequality in Australia too, it is just more concealed." She discussed during her interview how, once in a business meeting, an Australian man approached her to say that "Brazilian women have the best breasts." Viviana acknowledged that Australian men would never have the courage to say it to an Australian woman. She was highly offended by such remarks, as she is a businesswoman, married and dresses conservatively. This is a rare statement from interviews but demonstrates Australian discriminatory, stereotypical, and highly sexualized views towards Brazilian women associated with easy sex, promiscuity and Carnival.

you don't do what is immoral. And I was raised in a very Catholic environment like most Brazilians are very Catholic so there was a lot of this about how you carry yourself, how you dress, how you talk, why all this has this aspect of morality and honour, how are you perceived by society? It even questions a little, not how society perceives you, but how you behave regardless of what they think. Because the concept may be amoral for the other person, but for you it is perfectly within morality. So, to answer your question, yes, I was raised in a very Catholic family so this concept of moral honour was a very important concept.

Participant 12 ("Fiorela"), 28 years old

The word honour means respect. Something that is connected to personal relationships, what you have with someone. You honour your word; you honour what you do within your dignity. Yes, it was very important. The honour in my upbringing, in the relationship I had with my mother and my aunt. We always tried to make a relationship of great respect and honour, always fulfilling what we promise.

Participant 13 ("Poliana"), 45 years old

Stay true to your principles, what you believe, what you think is right and act that way towards other people and everything that happens around you... I learned more from my mother. Honour? The education part, my mother always said everything. My dad was a present person, but he was more about working and disciplining, helping my mom discipline when kids got out of line or did wrong things than having those conversations. Guidance has always been by my mother.

Participant 14 ("Laila"), 34 years old

Honour is living according to what you believe is right and what makes you happy, what keeps you on the right path, what brings you peace. Peace of mind, and that's it. And anything that hurts that feeling breaks your honour and your dignity. Within my family it wasn't something that was talked about much. Today as I am a grown adult, I can have a more critical view of how I was raised. I can't judge too much because my parents were very young when I was born. So, they weren't even formed that way, they didn't have a mature adult head.

Participant 15 ("Olivia"), 50 year old

Honour for me is difficult to explain in words. I feel that honour is something you revere. It is a set of attitudes that you need to have that will
determine, and a set of actions based on your behavior that will call you
someone correct, someone who has principles, someone who recognizes
something greater, for example, has a religion or respects a greater force
...Honour is much bigger than you, that's why you need to take care of
your attitudes. You turn around, in fact, you must have a standard that
leads you to good actions, good attitudes that lead you to be recognized
as an honourable person.

According to Brazilian Christian[8] women's views, honour as a "value," and a
moral compass, shapes Brazilian Christian women's honour consciousness,
providing the cultural lenses through which they understand the social world.
In some definitions of honour, Brazilian Christian women explained that honour consciousness and traditional values of the family, taught by religion, are
key elements of their value system. For Brazilian Christian women, honour
consciousness and traditional views of the family (within religion) are intertwined, and key to understand their lived experiences, and their notions of
womanhood. This is manifested even in the lived experiences of Brazilian
women who are not "church goers," practicing Christians or who follow other
religions such as *Spiritualists* and *Kardecists*. For Brazilian interviewees, their
lived experiences of honour consciousness are predominantly reconciled with
traditional views of womanhood, with women's rights and with female emancipation in the political sphere. According to their lived experiences, honour
consciousness and traditional family values (within religion) are transmitted
through their parent's values, views and moral values, as well as through the
values of their extended family – thus this is a consciousness which travels
down through the generations.

  Family life plays a central role in Brazilian women's lived experiences of
honour consciousness and traditional views of the family (within religion).
Honour consciousness as "a value" is internalised in their ways of thinking, as a

---

8 I include "Christian" in the sample group interviewed in this survey since Christianity and
   Christian values are an integral part of Brazilian culture. As explained before, some women
   taking part in this research were not practicing Christians. From the 15 participants, only
   samples 3, 8, 10 and 15 were "church goers." However, participants agreed that the values of
   the church influence even non-Christians. This is a result to what is referred to as Brazil's
   "cultural Christianity."

result of their family upbringing ("the way I was raised" or "the way my mother raised me") and shapes their lives, based on their parent's values ("what my family taught me" or "what my parents passed unto me"). These themes were explored in depth by several participants.[9] Although not a key theme, two participants[10] mentioned how to be "white" brought family honour in Brazil. For instance, Clara is *mulata* and was brought up to believe she was white.[11] She only had freedom to assume her "blackness" in Australia. Ana Gabriela mentioned in her interview how her father saw as something honourable to be of Italian descent.

Most participants agreed, and discussed at some point in their interviews, that honour consciousness and traditional views of the family (within religion) is not always experienced in the same way in Brazil. Participants agreed that there are "different" notions of honour, which can be shaped by the family's views, by the region where they come from, and influenced by how religious their families are. In all interviews participants agreed that each person has their own notions of honour, describing it as is something very "personal" or "subjective". Although there is a degree of subjectivity in individual notions of honour, some participants discussed in detail how honour consciousness and traditional views of the family can be experienced in what I classify an "extreme way." Women taking part in this research explained that their own notions of honour were different from "other notions", classified as "extreme" notions of honour.

The Brazilian Christian women interviewed predominantly held "moderate" notions of honour. "Moderate" notions of honour are manifested as follows: 1) Through reconciling traditional notions of womanhood (within Catholicism and Christianity) with women's agency, 2) Support towards women's rights, 3) Women's political emancipation, 4) Women's empowerment in political leadership, 5) Women's right to work, and 6) Protection against domestic violence and inter-partner violence. Conversely, extreme notions of honour consciousness are manifested as follows: 1) Through women's subjection (through strict views of religion, or traditional cultural views of female submission classified,

---

9   See Appendix, figure 2.
10   Participants 2 ("Clara") and 7 ("Ana Gabriela").
11   Clara's father was a black *Baiano* (an individual who is born in Baia, Northern Brazil) and her mother is of German descent. Her mother and the extended family were proud of their European ancestry – something which in Brazil increases family honour. Growing up, Clara had her hair straightened and was raised as a "white kid". Once she asked her mother if she was black (since her father is black). Her mother answered: "Are you crazy? Since when you ara black?"

or not, as "machismo"),[12] 2) Suppression of women's rights, 3) Absence of women's political participation and having a voice in the political sphere, 4) Absence of women's political leadership, 5) Women's lack of rights in the workplace (control by their husbands), or no rights to pursuit paid work outside the home, and 6) Domestic violence (in the name of honour) and femicides (a form of honour killings).

I will discuss women's stories illustrating the central role played by the family in shaping "different" notions of honour, and how the family's values are essential in shaping honour consciousness and traditional views of the family (within religion) as either "extreme" or "moderate" views of women's honour consciousness.

Another important theme emerging from honour as a "value" is that it is something which is taught or learned and is associated with your upbringing. Participants explained there are "other notions" of honour consciousness than their own (since honour consciousness is "subjective" and "personal"). They distanced themselves, "othering" these notions of honour which are different from their own. The "othering," and the differences between their lived experiences of honour from what I classify "extreme" notions of honour, were elaborated by most participants.[13] All the Brazilian women interviewed distanced themselves from religious views within Catholicism and Evangelical churches which preached on female subjection, and lack of agency. Brazilian Christian women interviewed for this study regarded "extreme" notions of honour as "the other." In their stories, they associated the manifestation of "extreme" notions with the Northeast of Brazil or with small regional cities, explaining that such views are less common in big city centres. Only few participants associated "extreme" notions of honour with a lack of formal education.[14] Brazilian women were predominantly critical of traditional views of the family which can lead to female suppression, as well as of those views within Catholicism and Evangelical churches which are "too strict," leading to "extreme" notions of honour, manifested through female suppression, and even violence towards women.

Laila, who comes from the Northeast of Brazil, explains she was raised by her parents to study and to be independent, to "don't depend on men." She sees

---

12   Machismo is a tradional form of hypermasculinity which focuses on male dominance. In *Machista* views of gender, men are expected to be strong whereas women should submit to their will. Men should also exert control and authority over all family members, be responsible for all decision-making as the sole breadwinners, and the defenders of the honour of the family, *in* Dengah et al.(2024).

13   See Appendix, figure 2.

14   See Appendix, figure 2.

honour as something you believe is right and "keeps you on the right path." She explained how her mother was a strong woman and worked, but was half *Amelia* (nickname to Brazilian women who accept anything from men). With critical lenses, Laila reflects upon the contradiction between the values taught to her by her parents, and her mother's subjection to her father's behaviour (arriving home drunk and going out with other women), as well as her mother's sole responsibility for looking after the home and children. She made the distinction between the abuse suffered by her mother and "other" forms of abuse such as physical violence, arguing the abuse was related to emotional and psychological abuse. Furthermore, she questions her mother's submission to her father's bad behaviour, and the Northeast notions of honour leading to female subjection, and acknowledges it had a negative impact on her previous choice of partners. In her words:

> Within my family, then, I was raised with both of them saying: go study so you don't depend on a man to be independent. But at the same time, seeing my mother being half Amelia, even though she was an independent and strong woman who subjugated herself to maintain a relationship... The division of household chores. I think the male role in a family in the Northeast of Brazil is very comfortable. Of course, there is the issue of providing, of providing food, a house...But there is no division of household chores. Nowadays everyone has to work, even because the cost of living is very high anywhere, both of them have to be providers... But I saw that my mother had a triple working day. She had to take care of the house, be a good housewife, she had to stay connected with the children, and the children's needs, both school and emotional and health. So, I saw that the biggest burden was on the mother's back and not so much on the father's.

Laila continues by explaining how the notions of honour learned at home have impacted her life, and how notions of honour in the Northeast contribute to "other" extreme notions of honour, leading to female subjection and acceptance of spousal abuse:

> (My notions of honour) have been influenced accepting abusive relationships. So not being aware that that relationship was being abusive. It's a society that kind of raises women to accept any behavior from a man, not just any, not physical aggression, but going out without talking, drinking and hanging out with other women and you'll be the last to know. Society in the Northeast, in general, is kind of growing with this culture and

it's not just there within families but listening to pejorative music that demeans women.

In Alice's story, she explains how notions of honour consciousness are values which are "taught" by the family. Although raised in one of Brazil's big cities, she had extended family originally coming from Brazil's Northeastern region. Alice explains how she was taught that honour is about not harming others and doing what is good, so it is something she sees as "positive." However, she acknowledges that what is honour for her might not be for the "other." With critical lenses, Alice distances herself and her lived experience of honour from "other" notions of honour which can "harm people". She also explains how there are "other" notions of honour in the Northeast of Brazil, where men use honour to justify their masculinity, for example as manifested through the rejection of a homosexual son, as well as killing in the name of honour. In her words:

> Since I was a child, I was taught the values that my family has always passed unto us regarding being honest, you not harming others, respecting yourself and others. So for us it was based on this vision... Usually [honour] I take it on the positive side and as soon as I learn...but depending on the consequences depending on what people do...it's quite complex. Because what is honour for me may not be for the other and suddenly the other is basing his attitudes on that and that is something that is not well seen by society or ourselves, so... Well (honour) can be used in a different way, in a negative form if the person has a perception of honour that only favors himself and but will harm someone else. Regions of the Northeast of Brazil where I have family, they use the question of honour to justify masculinity, in some ways. I can do this because I'm a man and for me it's a matter of honour, for example, not having a homosexual child, things like that. I saw this a lot, this culture of these regions. I don't believe it's still very common in big cities, and more common in the countryside I would say. And killing for honour too. For honouring the family. So, let's assume: Some case that you have a homosexual child and that you killed for honour, or if there was a situation where your daughter got pregnant. So, some people end up committing a crime because of that, honour. The family name was stained, for example, with this situation. So, it has this negative connotation.

Diolinda reflects upon honour consciousness in Brazil and "other" views of honour, religion, and traditional views of the family. In her words:

I think that honour in Brazil is more linked to the issue of the family, of honesty, the family they feel as if you have a responsibility for the name, you carry and with respect to honesty... But because of the question of religion (Evangelical Christians) for example: In the past he (ex-partner) was a person and said this and that. And then because of religion and politics (to support Bolsonaro), then the discourse now is different, understand? For the good morals and manners... I think it has a relationship with honour and religion, yes. Why before everything was all very beautiful, all very modern, all very open. Then he becomes Christian (Evangelical), then no. Out of a sudden everything is not so beautiful anymore, it is not so open anymore. Family first ... homosexuality (is forbidden) you know, is everything wrong? And before the vision was different, so in my head, it's confusing, I don't understand.

Diolinda was raised in the Northeast of Brazil, and her notions of honour consciousness learned from her parents are associated with the family name, good reputation and honesty. She distances herself from "other notions" (what I classify "extreme") of honour, traditional views of the family and religion. She is a nominal Catholic and distances herself from the notions of honour consciousness and traditional views of the family (within religion). She also rejects the values espoused by her ex-partner (the father of her daughter), who lives in Brazil, since he converted to Evangelical Christianity; he is also a supporter of far-right Brazilian President Jair Bolsonaro. She explains that before he became an Evangelical Christian he was accepting of differences, everything was "modern" and "open." She analyses critically the effects of Pentecostalism (and Brazil's Christian fundamentalism), as well as his support of Brazil's far right. She explains how for him now "everything is ugly and wrong" (behaviours not following traditional views on the family and religion), and that he is intolerant towards homosexuality (although one of his sons is homosexual). She finds it confusing how after his conversion to Pentecostalism his views drastically changed. But for her and her daughter, his strict religious views and his connection with Brazil's fa right are an embarrassment, bringing "shame" to their family name.

Clara explains "other" notions of honour leading to violence towards women, particularly the killing of women in the name of honour.

> But sometimes, other people's notions of honour terrify me. For example, in Brazil until recently, it was allowed for husbands to kill their wives in the name of honour. That was the honour defence. So, for me, which sort of honour that allows you to kill. So, this is my response.

Clara continues:

> Well, because my argument is based in what is saw in Brazilian newspaper headlines. Particularly in the 1990s and early 2000s because these days it sounds a little bit absurd, 15 years ago it was not. And it was extremely common to see it. Husband kills wife in jealousy rampage. Then the newspaper article was fully based on everything that woman did that was bad. They spent two paragraphs just describing and explaining everything bad she has ever done. In all that people used to say about her, then to spend at the end of the paragraph only two lines to describe that the husband, giving his full name, and that he was caught for killing his wife, then they [the newspaper] provide her full name too. And then this is it. It is like the guy goes murder his wife, then they spend the whole time explaining that she had one affair and that she had the second affair, that the neighbours said that she didn't look well after the children. For in the end to mention that then he killed her. It is like it is justified what he did.

Clara was raised in a Christian home where she was the only child of a white Brazilian mother with a black Brazilian father. She reflected critically on her upbringing: her mother was proud of her European heritage and raised Clara to believe she was not black, since past whitening practices see being black as something not to be proud of in Brazil. In her view, however, she was raised as a "tom boy" by her father, since she was big and strong, helping him out to lay bricks and cement on construction sites. Although raised to be independent, she inherited the honour code to dress modestly, to be pure, to be well behaved in public, and to be hard working and to study well. She acknowledges "other" "extreme" notions of honour which are, in her words, "well-known" in Brazil's media between the 1990s and 2000s dealing with the killings of women in the name of honour. Clara was critical of how media outlets would side with the men who killed their wives because they were having affairs. She finds "terrifying" that there are notions of honour ("extreme notions") leading to the killings of women to protect men's honour.

For Maria Paula honour is something of "extreme importance" which is protected through the use of violence. She tells her story:

> We went upstairs and there was a big table, and there were about in twelve chairs and girls were only me and my friend, all the rest of boys. It was just a coincidence. Not something that I was premeditating or had planned to do. And the other girls had not arrived yet. And about

one hour and a half after we arrived, then my dad arrived at the pizzeria unannounced. As a matter of fact, he let me go to this pizza party. But then he followed me to see what I was up to. He just turned up there. I remember him going upstairs and arriving there out of the blue. He looked at me when he arrived. And he said in front of everyone: Where are they are the girls, because here there is just man! Then he got me by the hair in front of everyone and dragged me out of the pizza place. He pulled me into the car and drove me back home. When I arrived at home, he slapped me across the face, accused me of having plotted to be in that party surrounded by boys, that I already knew that there would only have men in the party. When I was only a child! I was 11 or perhaps 12 years old, imagine...I was only a child.

According to Maria Paula, honour is a moral compass which she views as predominantly "positive," however she acknowledges it can be "manipulated" when used to justify "extreme" views of honour leading to violence, parental control and even femicides (the killings of women). She critically examined her upbringing, and how her father was very controlling and would not allow her to be around "just boys." In his view this would give her a bad reputation and tarnish his and the family honour.

For Maria Paula's father, who was not a Christian, Brazil's traditional views on the family and honour had to be protected and she should behave in a way to preserve the family honour. Although she sees her father's control critically, mentioning "she lived in a prison," and that she didn't "understand what his honour was all about" since she would do nothing wrong, nonetheless her perception was that she was not constantly under the threat of violence. She saw the pizzeria episode as "an isolated" situation. Maria Paula recalled that she only had to live within the parameters set at home, that her father was not inherently a violent man, and she didn't live in "constant fear." She explained, however, that in Brazil, "femicides are justified in honour, by men." In her view, it is absurd that someone can justify acts of violence and the killings of women to protect your honour.

When sitting down and talking to Brazilian Christian women in Sydney other key sub-themes emerged: The relationship between honour consciousness and Brazil's traditional views on the family (within religion), how it enforces the honour code, how it shapes individual behaviour, and how honour consciousness impacts the lives of women in Brazil, shaping gender politics in the country.

Traditional views of the family are an inherent part of Brazil's culture, transmitted through centuries of Catholic Portuguese colonisation. Until Brazil's Republic in 1889 the Catholic Church was the official church of the state (Holanda, 2007). Brazil is still a country influenced by Catholic values and Christian views of the family. These views uphold women's primary role as nurturer of the family and of children, in the light of the Universal Human Rights Declaration (*Familiaris Consortio*, 1981). Today religious teaching in Brazil's public schools continue to consolidate Catholic and Christian values in Brazilian children's consciousness – including those from non-Christian backgrounds.

This follows past whitening practices of Brazil's colonial period. Although religious teaching is not compulsory in Brazil's public school system, children who optout feel marginalised and singled out (Da Silva Gonçalves, 2019). The overwhelming socio-historical influence of Catholicism and Christianity in Brazil creates what I classify as "Brazil's cultural Christianity." Following the standards set up by cultural religion (Demerath III, 2000), individuals may be highly critical of the church's dogmas and its "strict views" towards sexuality, virginity, homosexuality and LGBTIQ+ rights, for instance. But, in broader terms, the religious values of the Church continue shaping their identities and their understanding of the social world (Demerath III, 2000). In other words: the values of the church continue shaping individual paradigms of right and wrong, morality and social justice, with Catholic values remaining as a key reference point, shaping their consciousness.

Brazil's "cultural Christianity" is manifested in the lived experiences of honour consciousness, and in traditional views of the family (within religion) of those Brazilian women who are not "church goers," practicing Christians or who follow other religions such as Spiritualists and Kardecists.[15] I argue that Brazil is deeply influenced by "cultural Christianity," influencing lived experiences of honour consciousness. Brazil's culture and traditional views of the Catholic church have been discussed by most participants, and how it is an important part of Brazil's culture impacting the lives of Brazilians – even non-practicing Catholics and Christians.

For instance, Clara reflected upon the interplay between honour consciousness and traditional religious views (of Catholicism) in Brazil. She elucidates:

> I would risk by stating that one hundred per cent (that honour, and religion are interconnected). Because we came, our culture came from the Portuguese culture. I will risk saying this. And since then, it was the church the one to exert dominion. The church, during the time that the Royal Family came to Brazil, it already controlled everything. And we know that the church is an institution to give advantage to men, since

---

15   Participants 4 and 7.

those times. Then, all our colonial legacy, how they felt that they had the right to enslave blacks because they did not have a soul, because they could not be baptised. And that thing, that the Catholic Church only has priests, and the Madres (nuns) are a level below them will never get to the priest's level. For me this is a good picture of what happens today. All these values: abortion, you know, you cannot do an abortion, why? Well, deep down inside it is the religion, it is because it is against God, it is a crime against God, it is a crime against life. Homosexuality the same thing.

Clara explained how honour consciousness can, in many ways, be conflated with Catholic values, and how these historically have been used as an instrument of masculine hegemony, as well as white Portuguese hegemony. Clara is not a practicing Christian but was raised as a Presbyterian in Brazil. She follows cultural Christianity paradigms by analysing Catholic views on traditional and family, female submission, and dogmas from the church such as the prohibition of abortion through highly critical lenses. In her interview, she also criticised the views of the Catholic church against homosexuality. By criticising these views within the church, she creates the "othering" of views which are deemed as "extreme" notions of honour consciousness. However, Clara acknowledges that honour consciousness is still an integral part of her moral compass, and values of right and wrong. For her, these encompass being hard-working, for instance. Her notions of honour consciousness can be regarded as "moderate."

In Laila's story she explains that honour and religion in Brazil are a family issue, a matter of identity, and something operating at the "subconscious level." In her words:

> Honour and religion are concepts that come from the family and operate at the subconscious level. I criticize a lot of things about the Catholic Church, but I keep following it.

For Laila honour consciousness and religion come from the family, from your upbringing and it operates at the level of the "subconscious," demonstrating intersections between honour consciousness, traditional views of the family within Brazil's Catholicism, and the key role played by the family in transmitting these values – which are an integral part of an individual's understanding of right from wrong, and their moral compass. She is a nominal Catholic, but asserts that she still believes in God, although questioning some key paradigms of the Catholic church such as forbidding abortion, and its views on homosexuals and the LGBTIQ+ community.

The interconnections between honour consciousness and the Catholic church (and values) in Brazilian society was also discussed by Alana. She elucidated that there is a relationship between Brazil's Catholic culture with Brazilian Christian culture. In her words:

> Yeah, completely, completely. I don't even think there are links to the Brazilian culture, I think they went to the Brazilian religious culture. So yeah, again, my grandmother was raised, and was practising Catholic. And my dad always loved that and was always a part of that, but he kind of come here from Brazil to Australia and converted to Christianity, to more practising Christianity. And so, he married my mum in Brazil, and they came here as Christians and kind of helped start a church here and stuff. So, I was born and raised very Christian, very much so. And honour is everything to us, because of the Bible, because of Jesus, and because of the church.

In her interview, Alana explained that Brazilian culture is embedded in Catholic views of the family and society which then influence Brazilian society more broadly. During our discussion, Alana explained that Brazilian Christians are different from Australian Christians. She was critical of Brazilian's Christian views on pregnancy out of wedlock and homosexuality. For instance, Alana elaborated: If a Christian girl falls pregnant out of wedlock or if a family has a child who comes out as being a lesbian or gay, Brazilian Christian families would see it as bringing shame to the family. In Alana's perception, Australian Christian families would have a more relaxed[16] approach to these issues, and not see it as shameful to the family name. Alana is an Evangelical Christian, the daughter of Brazilians, who was born in Sydney. She has never lived in Brazil and has visited their small country city only a few times. Her parents transmitted their notions of honour consciousness and traditional views on the family (within religion) to Alana and her sisters in Australia. Her Evangelical Christian views see submission to her parents and to the church as key to her notions of honour consciousness. She is a university student and acknowledged that she enjoys the freedom to ask questions, and to express her views. Alana's parents'

---

16   In Australia, there are ultra-conservative views within all Christian denominations and particularly within Pentecostal Churches. The notions of honour and shame associated with ultra conservative Christian groups in Australia are manifested differently from those in Brazil – which is a collectivist/ family-based society. Moreover, the shifting and negotiation of Brazilian Pentecostalism with Australian Pentecostalism (which is more focused on the individual) reshapes how those views are seen in the migration setting.

expectations, however, are that she will live within the boundaries of the Christian belief and the honour consciousness.

Brazil's cultural Christianity and traditional values of the family within honour consciousness are experienced throughout Brazilian society, influencing the lived experiences of honour of Christians, non-practicing Christians and non-Christians alike. Maria Paula explained the key role played by honour, as part of Brazil's culture, history and religion, and how this is hybridised, suffering intra-cultural variation depending on the region where you come from. In her words:

> Notions of honour in Brazil are well related to culture, history, religion as well. It has a lot to do with the different regions of Brazil. Where do you come from? In the South, maybe it's a more rational question, but I don't know, the Gauchos are also very honourable…and in the North, maybe something more visceral, the Northeasterners resort to the "peixeira"[17] to solve matters of honour.

In Maria Paula's story, honour is a moral compass of right and wrong, and is still strongly impacting her lived experience of honour consciousness and gender. She understands that honour is an integral part of Brazil's culture and history, which is also influenced by Catholic views of the traditional family. Maria Paula is not a Christian – she is a Spiritualist Kardecist, but honour consciousness and traditional family values as taught by the Catholic church and Christianity through cultural Christianity, have shaped her lived experiences of honour consciousness and gender.

Thus, Brazilian women's lived experiences of honour consciousness are embedded in Brazil's cultural Christianity (traditional views of the family taught by the church), with their identities still being shaped by religion (Catholicism and Catholic values on the family) even after participation in ritual and belief have lapsed. Cultural Christianity also makes Brazilian women taking part in this survey more critical of practices, dogmas, issues related to sexuality and female subjection within Catholicism. However, Christian values still shape Brazilian women's lived experiences of honour consciousness and their notions of womanhood, which I classify as predominantly "moderate".

Interviewees distance themselves from "strict" religious views within Catholicism or other Christian Evangelical denominations, which I classify as "extreme" notions of honour consciousness and traditional views of the family (within religion). However, honour consciousness and traditional views of the family continue shaping Brazilian women's notions of womanhood. Their experience

---

17   Northeastern knife popularly used to "defend honour."

I classify as "moderate" notions of honour consciousness. They distance themselves from "other" notions of honour consciousness in Brazil leading to female suppression and violence towards women. They also create the "social other" of "extreme" or "negative views" within Catholicism or Evangelical churches, which lead to female suppression, lack of agency, lack of voice and lack of empowerment within the home and society. In the religious context, participants "blamed" Catholic and Evangelical teachings on female submission.

Viviana explains how traditional views of the family (within the religion) reinforce the honour code, which is something cultural. She said she doesn't know any families who are atheists in Brazil, but that these views of what women and men should do seem cultural. She acknowledged that her mother and other mothers in Brazil are sexist (*"machista"*) and that Brazilian mothers tend to give privileges to their sons. For example, she elaborated she had to do the dishes and help in the house, but this was never asked from her brother. In her story, she tells that one day, she arrived at a friend's house, and she was ironing her brother's and her father's underwear. In her words:

> Yes, there was and still is a very different treatment for the male child from the female daughter. I remember at a friend of mine they were five children. Three girls and two boys. I looked at it and didn't understand. She is ironing her brothers and father's underwear. What and why? And I'm talking about something, like, our generation, you know? And very unacceptable... She was passing by, and even a very wealthy family, very well off, but finally the maid was absent. I do not know... And family lunches in the interior of Minas. I've never seen men in the kitchen, neither to cook nor to wash the dishes. I never saw. I lie. Sometimes, I don't know, if there was a barbecue, yes. They were there making barbecue and such. But the rice, the feijoada, there in the kitchen they didn't put their foot. Not to wash the dishes, not to cook or to wash anything. I think this is a cultural problem because I also think it has nothing to do with social class. This example I gave of my friend was a very wealthy family. But man and woman clearly have different positions, and you have to respect, and you have to accept. That's why I think it's very cultural.

Alice explains how religious teaching on female submission conflated with traditional views of the family might lead to "extreme" notions of honour. In her words:

> That influence would be in what is expected, in the way you should behave perhaps. As the woman should do in her role and the man also according to religion. What do you believe in your faith? If you believe

that a woman's role is to serve the family, serve the man and the woman doesn't want to do that and the person you are relating is extremely religious or extremely sexist, this will create a problem with this situation, this relationship, and this will be reflected in society…Because they (who are very religious) will expect, exactly, that you have the same attitude, and you will not, and suddenly you will not follow that norm and follow what is being said by religion…I believe that it is expected that the man is responsible for everything, for the family, for providing for the family, and the woman is responsible for serving. In the case of religion, it would bring this vision to the relationship of man and woman.

Similarly, Marielle, who is a practicing Evangelical Christian, reflects upon the negative effects of the church's preaching on women's submission. This might lead to "other" ("extreme") notions of honour consciousness as manifested through female suppression and lack of agency. In her story, her friend, in order to honour church teachings and to submit to the church, had to marry another Christian. This man controlled her friendships and would tell her to "shut up" in public. In her words:

> The person met someone who was not from the church and fell in love with the person who was not from the church, from the same religion, and not believing in the same things the person had to stop liking, or not having a relationship with that person anymore because the church and parents said she couldn't relate to that person because he wasn't a Christian…Negative for the person and positive for authority…We were friends until just before they got married. A few days before they were married her husband forbade her to talk to me. She said: Look, my husband doesn't want me to talk to you anymore. Really? Because even though I was at church I saw him telling her to shut up in front of everyone. Why can't women talk in public?

Discussing the effects of honour consciousness on lived experiences of gender, Carina explained how her father was very "controlling," monitoring where she and her sister went, where and with whom. However, she was taught to have an opinion and had an education. She had no brothers and worked with her father in Brazil and would inherit their business if she had stayed in Brazil. She acknowledged that things are different in this generation and women have a voice. In her case, her father had to adjust to only having daughters, and not a son. In her view, it made it easier for them to have a voice and "gain space." She explains how her father "was controlling," but also gave her and her sister a platform to discuss their opinion. In Carina's "moderate" notions of honour consciousness she "resisted" women's suppression by having an opinion, a voice and education. Still, she and her sister had to submit to their father's control.

> My father and I we are very close, but he has always been a very con-
> trolling father of two daughters, me, and my sister. I think he did all he
> could to create a dome sheltering all we did. He always controlled every-
> thing he could, where we were, what time, with whom, everything he
> could while he could, you know... Because I think is in this sense of strong
> values, like honour as a value, in general. I think that in my family, despite
> the fact that it is this very traditional family, and sexist, but at the same
> time is a very open family...So even my father always being very sexist, me
> and my sister always spoke our minds...We always discussed everything.
> It has always been very open to discussion and dialogue...So for us, like
> when we were teenagers, we always have those discussions because he
> was controlling, and we wanted to do things and go to places. We never
> did anything wrong and hidden from him. But we never accepted things
> quietly. Because he opened a platform for dialogue.

Olivia shares her story, and how being in "bad company" or out and about late at night could get her in trouble with her father. In her words:

> Ah...but that was on a birthday. Ah, but I saw you in the car. I couldn't
> talk I think you drank, because it wasn't me. But he took it and said now
> you will catch it, and if it wasn't for my sister to persuade him to don't hit
> me...Why? he said...you lied. Why? I saw you in the car with that girl who
> goes out with everyone, who sleeps with everyone, and you were there
> with her. I said, I wasn't. But he didn't believe me, my father. He thought
> he saw me in the car. There, in a car at night...it wasn't me! So, if it wasn't
> my sister...I remember...he would hit me with a whip, just like he did with
> my brother, leaving the whip marks on his back.

In Olivia's story, her father was a man of no education, born and bred in Brazil's Northeast region, but "hard working, a man of honour." He would not allow her to be in the company of girls of bad reputation or out late at night on her own. Her father also controlled her brother, having used a typical Northeastern whip ("chicote de rabo de tatu") once, leaving scars on his back. "Olivia's" father nearly hit her with this whip for suspecting that he had seen her in the company of a girl of "bad reputation," well-known in the neighborhood for sleeping around and for her bad behavior. She explained that only her sister "saved her" from getting whipped by witnessing she was not out late at night with "that girl," and was back home on time.

Ana Gabriela, who was not a practicing Christian, and who lived in one of Brazil's big city centres explains how women in Brazil can be ostracised after a divorce. She shares her story:

> I had problems with marriage, divorce and it was very difficult I lost friends. Because being a woman when you get divorced a lot of friends dump you because you were with that person, you were part of a pair. From the moment you're alone you end up being...people already look at you differently and you lose a lot of friends, which weren't really friends. So, it hurts your honour or your identity a little and then the honour and pride of that being, let that friend go, who was not a friend, those are my friends. This identification is that this exchange that you start to perceive how people see you just because of a social situation is the time that pride and honour take shape...I heard other stories from other (divorced) women, that they were no longer invited to parties, that no one invited them anymore because people were afraid to invite them because they were people who could cause something or mess up with the group's relationships. In a way that people are afraid to change if anything...But it's a very common thing.

In Ana Gabriela's story, the fact she was divorced made others "uncomfortable" and "afraid" of a strong woman who is "not submissive," or who "might steal their husbands." She explained in her interview that not having a man by your side brings social ostracism (and "loss of honour"). She acknowledges that things might be changing in Brazil, since this episode was a long time ago (mid 1990s). Being divorced also increases the likelihood of a woman experiencing sexual harassment, even within her circle of friendships and acquaintances. During her interview Ana Gabriela explained that soon after her divorce, she went to a party and one of her male acquaintances "hit" on her. He was married, and when his wife arrived at the party, all guests sided with him. The only person who supported her was the host, in her words: "because he knew her." She was seen as someone "trying to steal" another woman's husband. She acknowledged in her story that she lost many friends after the divorce, because it is like a "loss of identity." She also explained how divorced women "no longer" are invited because they can "disrupt" the group's dynamics. Participants 9 and 10 shared similar stories.

Family unity is central to consolidate honour consciousness. One of the consequences for a woman who challenges the honour code, by filing for a divorce or separating from their husbands, is social ostracism. A divorced or separated woman loses honour (and social respect) for not having a man to protect them from harassment. Through the cultural lenses of honour consciousness, women play a vital role in the family as nurturers and home makers, and single women, particularly divorced and separated women, have compromised their primary social duty: to look after a husband and a family.

During interviews, the Brazilian Christian women explained that honour impacts individual behaviour in ways that are applicable to both men and women. Nevertheless, as mentioned in the previous section dealing with honour consciousness and family, there are also gender-specific guidelines applicable to women only.

Dealing with honour consciousness' gender-neutral guidelines on behaviour, there are several behaviours which "brings honour." Brazilian Christian women explained that to uphold the law and be honest by not using Brazil's *jeitinho*[18] *or the Brazilian way*, telling the truth, fulfilling your promises and keeping your word, respecting your parents, as well as working hard, putting the best effort in what you do, and striving for excellence, are all behaviours which bring honour to an individual. These behaviours are gender neutral, since both women and men should aim to have a "good name" and uphold the family name. This was discussed in detail by most participants.[19]

Diolinda reflected upon honour being honest (having a "clean" name):

> For example: If you are corrupt and it comes out, then it stains your honour and not only yours, but the honour of your whole family – at least in the Northeast where I come from. And it's shameful to do something like this and people to find out, something dishonest for instance. And the consequence is that the whole family suffers from an act of one person, right?...Oh, he was an honest man, he was a very correct man. So, this for us, makes us very proud. Imagine if it were the other way around, right? You know, if there was anything that someone in your family did that

---

18   The *"jeitinho Brazileiro"* or the *"the Brazilian way"* is a medium to gently bypass the law without harming people around you, but still not complying with the law. In other words, *"the Brazilian way"* is a friendly way to bypass the law, but still doing something blatantly illegal.

19   See Appendix, figure 2.

wasn't good…You might be a little embarrassed, let's say right? Having a
person in the family who was not worthy, who was not honest.

Diolinda explained how being corrupt (dishonest) brings shame and stains the
name of the whole family. In her interview she reflected upon how being honest brings a lot of pride to the family, and she is proud of having a family which
is honest and obeys the law. Honour for Diolinda is very much connected with
her family name, good reputation, honesty, and obeying the law, and by not
using *Brazil's jeitinho*. For her, is dishonesty brings family shame and dishonour. Other participants sharing similar stories are participants 1 and 13.

Aurea reflects upon how she and her siblings were raised to study, to be
honest, and to have a career. In her view this is something honourable. In her
words:

> My mother created me and my sisters and my brother, we were all created
> to be honourable people. People who work with dignity, and work hon-
> estly, to be able to achieve the things they have (professionally).

Ana Gabriela, for instance, was bred and raised one of Brazil's big city centres.
She explains that in her lived experience honour is to be proud of your work
and career, in her words:

> So, you are honoured to work at that place because you are proud of that
> place. You think that place gives you a good image, I mean, a personal
> satisfaction.

A behaviour which brings honour is to have a job and to be hard working,
earning money honestly by not stealing from others, and not being corrupt
or taking advantage through the *Brazilian jeitinho*. Professional jobs such as
doctors, lawyers, and other professional careers, bring greater honour to an
individual and their families. To be hard-working, to study and to have a professional career is seen as something bringing honour, making you and your
family proud, which was discussed during interviews by most participants.[20]

Nonetheless, honour consciousness consolidates gender specific guidelines disproportionally affecting the lived experiences of Brazilian women.
According to Brazilian Christian women's lived experiences of honour, honour

---

20   See Appendix, figure 2.

consciousness and traditional views of the family (within religion) shaped the way they should behave socially so that they were seen as "a good girl." For a woman to be honoured, there are several "boxes" they should tick, whereas for men they can do "whatever they like." Although not focusing on the impact of honour in Brazil's gender relations, literature suggests that Brazilian women have increasingly gained the right to earn an income and participate in Brazil's workforce. However, they continue to struggle to break down gendered norms within the home and are predominantly overburdened with domestic work (Sardenberg, 2010). According to interview results, honour consciousness and traditional views of the family (within religion) are key drivers consolidating gender politics, and Brazilian women's role as good mothers, daughters, wives and homemakers.

If a woman is to be honoured, she needs to behave and dress appropriately. This was discussed during interviews by most participants.[21] This is prevalent in the countryside and amongst more conservative families living in major city centres who may or not be practicing Christians.

Poliana observes how an honoured woman ought to be a good wife, a good mother and faithful. In her words:

> It seems that honour is different for male and female. Which is a very divided society. As much as the woman is seeking, she is still learning, I think there is a lot of difference. In women it is more linked to that thing of being the ideal woman for men and something more beautiful, you know? With honour and family principles. As for the woman more...For example: the man who is a worker...the man who is a husband, father of a family, worker he is already seen as an honourable guy. He has his job, and he proves it to his family. The woman, so what is her honour role? She has to be faithful; she has to take care of the kids so she has to honour the role of wife. So, the role of man (and woman) seems to be different plans.

Fiorela elucidates how a girl with a bad reputation affects the whole family. This is because the family should have raised her to be "pure and correct." And if she has a bad reputation, she will never get married. Conversely, this is not a problem for boys. In her words:

---

21   See Appendix, figure 2.

There was a friend of mine that we used to joke that he was with several girls, and that was super normal. Of him sleeping with several girls. If people found out that a girl (sleeps with lots of guys) she would be talked about as perverted, a bitch...Because in our society women cannot do that, within Brazilian society. And her parents should have raised this girl as a pure, right, right girl for her to marry. Because the Brazilian woman has to get married, have children and have a perfect family...So, she wouldn't be able to marry, she wouldn't have a good reputation to marry, how corny!

Honour consciousness and traditional views of the family (within religion) is intrinsically gendered, consolidating gender power relations (gender politics) in Brazil. Through Brazilian Christian women's lived experiences of honour, this chapter demonstrates how honour consciousness, as experienced by those women taking part in the interviews, demands far more from women than from men. For women to be regarded as honourable by their families they ought to obey curfews, obey their parents, to be married (be good daughters, wives and mothers), as family plays a central role in the consolidation of honour consciousness and gender relations. Notwithstanding, there are several "boxes" women ought to tick, when dealing with social behaviour: they need to dress modestly and behave in ways that are modest. If women "breach" the honour code, it will be impossible for them to regain it. Conversely, it is nearly "impossible" for a man to lose honour. Even if he commits murder, he will eventually be "forgiven" and move on with his life (as if nothing had happened). These factors all promote male hegemony and privileges, consolidating gender politics in Brazilian society.

The table below shows, and the gap between women's and men's lived experiences of honour. The table also sets out the distinction between moderate and extreme manifestations of honour consciousness in the lives of men and women, as well as how women are disproportionally affected by the honour code.

In this section I will discuss Brazilian Christian women's stories and how honour consciousness and traditional views of the family (within religion) continue shaping their lived experiences and gender politics in Australia.

When discussing lived experiences of honour in Australia, Brazilian Christian women explained how traditional views of the family (within religion) still play a central role in their lived experiences, which shift and adapt to the Australian environment. Although more recent waves of Brazilians have migrated to Australia as single individuals, there are also professional couples

TABLE 2.3   Honour consciousness's key ideas regarding behaviour and family relations

Honour consciousness	Behaviour	Family Relations
Intrinsically gendered	**Women have more duties:** – they need to behave well – dress modestly – be pure – have curfews – they uphold the family honour	– to be married – be good wives – be good mothers – family must approve choice of spouse – house chores still predominantly their duty
	Men can do whatever they please: – no curfews – no need of purity – no restriction to dress code	– they are the breadwinners – they are the head of the household
What brings honour equally to men and women?	– education – professional career – ethical values – moral values – be hard-working	– respect of the parents – respect of elders – good family name
Moderate notions	– tradition coupled with women's rights – women's rights within religion (Islam) – fight for the protection of women's rights	– taught by the parents – values of the parents – where you came from – predominantly city centres
Extreme notions	– female suppression – female control – forced marriages – violence towards women – honour killings	– taught by the parents – values of the parents – where you came from – predominantly rural areas

resettling and starting their families in Australia (Rocha, 2014). Brazilian women's honour consciousness and views on the traditional views of the family (within religion) translate to Australia and continue to shape first generation Brazilians and the Brazilian community in Australia.

Brazilian Christian women interviewed in this survey explained their lived experiences of honour consciousness in Australia, acknowledging that their parent's values, upbringing, and their views on the family are key in shaping their notions of honour (as well as the notions of honour of other members of the Brazilian community) in the diaspora. Thus, the family's values and notions of honour are transmitted via the parent's values, with the family being central in internalising their notions of honour and traditional views of the family (within religion) in Brazilian women's consciousness. This also impacts on those Brazilians born in Australia to Brazilian parents living in Sydney, New South Wales. For example: parental control and code of behaviours ("not get drunk or go partying") enforce Brazilian honour consciousness and familial views in Alana's lived experience. She is a first-generation Brazilian born in Australia. Her parents migrated to Australia in the 1970's in the first wave of Brazilian migration (Rocha, 2014).

Honour consciousness and traditional views of the family (within religion) in Australia are more "relaxed" than in Brazil, but women are still concerned with "non-traditional" dress code in the workplace, for instance. Traditional views of the family and gender roles can be more "flexible" but, still, women do more household chores than men. They have internalised the honour code and home duties continue to be their responsibility, particularly after having children. After having children, and due to high childcare costs, women tend to work part-time or to leave their jobs. Their husband's work is seen as a priority, "as they tend to earn more." There were reports of domestic violence towards Brazilian women within the Brazilian community in Sydney, with some incidents perpetrated by Brazilian men[22] and others by Australian or men of other nationalities.[23] For Brazilian women living in Australia, although their extended family and parents live overseas, honour consciousness and traditional views of the family (within religion), continue shaping their lives and gender politics within the Brazilian community in Sydney, New South Wales, albeit changing and adapting to the Australian culture.

Most Brazilian women interviewed have migrated to Australia on their own. However, to dressing "conservatively," in the way it was taught by their family and parents in Brazil, continues in Australia. When considering behaviour and dress codes, participants 4 and 9 shared that they "still think about their fathers" if faced with a situation where they could breach the honour code and behave in a way which is "dishonourable." Maria Paula explained that the way she was raised by her father still affects her "a lot" – even after living in Australia for about 20 years. She sees her experience as overall a positive one, although she was in fact controlled and subjugated by her father.

---

22   Participants 5 and 8.
23   Participant 4 and 13.

Maria Paula, however, is critical of Brazil's women's "empowering" movement, which preaches women's sexual liberation, encouraging them to have
as many sexual partners as they wish, and to dress immodestly (Coutinho,
2021). This branch of Brazil's women's movement is new and highly criticised by women in Brazil. It is manifested by women in *Funk* music, representing a grassroots movement amongst women from favelas (*shanty towns*).
The new movement within Brazilian *Funkeiras* is what is classified as *Funk
Putaria* ("Funk of Whores"). Their advocacy is around sexual liberation ("I do
whatever I want with my body"), to have casual sex on demand and to wear
tight shorts as being "empowering." These are women systemically oppressed
who want to express their sexuality and the reality of marginalised coloured
groups "on their own terms" – "breaking away from oppression." The singer
"Anitta" is an example of this new movement. Most Brazilian women, however, would see this as not empowering but "doing actually what men wants."
The contrasts between women reconciling tradition with women's rights, and
having a voice in the political arena, with the women's "empowering" movement highlights how social class and race impacts Brazilian women's lived
experiences of honour and gender.

   In Maria Paula's lived experience, the honour code continues in her life, even
as she criticizes Australia women's dress code in the corporate sector (short
skirts, no stockings and with cleavage). Gendered lines of honour establishing
how women ought to be well-behaved (and be pure), influence Maria Paula's
view of the social world. This is manifested when she critiques Australia
women who dress immodestly in the workplace, and who then complain that
they have suffered from sexual harassment (they are "victimising themselves").
In her words:

> The way my father raised me affects me a lot, to this day. But I don't think
> it affects me in a negative way. I felt like a negative thing when I was being
> subjugated, I felt like I was in prison. But I think it affected me in a more
> positive than negative way in my life today, because there was no vio-
> lence – apart from the hair pulling, the fear I had of him, but I didn't live
> that way. They were isolated cases... I think this female empowerment in
> Brazil... The question of honour, the bar is a little low these days. Women
> want Freedom to do everything I want, to dress, to act in all the ways I
> could never do before there were social barriers before. I remember here
> in Australia that I saw in the corporate environment that it was unpro-
> fessional with a very low neckline showing the chest, short skirt without
> stockings...Then women complain about sexual harassment and bullying
> but I think they victimize themselves.

In Australia, most Brazilian women continue to see housework as their responsibility.[24]Viviana, for instance, discussed that Brazilian men "participate" more in the upbringing of children in Australia (which doesn't happen in Brazil) because there are no house maids or babysitters (*empregadas* e *babas*)[25] as there are in Brazil. She acknowledges that women with children might struggle more with balancing their home responsibilities, as Brazilians (and Brazilian men) are raised by Brazilian mothers, who teach women to serve (be good mothers, good home makers and wives), whereas men are raised to be served (and "never put their feet in the kitchen"). Viviana critically examines her friend's situation, although acknowledging she doesn't have kids. In her view, if she had children maybe she would also struggle, ending up seeing home duties and looking after the kids as "her duty." This is an issue even for professional couples in Australia. In her words:

> But I still notice that a friend of mine who is married with children, he is an economist, her husband is an engineer, both are highly sought-after professionals. And she was talking like this: Why my husband can help me. I said: you are using the wrong verb! It's not help. You two have the same role. He has the same obligation to take care of children, to educate and to take care of domestic services. I think if she didn't work there, yes. Because work is either you go out to work or you stay at home. But both working, why is he going to "help" me around the house? So, it's 100 percent yours the housework and... It's very embedded in our woman's mind and it's something from centuries and centuries and you don't change. Because the Brazilian Married to a Brazilian, he was raised by a Brazilian mother, you know? I don't think my mother was an exception. I think it's typical of her generation.

Aurea, who lives with her partner and is not married to him and does not have children, tells her story. Although she doesn't put her partner's emotional needs before hers or accept emotional abuse as she did with previous Brazilian partners, she does iron her partner's clothes. And if she is running out of time,

---

24   See Appendix, figure 2.
25   In Brazil, *empregadas* e *babas* stay over at your home and usually sleep in a room at the back of the house/apartment, having one day off work weekly. They are predominantly women of colour, do not share meals with the family and only eat after serving their bosses (and in the kitchen area, not the main dining room). Although this is paid work, the wages are extremely low, and it reflects traces of Brazil's African slavery and what Freyre (1946/1956) regard as the system of "master and slaves."

she will prioritise her partner's ironing rather than hers. Her partner is not Brazilian but of Anglo-Celtic background. In her words:

> I don't put my partner's things above mine. For example: If I need to (ironing clothes). I only have 30 minutes to iron an outfit and I have to iron mine or my partner's, I know that in his work they are stricter about the uniform issue. Then I would iron his shirt not mine. Mine I find a way and find something else or do whatever.

According to field work notes, most Brazilian women, after they have children, are stay at home mothers, or they only work part-time. Poliana explains: "why to put a young child in Childcare? For her (the mother) to be waiting tables? Doesn't make sense, even financially." Brazilian men have better paying jobs and some women will never return to the workforce, thus "depending" financially on them. Poliana elaborates:

> There were a lot of people who had their second child, so they are still at home because the cost of Childcare is very expensive here in Australia. So sometimes it is cheaper for you to stay at home and take care of the children than you go out and work; why do you leave, do you work, do you receive, but practically everything goes to Childcare and then the house still goes back. So, there is yet another commitment...but it is the financial question. But if you didn't already have a dialogue before, when a situation makes it difficult or worse, then you won't have it. So, if the person doesn't talk before, let the thing arrive at that time, and doesn't have that dialogue, and the husband already has the power, so to speak... Because who needs the argument if they want to change something? And that person who wants to make the change. She must have argument. He already has his argument: I work outside, look here the money is here. He doesn't need to create an explanation. I think that is why these women go, who do not know how to impose themselves... Society does not help. It is not just the husband but is also the society. We don't have much support. They don't bring the money; they need to obey.

In her lived experience, she quit her job to look after her daughter, but later she started working part-time. She runs her own business from home and works part-time so that she can look after her daughter. But this had to be negotiated with her husband, as he would need to "help" sometimes. She explains how the financial situation of couples, and the fact that men earn more, keeps women at home, and that it is convenient for men to have women looking after everything. They work outside the home and are the breadwinners, so it is up to women to alter the distribution of domestic duties and work outside the home after having children. When women stay at home and don't have their own income, they have to "submit" to and "obey" their husbands, having no other options.

Based on field work notes and conversations with Brazilians and Brazilian community leaders during field work in Sydney, it appears that inter-partner violence towards Brazilian women in Australia is endemic and widespread. For instance, service providers to the Brazilian community in Sydney such as BRACCAMIND, which provides Medicare funded psychological assistance to Portuguese-speaking students in Australia, reported high incidence of inter – partner violence towards Brazilian women who had come to Australia as international students. Participants 4, 5 and 8 discussed cases of Brazilian women in Australia who were victims of inter-partner violence.

During the interview with Maria Paula, she discussed the femicide of Japanese-Brazilian Gold Coast woman Fabiana Palhares, 34, who was 10 weeks pregnant when she was murdered by her former (Australian) partner in Queensland: Brock Wall, also 34, allegedly bashed her with a tomahawk. In her interview, Maria Paula shared how other Australian men knew about his intention to kill his ex-girlfriend, but they did not report him to law enforcements agencies.[26] Although Fabiana's boyfriend was Australian, her notions of honour consciousness, and "extreme" views of honour leading to female submission and lack of agency could have led her into an abusive relationship with an Australian man, who ended up killing her.

Alice shared a story of a Brazilian couple who had recently arrived from Brazil. The Brazilian man "pushed his girlfriend against the wall" due to his jealous rage. She explained how she and her friends strongly condemned his actions and cut ties with him, refusing to give him shelter. They helped her by letting her stay over, but later the Brazilian girl got back together with her boyfriend. She believes they have split up now. Marielle also reported a friend that was constantly suffering emotional abuse ("he would yell at her") from her Brazilian boyfriend. She offered help and said she could live with her, but her friend would always go back to her abusive boyfriend and refused her help.

Poliana explained that most Brazilian women she knows, who don't work after having children, "they need to obey to their husbands." For example, she shared that with regard to her Brazilian customers who don't work, as she explained, the husband treats them "like children" and controls the family's

---

26   This case study highlights the vulnerability of domestic violence victims in Australia and the difficulties to enforce protection orders such as Restraining Orders.

finances and how they dress in public, and they have "no voice." When they want to buy a product or purchase her services, these women need to "ask permission" from their husbands. Poliana did not acknowledge this as violence, but thought it was "something unacceptable" and "sad." Following the Australian Human Rights Commission, based on the United Nations Declaration on the Elimination of Violence Against Women (1993, p. 2), violence against women is defined as: "Any act of gender-based violence that results in, or is likely to result in, physical, sexual or psychological harm or suffering to women, including threats of such acts, coercion or arbitrary deprivation of liberty, whether occurring in public or private life." According to this definition, financial control is a form of psychological harm and coercion, classified as a form of violence.

When dealing with "extreme" notions of honour in Australia, another case discussed during interviews was the Christian Evangelical preaching on female submission, and how this might lead to "extreme" notions of honour consciousness as manifested through female subjection, lack of agency and violence towards women. During field work in Sydney, when discussing the condition of women with community leaders and other members of the Brazilian community, they mentioned a Brazilian women focused Facebook page jocosely named *"Papo Calcinha"* (*chat panties*). On this Facebook page Brazilian women can network, discussing several issues, including job opportunities in Sydney and, through anonymous posts, everyday life challenges in Australia. This page is a popular networking platform for women in Sydney, managed by Brazilian women in Australia, and all posts are written in Portuguese. On this page there are also several posts by Brazilian women in abusive relationships disclosing the abuse, and asking for advice and help from the community in Sydney. Sometimes, Brazilian women post asking for advice, but are unaware they are in an abusive relationship. This online network supports the disclosing of abusive relationships, helping women to leave controlling partners. This page calls out Brazil's perceptions on female suppression (and lack of agency) as something "not ok."

Poliana reflected upon a *"Papo Calcinha"* Facebook post, where a Brazilian woman in Sydney regularly suffered physical violence by her partner. He happened to be an Evangelical Christian, according to her words "from a fundamentalist church." Allegedly, the couple married outside the church, without her husband's parent's permission, leading to him being "expelled" from his family and from the church, because he married an "unbeliever." He had a drinking problem and after they had their first child, he begged to be accepted back by his family and by the church. He started attending church again. In Poliana's story, this Brazilian woman was physically hurt by her partner to the point of "getting disfigured," miscarried her baby and being hospitalized. In her words:

> Everyone in the church knew that the husband drank and beat his wife. This was a [chat panties] post of the girl asking for help, who was in the hospital, something like that. Who was beaten a lot by her husband, who miscarried the baby...who was pregnant, and he beat her so much that she lost her baby. So, I remembered. It was a post (on Facebook). She, married to her husband for many years, being beaten by her husband. Later he apologized and went back to church, and everything was fine. Then there was a situation that she was pregnant, he knew she was pregnant. He told friends at church that she was pregnant, but he hit her so badly that she lost the child. She got disfigured and everything.

Poliana elaborates further how other church members "judged" the Brazilian woman, who got beaten by her husband and lost the baby. In her words:

> The church people went to visit her judging her. What did she do to lose the child? What she did to deserve...in the sense of judging, not of comforting. So, besides being beaten up, losing the children, she was still being judged by women, not just men, right? From the church community itself. Oh, this is horrible.

According to Poliana the motives behind the violence were trivial, such "as arriving home late," and "disagreeing with her husband." I argue that "strict" Evangelical Pentecostal teachings on female submission, which are disconnected from the broader Christian tradition,[27] might lead to "extreme" notions of honour consciousness. These are manifested through female's lack of agency, violence towards women and femicides (a form of honour killings). In Australia, however, Evangelical preachings on female submission and how it impacts women's rights not a problem found exclusively within Brazilian Evangelicals. The University of Queensland conducted a study exploring what Christian women in Australia are being taught in Christian churches. This study uncovered the truth that Evangelical women are being taught to submit

---

27   Other Traditional Christian faiths (and the Catholic faith, for instance) preaches female submission within the context of the family and the protection of fundamental Human Rights and the dignity of Human life (*Evangelium Vitae*, 1995; *Familiaris Consortio*, 1982; *Dignitatis Humanae*, 1965). There are "extreme" notions of honour consciousness within traditional Christian churches, but predominantly reconciled with women's traditional roles, agency, the right to participate in the work force and political activism.

to their husband's authority at all levels of their lives, from finances to where and when they work. This study points out how this preaching is leading to increasing rates of women's abuse and domestic violence victimization (Lowik & Taylor, 9 December 2019).

In Australia, honour consciousness and traditional views on the family continues, with women's role still being seen primarily as the carers of children, of their husbands and their homes. Brazilian women usually work part-time or do not work (as there is no domestic help), so that they can look after the children and manage domestic life, allowing husbands to substantially progress in their careers.

Women's primary role is still concerned with family duties (for example, minding the children, making sure dinner is ready for husband and children). They can work as long as they can successfully manage their family duties combined with paid employment – these duties are the main reason for them working predominantly part-time (when they do have paid work), or for them to simply leave their careers to look after their husbands, the home and the children. There is a continuum given to honour consciousness and the traditional family, translating to Brazilian lived experiences in the diaspora. In Australia, Brazilian women's primary role is still to be good mothers, wives and caregivers, even if they work outside the home, continuing social reproduction in Australia, although shifting and changing to Australian culture.

Honour consciousness and traditional views of the family (within religion) can be manifested via "moderate" or "extreme" views, and these are internalised in the way they see the world – the "cultural lenses of honour." For instance, while Brazilian women may feel liberated and will not submit to abusive relationships, they may still iron their partner's shirts even if they work outside the home (they have internalised home duties as being their responsibility). Married women with children, who have professional careers, are grateful when their husbands "help" with something at home or to mind their children. They have internalised the honour code and feel that it is their responsibility to look after their children, the home and their husbands. This continues to impact Brazilian Christian women's lived experiences and notions of womanhood in Australia. In my view, honour consciousness and traditional views of the family (within religion) frames Brazilian women's primary role as "home makers," "mothers" and "good wives" (who "looks after" their husbands). By internalising honour consciousness's gendered lines and notions of womanhood, they allow social reproducing processes in the home, impacting their financial independence and the advancement of their careers, as men's careers are prioritised, and women are more likely to quit their jobs to look after their husbands and children. Conversely, their husband's privileges as "breadwinners" consolidate Brazilian Christian men's privilege in Australian society.

Summary:

Honour consciousness	Social reproduction	Family Relations
Intrinsically gendered	– Women still seen as primary care givers of children, of their husbands and homes – Men can help minding the children, but this is not seen as their primary responsibility – Men's work is prioritised – Women sacrifice their careers after having children (work part-time or don't work at all)	– If women work (which is common in Australia) they still prioritise their children, husband and home duties – Men need only to be good breadwinners. This makes them honourable before the family and the community – A good and respectable woman is a good wife, mother and a home maker (looks after her husband).

2   What Changes in Brazilian Christian Women's Lived Experiences of Honour and Gender in Australia?

Honour consciousness and traditional views of the family (within religion) continue in Brazilian Christian women's lived experiences in Australia, with values, morals, and respect for tradition and family translating to Australia. Consequently, "moderate" or "extreme" notions of honour both are transmitted to Australia – depending on an individual's upbringing and the values internalised by the parents, as well as on the region where they spent their formative years. In Brazil's big cosmopolitan centres, individuals are exposed to more progressive and modern views, manifested through "moderate" notions of honour, whereas in Brazil's Northeast and in small country cities people tend to hold more conservative views, predominantly leading to "extreme" notions of honour.

Participant stories demonstrate how honour consciousness's cultural lenses continue giving meaning to Brazilian Christian women's lived experiences in the diaspora. But their notions of honour shift and change, creating new meanings when interacting with the broader Australian society, as well as with other cultures and faith groups living within Australia's multiculturalism.

In the lived experiences of Brazilian Christian women, honour and traditional views of the family (within religion) are still their bedrock of "right and wrong," shifting and adapting to the Australian context. In some stories, however, their perception is that their views of honour and traditional views of the family have not changed (or just changed "little") in Australia. It was a common perception during interviews that some members of the Brazilian community in Sydney, New South Wales "do not change" or just "continue the same." However, their views also morph into new versions of honour consciousness and traditional views of the family (within religion) in the diaspora, due to exposure to both Australian and other cultures, and different ways of living. Participant's views of honour consciousness and traditional views of the family might be more malleable, shifting, adapting and being negotiated with the values of the host country. The lived experiences of Brazilian women's negotiations in Sydney, New South Wales, illustrate the findings from Stirling (2013), and her thesis discussing the shifting, negotiating and remaking of religious and cultural identities of Iranian and Turkish Muslim Women in Brisbane, Gold Coast.

According to interview results, individual responses to the host culture's impact on lived experiences of honour consciousness are not homogenous. Interactions with the host culture can either lead to "lighter" or "more relaxed" notions of womanhood, or, conversely, to stricter views on gender roles, family life and lived experiences of religion in Australia. For example, some interviewees believe "other" members of the Brazilian community with "extreme" notions of honour consciousness "just don't change," and that after they have children women become "more submissive" to men, as there is no home help, and they cannot have an income. Lived experiences of honour, and cultural negotiation, reflect on how migrants conceptualise "home" and how they manage the on-going negotiations between migrant identities, culture and the host culture (Erdal, 2014). These negotiations reflect on the ways in which gender politics manifest in the Brazilian community in Sydney, Australia.

Poliana explains that not using *Brazilian jeitinho* is something which brings honour. However, she acknowledged that she had done it sometimes in Brazil, whereas in Australia, due to the strict rule of law, she adapted and never tried to take advantage of others. She explained that some other Brazilians still try to take advantage and break the law. In her view, it "all depends on the luggage you bring" (your background), and some people change more than others in Australia. She distances herself by "othering" Brazilians who use *Brazilian jeitinho*, as this is not honourable behaviour. According to her story, her notions of honour "are even stronger" in Australia, which, in her lived experience of honour consciousness, is associated with her principles and with respecting others. In Poliana's words:

> I think it depends a lot on the person, the baggage you bring with you and how you decide to live here. I lived in Brazil. Like all Brazilian people, I had the Brazilian jeitinho of getting things done too. Simple things also from day to day. Then I also saw that I came here and there are other people, there is the other society, right? There is Brazilian society and there is another society that is not Brazilian. So instead of getting here and wanting to impose my way, I tried to adapt, because what I saw here, I liked. So, I think there are Brazilians who come here and try to enter the community like her and there are some Brazilians who try to take advantage of things. For example: Simple things, ok? Go to the supermarket, ok? You can go in those that you will pay for your own purchases. So instead of picking up a tomato that costs 12 dollars a kilo a year to buy because it is very expensive, I go there and pass it like a potato because it is 3 dollars. So, I've seen it, I've seen it, I've seen people telling it as an advantage and laughing, because they managed to circumvent the system. No, you are not circumventing the system, you are using a good thing that is a respect for the citizen, I am recognizing that the citizen will be honest and will do the right thing. In this case a simple thing. You will get the groceries; you will pass and go to your house. A simple thing. No, you need to have someone check that you're going to do it right. When you don't really need it. If I have principles, I am a correct person, I am an honourable person, so I don't need anyone monitoring me, for me in my day-to-day, in my shopping, to do everything right.

Alana, who was raised in Australia, explains how honour and traditional family values are an important part of her life in Australia, and that she wants to obey her parents, bringing them honour. In her words:

> I'm trying to think, my whole family this relates to one of the other questions, but I will just come back at it later again. But for me, honour is like the biggest example and way of showing that you love someone is to honour them and to respect them. And it's such a big part of my family, because personally for me growing up in my family, all I ever wanted to do was to honour my parents and everything. And so I was never that the child or teenager that would deliberately go away and disobey my parents and rebel against them, because I always wanted to honour them...But they, yeah, so both, each two of my uncle's, they both have an

LGBT daughter. And one is in Brazil, the other is in the UK. But they when they found out they were so disappointed, they were scared to tell anyone else, because they were like this will shame the entire family. And they did not support their daughters at all, did not listen did not understand kind of just keep them home and did not want anything to do with them. And the girls also just wanted to leave because they didn't want to live in that environment anymore. And so that line was always very clear and unspoken, of what you shouldn't be. And then I look at my parents. And I'm like, I have only I honour you guys and you guys honour me. But there's such an understanding of mutual respect. It's so healthy. I'm so thankful for it. But what if I was, you know, my cousin? Aren't we related by the same blood?

Nonetheless, she critically examines her extended family (who live in Brazil and in the UK) and her family's views on children born out of wedlock, and particularly the LGBTIQ+ community. She explained there are some "unspoken" rules about it, and if you break these you would be "banned" from the family and bringing family shame. She explains how her lesbian cousins were poorly treated after they "came out." Her lived experience of honour in Australia is "moderate" and "positive" in her words. In her view, "other" (which might be "extreme") notions of honour consciousness might be associated with Brazilian Christian culture. Alice never lived in Brazil, she is an Evangelical Christian, and her notions of honour consciousness were transmitted by her parents. Since she has lived in Australia her whole life, they are "more flexible," shifting and adjusting to Australian culture and Australian Christian culture.

During interviews, most participants discussed how lived experiences of honour consciousness and traditional views of the family (within religion) are "more relaxed" and they "feel lighter" in Australia.[28] These participants have migrated to Australia on their own and their families, both nuclear and extended, are in Brazil, therefore there is less familial pressure in Australia. They explained how it is "lighter" in Australia, as you "don't need to meet" familial expectations and you have freedom to be "who you want to be" and "live things they would never even think of living" back in Brazil. Most of these participants have lived with their partners in Australia, without being married – something they regard as "unthinkable" back home,[29] particularly if you are originally from a traditional family or from a small country city.

---

28   See Appendix figure 2.
29   See Appendix figure 2.

Still, there is huge familial pressure for these women to marry their Australian (or Anglo-Celtic) partners in Australia. For instance, few participants co-habited with their partners before marriage,[30] but felt strong pressure from their families for them to get married. Their families see it "as not right" and that they should "get married," since it "gives more respect."

Based on Laila's field notes, her mother is regularly in touch with her and her Australian partner via WhatsApp messages and calls. Recently, she sent Laila's partner a private WhatsApp message asking him when he would propose. Laila explained this was a huge embarrassment, but her partner understood it as being a cultural issue.

Brazilian women in Australia are also not so concerned with suffering discrimination for being divorced, separated or not being married. They become less accepting of abusive relationships.[31] Aurea shares how for her "marriage is sacred." Although she is not married on paper, she works daily on her relationship. She is not afraid to be "dumped" by her partner and is clear that she will not accept emotionally abusive relationships in Australia. In her words:

> Marriage is a sacred thing. We must work on our marriage. I work for my relationship every day, we are not yet married on paper, but we live like this (together as if married). I work for my relationship every day, but I love myself first. I'm not afraid of my partner leaving me...So, in that I would put him above (iron his clothes instead of mine), but I don't put him above my emotional needs, you know? I learned this the hard way from previous relationships.

Clara also reflects how Brazilian women and some members of the Brazilian community have more freedom in Australia and are "more open minded," particularly if their partner is Australian or not Brazilian. This shows how cultures adjust and adapt in Australia. In her words:

> It changed the whole commitment thing in a relationship. I travel without my husband. That doesn't mean I want to cheat on him, that I don't like him, that it's unacceptable or, at the same time, for him too, you know? Of him having this freedom to go out and do things. And for me it is still a shock, because here I see that this is very common. You go out, sleep outside. You know, occasionally I go to the other side of town, I go with my female friends and it's going to be really hard for me to cross town

---

30   See Appendix figure 2.
31   See Appendix figure 2.

so I'm going to sleep at their place even if I'm married, no problem. This is something you don't even think of doing (in Brazil).

Clara explained how her Brazilian friends who live in Brazil were shocked to hear that she travels on her own, and how her husband is fine with her staying overnight at a female friends' house.

Noemia shared how her notions of honour consciousness associated with the values taught by her parents "are still the same" in Australia, but it changes "a little." She explained that the relationship with your extended family changes because you are living in Australia, and that you become "more independent." In her words:

> It changes a little, if you think about honour, and who you are. So much so that it changed a little for me here, my professional and sentimental life. For me, personally, nothing has changed, since my values came from my parents' upbringing and they had religion and everything, it hasn't changed. But, my people in my attitudes, because I even push myself, because sometimes I want to do things here that I did in Brazil, but I can't...The values change a little, they become more independent from the family...Those who are here in Australia for a short time have this side of honour connected with the family.

In her story, Noemia elaborates how her family resents the fact she lives in Australia and cannot participate in family gatherings as she used to and spend more time with them as in the past. She explains that Brazilians who have recently arrived in Australia are still very connected with their families back home and have not "changed yet". She shared that she "feels guilty" because she is not participating in family gatherings as much as she did previously. Carina shared a similar story, of how her family back in Brazil "complains" and "doesn't understand" what she is doing so far away from them in Australia, and how they pressure her to return home. This can make her feel, sometimes, guilty.

When dealing about the impact of familial views in honour consciousness and religion, Marielle shares her story:

> My mother was always very flexible. My mother never believed in sub-mission. The church said you need to be submissive to your husband. But my mother never really believed that. Even because my father was pas-sive so to speak. Everything my mother solved. So, there was no way she could submit to her husband's authority if my father behaved that way. So, despite believing and trying to follow everything the bible said, which

church determined, she was always a little more rebellious in the sense. Things are not quite like that. The positive influence on honour was my mothers in that sense. The negative was so...someone tell you must do this and this and that and you kind of mix the values and you can't separate what's right and what's wrong anymore, because you follow everything literally (Christian church teachings). And that creates a conflict. And I only get to see it when I came to Australia. And that was a shock to me when I arrived here because of the cultural, religious diversity. That I didn't have as much contact in Brazil as I have here. My mind opened and things started to become clearer in that regard.

She is an Evangelical Christian and her mother always taught her to "don't be too strict" and take the teachings of the church too literally. But when she left her home church and moved to Australia, being exposed to other ways of living made her more open minded and question religious fundamentalism. However, her parents' notions of honour, and the notions of honour consciousness taught by her mother are "moderate," teaching her to be open to different views and question religious fundamentalism, in particular teachings of female submission. Moving to Australia helped her to reconcile her faith with "moderate" notions of honour consciousness, manifested via women's agency, the right to have a voice, and greater freedom to choose a partner outside the church.

Although most interviewees moved on their own to Australia, honour consciousness and traditional views on the family continue to "haunt" them. Participants 2, 4, 9 and 14 explained that the values taught by their families continue to guide them in Australia – even though the families are back in Brazil ("they are not here to see"). Participant 4 and 9 shared how they still think about their father when they need to choose between "right and wrong," and how a wrong choice might impact their father or their reputation – even though their fathers are back home in Brazil. They acknowledged he "would never know" or "cannot see what I am doing," but still they would follow honour values taught by their fathers. Honour consciousness and traditional views of the family, therefore, continues impacting their lived experiences in Australia.

According to interview results, honour consciousness and traditional views of the family (within religion), translate to Australia but shift and change, adapting to Australian culture and through exposure to different ways of living. For instance, women who lived with their partners in *de facto* relationships would nonetheless rather get married. Brazilian Christian women's notions of honour consciousness become more "flexible" in Australia (as they live with their partners and are not married). Nonetheless, they still want to transmit the values of honour to future generations. Male partners also "help" in Australia.

Brazilian women, however, still regard home making, child minding and "looking after" their husbands as their duty, particularly after having children. When they have Australian partners, the men "participate" more in the upbringing of children. Although Brazilian Christian men "participate" in the upbringing of children, this is still seen as a woman's responsibility. Brazilian Christian women may become more accepting of men looking after children, but at the level of consciousness they still struggle to accept it when men are not the family's "breadwinners."

Brazilian Christian women have greater freedom in Australia, and can live with their partners without being married. This is also becoming more common in Brazil, but is still not acceptable in more conservative families and small regional cities. Even for women living in Australia there is pressure from their families overseas for them to get married. Olivia, for instance, feels that to be married gives greater stability and respectability. In Olivia's words:

> I came here and lived with my husband, and I made a bit of pressure to get married. I didn't want to miss the opportunity to live together to see if it works out for the rest of my life. Then we can marry or not. Until I made a deal with him. Because it was indifferent to him to marry or not. But then he agreed to marry, because it was more of my satisfaction. Because I like this ritual thing, a ceremony, being married. I used to be married. My son was happy. Before he said: But mom, do you live with him? Do you intend to marry him or not? Oh, my son, I intend to get married. I think it's a security for the male child. No, really, I don't know him well. Will he take care of my mother, right? Nah, that thing...I noticed that after I got married, he relaxed. Oh, my mother got married. He came here for the ceremony. It was like a guarantee for him.

Although they feel lighter, honour consciousness continues, shifting and adapting to Australian reality. Aurea shares how she will teach her children to be honest and honourable. In her view honour and the issues associated with the way you dress and your relationship status, and whether you are married or not to your partner and father of your children, are not important. However, she acknowledges that they are important for her family in Brazil. Aurea wishes to transmit to her children the values of honour which are associated with being honest and having good principles. In her words:

> I think you teach your children to your future generations, you teach the question of honour hoping to create people who are going to be healthy for society. And so at least I imagine. They may have the differences in

their thoughts as I do with my family for example. For me…clothes and relationship status, those things don't influence honour, for my family maybe they believe it does. My children will probably have slightly different ways of thinking. It won't be exactly the way I taught them. But they will have some principles that I have taught them, and they will determine whether they are honourable people or not.

In Australia, Australian partners help more around the house and minding children. Brazilian Christian women acknowledged they were "shocked" when they first saw men looking after children and staying at home. Clara shares her story, and how her notions of honour and gender changed in Australia, although she struggled to accept men not being breadwinners. In her words:

> It changes a lot and continues to change. A basic question that we all discuss a lot. All of us who have a foreign partner, mainly from the countries here (Anglo-Celtic). Many of us see the distribution of household obligations is something you don't have to ask him to do, he helps you. He's just doing things, you know? You don't have to delegate things to him. He really will. One thing we see here is the father staying at home taking care of the family. Still a shock to me when I see it. Despite looking at it like that and thinking, what a cool thing. I still catch myself, deep inside, turning over (judging). And that unconscious thing. Despite all the information of all the access I have, there's still that primitive thing of mine about him not being the provider of the house. And here is already an acceptable behavior.

Diolinda explained how her notions of honour and gender changed in Australia, as her partner does his laundry, for instance. He is Australian. She explained that some people in the Brazilian community continue the "same," particularly if they are a Brazilian couple. Olivia, who is married to an Australian man, explains how they "help" around the house and say "thank you" when you prepare a sandwich. In Brazil, this is seen as your responsibility, and men would not acknowledge your work.

Viviana critically explains how Australian men are raised to "help" around the house, whereas Brazilian men were raised by sexist mothers and "to be served." She reflects upon how women still do more housework in Australia. Men "participate" more only because there are no maids or household help. Still, she acknowledges that, if she had children, probably she would also see home making, looking after the children and her husband as her responsibility. In her words:

> I think it changes. Maybe because you are immersed in a different culture, so you are molding yourself to that culture. I think the question of the mother, who clearly raised her children in a different way. So, I cannot speak for all families and all Brazilians. But I see here that the Brazilians, my Brazilian friends who are married to Brazilians, I see the most active husbands in the matter of children and domestic work. But I think there is also the issue that in Brazil you can count on help, you can have a babysitter, you can have a maid and that relieves the family more, and here it practically doesn't exist. So that's why the husband ends up participating more... But I think when you have an Australian husband or partner, he is naturally more participatory, because he was raised that way. He was raised doing his own laundry, vacuuming his own room, cooking. So, he was created differently. More so, I don't have children. Maybe if I had kids, it would be different.

In the Australian experience, honour consciousness and traditional views of the family (within religion) continues shaping notions of womanhood, and gender politics within the home and the broader Brazilian society. Women continue to see home duties and looking after the children as predominantly their responsibility, with Brazilian men's careers taking preference over women's. Unaffordable childcare and the lack of home help (paid maids and nannies) makes it hard for women to return to the workforce full-time after giving birth. Most Brazilian women, after having children, only work part-time or, depending on her husband's salary, leave their jobs and are stay-at-home mothers. After having children, Brazilian women's primary role is predominantly to be a good mother, look after the house and the husband.

Thus, Brazilian Christian women's lived experiences of honour in Australia, and that of the Brazilian community, continue the reproduction of gender politics in Australia, although with changes and adaptations to Australian culture. For instance, although women still do more housework than men (and some of them iron their partner's shirts), Brazilian and Australian men "help" with home duties (cooking and cleaning, which they do occasionally) and child-minding. But homemaking and child minding is still seen as women's priority, even if they have paid, full-time, work. This has an impact in social reproduction in Australia. Honour consciousness and traditional views of the family (within religion) continues to give men privileges, and they are still seen as the primary breadwinners in Australia.

In Brazilian Christian women's stories of honour consciousness and traditional views of the family (within religion) there are changes in their lived experiences in Australia, and these are mostly positive: 1) In lived experiences of honour and traditional views of family and religion in Australia, there is more tolerance towards different views and different religions, 2) Brazilian women can live with their partners without being married, and they don't suffer discrimination if they are divorced or separated, 3) Brazilian women have freedom to travel on their own and sleep over at a friend's house, even if they are married, 4) Brazilian Christian women are exposed to different ways of living and literature, becoming more "open minded" and "lighter" as most of them are away from their families in Brazil. They become more "flexible" when dealing with honour consciousness and traditional views of the family (within religion), notions of womanhood and society, 5) Individuals developing ties of friendship within the Brazilian community tend to change less, than those developing friendships with Australians and people from diverse backgrounds living in Australia. The cultural lenses of honour consciousness adapt, shift and change for these individuals, but to a lesser degree than for those Brazilians who mingle with the Australian broader community. Participants described them as "the same" "they don't change," whereas exposure to different ways of living in Australia encourages adaptation to Australian culture. However, their views on gender and the role of women continue to be very similar to those you might experience in Brazil, and could tilt towards "extreme" views of honour, manifested via women's suppression, lack of agency, lack of having a voice, domestic violence and even femicides (a form of honour killings).

3   Aspects of Honour Consciousness, Religion and Gender "Changing Less" in Australia

However, Brazilian women discussed that, in some ways, honour consciousness and traditional views of the family (within religion) "continue the same" in their lived experiences in Australia: 1) Honour consciousness continues shaping gender roles within the family: and home duties and child minding are still seen as women's priority, particularly after having children. In such case, they usually leave their jobs or work part-time, whereas men remain predominantly the breadwinners, 2) Notions of womanhood and family: participants can live with their partners without being married, but there is pressure from their families back home for them to get married. Also, there are members of the Brazilian community less accepting of living together without being married, as some members of the community "do not change" or "are just the same." The diasporic experience softens some views of the Brazilian community, as they need to adapt to Australian culture. Daily exposure to other ways of living has an impact in individual's lived experiences of honour in Australia, but some members of the community may change more than others.

In the next chapter I explain honour consciousness in Pakistan and lived experiences of women. It illustrates how this is manifested through gender power relations in Pakistani society. This chapter explains the evolution of honour consciousness through Pakistan's state formation, the interplay between honour consciousness, *izzat* and religion, and the effects of class and race in lived experiences of honour consciousness and gender.

CHAPTER 3

Pakistan's Honour Consciousness and Women's Lived Experiences of Gender

Indian Muslim frustration with under-representation during British rule led to the creation of the state of Pakistan in 1947. British trained lawyer, Muslim nationalist Mohammed Ali Jinnah, was the leading architect of Pakistan's fight for political rights and independence (Jalal, 2014). By evoking Indian Muslim rights of self-determination, Jinnah fought for an undivided Punjab and Bengal for Indian Muslims (Jalal, 2017). In 1947, the Pakistani state was established in the Muslim majority regions of Punjab and Bengal, in Western and East Pakistan. Though East Pakistan seceded after the third Indo-Pakistani War in 1971, thus forming the state of Bangladesh, Indian Muslim nationalism is an important factor in Pakistani identity formation. Scholarship discussing the genesis of Pakistan ascribes a central role to religion in relation to Indian Muslim nationalism (Cohen 2004; Talbot, 1998; Verma, 2001). More recent perspectives unravel a secularist view of Muslim nationalist aspirations, with deep governance divides over representation in post-colonial India being the key drivers for the creation of an independent state (Jalal, 1994).

According to the World Population Review (2021), Pakistan has a population of over 226 million people, with one of the highest birth rates in the world (World Population Review, 2021). Pakistan is also a state suffering various security challenges (Malik, 2018), including political extremism, secessionist, interfaith and intrafaith extremist violence, and ethnic tensions (Yamin & Malik, 2014). Even though it was created as a state for Muslims, Pakistan is characterised by diversity in its religious and ethnic composition. The leading religion is Islam, with Muslims making up 96.2 per cent of the population (2017 census). But the country also encompasses other religious minorities. Accordingly, Hindus comprise 1.6 per cent of the population, followed by Christians 1.59 per cent, Scheduled Castes 0.25 per cent, Ahmadis 0.22 per cent, and other minorities 0.07 per cent (2017 census). The main ethnic groups in Pakistan are Punjabis, Sindhis, Balochis, and Pashtuns in the Northwest Frontier and the formerly Federally Administered Tribal Areas, near the border with Afghanistan. Each ethnic group represents, respectively: Punjabis 44.7 per cent of the population, followed by Pashtuns 15.4 per cent, Sindhis 14.1 per cent, Sariakis 8.4 per cent, Muhajirs 7.6 per cent, Balochis 3.6 per cent, with 6.2 per cent representing other ethnic groups (World Atlas, 2021).

© FLAVIA BELLIENI ZIMMERMANN, 2025 | DOI:10.1163/9789004711242_005

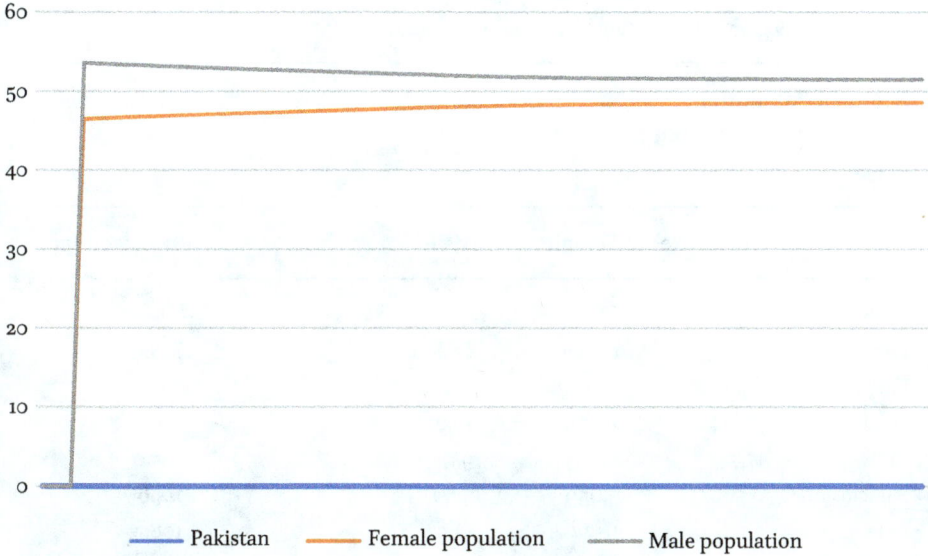

FIGURE 3.1   Pakistan gender distribution
SOURCE: THE WORLD BANK, PAKISTAN (2020). FIGURE 3.1 ABOVE SHOWS THAT
SINCE THE CREATION OF THE PAKISTANI STATE IN 1947 THERE ARE FEWER
PAKISTANI FEMALES THAN MALES, ALTHOUGH THE GENDER GAP HAS BEEN
CLOSING IN RECENT YEARS.

According to the World Bank data (2020), of the total 220,892,331 million of
the Pakistani population, 48,5396317 was accounted for Pakistani women and
51,4614171 for Pakistani men (World Bank Pakistan, 2020).

Figures from the Compendium on Gender Statistics of Pakistan (2019) indicate that between 1998 to 2017 over 50 per cent of women live in the Punjab
area, with men's numbers slightly higher than women (Table 3.1). The second
highest population centre is situated in the region of Sindh, with approximately 22 per cent of women living in this region.

Table 3.2 indicates that between 2018 and 2020, 138.7 million Pakistanis lived
in underdeveloped rural areas, with 73.8 million people living in urban cosmopolitan centres. According to the World Economic Forum's Global Gender Gap
Index Report (2020), Pakistan rated 151 out of 156, with one of the highest gender gaps in the world. In the following year, Pakistan slipped two points, currently ranking 153 out of 156. The report stated that few women participate in
the workforce (22.6 percent), and even fewer women currently have manage-
rial positions (4.9 percent), translating into huge income inequalities between
men and women. A Pakistani woman's income is on average 16.3 per cent less
than that of a man. Other inequality issues contributing to women's worsen-
ing conditions are unequal access to justice, ownership of land, non-financial

TABLE 3.1   Regional distribution by gender (1998–2017)

Regional Population Distribution of Pakistan Areas	Population				
	Both Sexes	**Female**	**Male**		**Transgender**
1998					
Pakistan	1,32,352	63,479	68,874	-	108.5
Punjab	73,621	35,527	38,094	-	107.2
Sindh	30,440	14,342	16,098	-	112.2
KP	17,744	8,655	9,089	-	105.0
Balochistan	6,566	3,059	3,507	-	114.6
FATA	3,176	1,524	1,652	-	108.4
2017					
Islamabad	805	371	434	-	117.0
Pakistan	2,07,775	1,01,325	1,06,439	10	105.0
Punjab	1,10,012	54,047	55,959	7	103.5
Sindh	47,886	22,956	24,927	3	108.6
KP	30,523	15,065	15,457	1	102.6
Balochistan	12,344	5,861	6,484	0	110.6
FATA	5,002	2,445	2,556	0	104.5
Islamabad	2,007	951	1,056	0	111.0

Note: Provisional

SOURCE: PAKISTAN BUREAU OF STATISTICS, IN COMPENDIUM ON GENDER STATISTICS OF
        PAKISTAN 2019

assets, or inheritance rights. In the United Nations Gender Inequality Index
(2019) figures, Pakistan rates 135 out of 162, reflecting high levels of gender
inequality when dealing with women's reproductive health, empowerment,
and economic freedom (UN Human Development Report, 2020).

In Pakistan, boy babies are seen as preferable to girl babies. This is reflected
in a persistent gender gap between the number of females and males
throughout the country (World Bank Pakistan, 2020). Women tend to have
several children, are fed less, and not taken to the hospital as regularly as they
should. Although the gender gap between females and males has closed in

TABLE 3.2   Pakistan's urban and rural distribution (2018–2020)

Pakistan urbanisation: Urban population	Rural population
– There has been a growing urban cosmopolitan population – In 2020, 73.8 million Pakistanis lived in rural areas (37.17 percent) – Migration flow from rural areas increasing population urban population	– But the majority of the population still live in rural areas – 138.7 million Pakistanis still live in rural remote ares of the country – Migration flow from rural areas decreasing the rural population

SOURCES STATISTA PAKISTAN: URBANISATION FROM 2010–2020 (2021) AND MOHSIN
HASSAN (2018)

recent years, there are still persistent views towards gender, and male preferential treatment, that prevents the full realisation of women's fundamental rights in Pakistani society.

1   Views on Islam, *Izzat,* and Honour Consciousness

Cultural notions of *izzat* are key in shaping regional notions of honour consciousness, influencing regional perspectives on the condition of women. According to Takhar (2005, cited by Gunasinghe, 2015, p. 12), *izzat* can be framed as "honour, self-respect, and prestige." The cultural notions of *izzat* (honour) affect not only the individual, but an individual's entire family. The South Asian concept of *izzat*, however, is not confined to individuals from a Muslim or Pakistani background, but it also affects the lives of Hindus and Sikhs throughout the region (Gill & Brah, 2014).

In the Indian context, female behaviour is framed by *izzat* standards. In other words, a woman should not pursue her dreams, but should live in accordance with what her family envisioned for her. A woman who goes against her family's wishes would risk losing their support. Takhar (2005) argues that South Asian women sacrifice their lives and desires for the sake of their families, as "all measures are taken to preserve the *izzat* of the family...whatever the cost" (cited in Gunasinghe, 2015, p. 12). The loss of honour can impact a woman's extended and immediate family, so she has to behave in an honourable way. The way *izzat* shapes the lived experiences of honour, and honour consciousness throughout South Asia, is a key variable in seeking to understand Pakistani honour consciousness and religious consciousness.

Izzat plays a vital role shaping honour consciousness gender roles, setting out how women should behave socially and within the family, how they must perform the domestic roles of good mothers, daughters, sisters, and wives, as well as how they are perceived socially. Women ought not only to be honourable: they ought to be perceived by society as honourable (Ortner, 1978). *Izzat* is fundamentally gendered and experienced differently by women and men. For instance, parents look for suitable spouses for their children to uphold their family's *izzat* (Sanghera, 2009). A son's marriage is important for the family's *izzat*, but a daughter's good marriage is essential for the family's *izzat* (Fisher, 1991), since women's good reputation is a central point to the family's *izzat*, women are seen as the "bearers of honour."

The gendered nature of *izzat*, and honour consciousness, not only regulates who women should marry, but also how they should behave to uphold their husband's family honour. There are certain sets of behaviours expected by a girl after marriage. She should submit and obey her husband's family, as they are now responsible for her "good behaviour" (Fisher, 1991). If the in-laws are not successful in controlling their daughters-in law behaviour, her bad reputation will impact both her immediate and extended family. Her family of origin must take the blame for the girl's bad behaviour, since it was their duty to teach her the ways of *izzat*, and those values associated with honour consciousness: in effect, how to be a good wife and a good daughter-in-law, and how to behave well socially. If the girl's behaviour is not corrected, and her bad behaviour continues, she has clearly married into a bad family who failed to constrain her, and her family will then be seen, socially, equally as bad for associating with them (Fisher, 1991). A girl's immodest and bad behaviour could include abandoning her husband or committing *zina* (having an extramarital affairs). It is her in-laws or her family's responsibility to bring her back to the ways of *izzat*, upholding honour consciousness.

When dealing with *izzat* and honour consciousness, and the gendered nature of honour, the leading issue with loss of honour is that it brings family shame (Kushal & Manickam, 2014). Gilbert et al. elucidates the effects of women's loss of honour on men. Seen from the male perspective, women bring family shame upon men for their failure to control their behaviour and their bodies (Gilbert et al., 2004). Following this line of thought, *izzat* gendered rules and regulations are strict when they are applied in order to control women's behaviour, but lenient when dealing with the behaviour of men.

Arguably, *izzat* (honour consciousness) reproduces societal norms which have been constructed by men, for the benefit of men. The gendered norms set up by *izzat* are designed to protect male honour and to avoid shame, through the control of women's bodies and sexuality (Lindisfarne, 1998). Men lose honour if they fail to protect the honour of the women within their immediate or extended family (Lindisfarne, 1998). *Izzat*'s gendered norms consolidate Pakistan's gender power relations.

The role of men is to protect women's honour, and that of the extended family, and in a case of female insurrection with regard to honour consciousness, to steer her back into the path of *izzat*. A woman's rebellion against *izzat* and honour consciousness is a direct affront towards her family, and if she is married, also to her husband's family wishes, leading to a loss of honour. In a desperate attempt to recover the family's reputation, this can lead to "extreme" measures taken by the men of the family, and other family members, such as acts of domestic violence or even honour killings. This can be deemed as "extreme" notions of honour consciousness. These strict notions of *izzat* (honour consciousness) sets up gendered norms which suffer intra-cultural variation, depending on the region women come from. For example, "extreme" notions of *izzat* and the role of women, and how they should uphold family honour, are predominantly manifested in the lives of Pakistani women living in rural Pakistan.

"Extreme" notions of *izzat* (honour consciousness) may be consolidated through another regional cultural practice called *purdah*, literally translated as "curtain" or "veil." This cultural practice secludes women from the public eye in order to preserve female purity and modesty (Papanek, 1971). *Purdah* is a practice throughout South Asia and Pakistan, affecting the lived experiences of Pakistani women from Hindu, Sikh, and Muslim backgrounds, and is predominant in Pakistan rural and remote areas, regions lacking education and access to information.

As argued by Papanek and Minault (1982, p. 160) "purdah is a system of ideas, actions, an important part of the life experiences" in South Asian countries such as India, Pakistan and Bangladesh, and is closely associated with other societal aspects in the region. *Purdah* is a social process where women are educated to comply with submission, and where the next generation of girls is taught to accept restraint and suppression by the patriarchal system. For instance: young girls learning to comply with strict rules of modesty and concealment might struggle to accept these rules, but once grown up and raising their own children, they will be the ones enforcing modesty codes in their daughters (Papanek and Minault, 1982).

Purdah, and the symbolic notion of "shelter", develops a division between the domestic realm of kinship and the outside world. The role of women is ambivalent, as they are seen as very important within the family unit but seen as vulnerable when they step into the outside world (Papanek, 1971). The cultural notion of *purdah* shelters women in the safety of their families, protecting them from sex and external aggression (Papanek, 1971). *Purdah* operates within a system of shame and guilt, with *izzat* and family honour being key notions that should be protected. In the Pakistani region of Panjgur in Baluchistan, for instance, the Baloch values of *izzat* (honour) and *laj* (shame) are key elements in the regulation of relationships between kinsmen and strangers, in the absence of a more organised state structure.

In Pakistan's case, traditionally the use of hijabs and headscarfs was not observed by most women; however, in the last twenty years this trend has been on the rise (International The News, 2019). And even for women not observing *purdah* practices, the embedded values of *izzat* (honour) have been internalised in their lives. This can be manifested through preserving the family's *izzat* by not mixing with unrelated men, as well as by adopting a modest dress code. In order to uphold the family's *izzat*, Pakistani women must behave within the boundaries of tradition and respectability (Weiss, 1985).

Izzat is a cultural notion operating independently of the practice of *purdah*. Scholarship contends, however, that *purdah* plays a key role in social organisation and reproduction of culture, social and gender roles (Pastner, 1982). Consequently, purdah consolidates *izzat* and honour consciousness across the region, and remote areas of Pakistan. Honour consciousness and the observance of *purdah* suffer intra-cultural variation throughout Pakistan, with class, ethnicity, geography (if women live in city centres or remote rural communities) playing a key role on women's experiences of *purdah*.

Notions of Islam and women, *izzat* (honour consciousness) are also key drivers in shaping lived experiences of Islam in Pakistan. The sub-continent's cultural notions of *izzat* (honour consciousness) sheds light on interpretations of Islam in Pakistan. These two variables, honour consciousness together with religious consciousness, are instrumental in societal perceptions of women and can lead to two diverging outcomes: 1) The protection of women's fundamental Human Rights, and agency, 2) The consolidation of female oppression in Pakistan and throughout the sub-continent. In this light, there are two leading interpretations of Islam in Pakistan, shaping social expectations towards the role of women: 1) One interpretation consolidates *izzat* (honour consciousness), leading to women's suppression and violence towards women, 2) The other reconciles *izzat* (honour consciousness) with religion (Islam) and traditional gender roles with women's agency and the protection of women's fundamental rights in Pakistan.

When considering those readings of Islam embedded in cultural notions of *izzat* (honour consciousness) which contribute to female submission and oppression, one ought to contextualise views of honour and dignity within Islam. Honour and dignity can be conflated as synonyms within Islamic texts, but it can be argued they have different meanings (Andisham, 2019). Nonetheless, several Muslim scholars neglect this distinction between honour and dignity in the Qur'an, reconciling this section of the Qur'an, as well as Islamic teachings, with modern views on human dignity connected to the universal protection of Human Rights. Andisham (2019) suggests that the verses discussing honour in Islam are the ones explaining the genesis of man. In these verses, Allah discusses the creation of man, creating man by his hand (Qur'an 38:75), inflating his soul into man (Qur'an 15:29), and because of these privileges man will rule over the Earth (Qur'an 3:30) and be honoured above all species. According to Andisham (2019) the literal English translation of *karama* is honour, and the most accurate translation for human dignity being *e'tibar*. Qur'anic verses say that God will honour man, and that this is not intrinsically an attribute of human beings. The translation of *karama* as honour is consistent with the Islamic worldview, following other Abrahamic religion's perspective that God is the ultimate source of value. The Holy book sees that any kind of worth must be traced back to Allah, with Allah giving value to man (Andisham, 2019).

It is not only a semantic confusion between honour and dignity which creates interpretations differing from an Islamic worldview. In South Asia and Pakistan, the Qur'an's views on *karama* (honour), instead of being contextualised holistically with Islamic principles of the Holy book, are given an interpretation which is embedded in cultural views of *izzat*, and how *izzat* perceives honour in the lives of women. Religious perspectives as seen through the cultural lenses of *izzat* consolidate Pakistan's gender norms of female oppression and male privilege in the name of honour.

Sura 4, verse 34, is a contested Qur'anic verse, giving rise to an Islamic interpretation that gives husbands the right to physically chastise their wives in case they behave "disrespectfully" or are "rebellious," since they are the "head of the household" and the family's provider. Hajjar (2004) argues that interpretations of Shari'a have historically endorsed patriarchal views and men's status as the head of their families and as guardians over women (Sonbol, 1998). The hierarchical and highly patriarchal interpretation of Shari'a is based on the Qur'anic principles of *qawwama* (authority and guardianship) and *ta'a* (obedience), condoning gender specific roles and duties inside and outside the home (Sonbol, 1998). The primary source of the Qur'anic principles of qawwama and ta'a is Sura 4, verse 34, with this verse being regularly quoted as allowing men a religious prerogative to beat "disobedient" wives (Hajjar, 2004).

Sura 4, verse 34, when read through the cultural lenses of *izzat* (honour consciousness), legitimises views in support of the use of violence against women.

Although views of Islam are influenced by honour consciousness throughout South Asia and Pakistan, regional interpretations of Islam, supporting violence towards women, are predominant in rural remote areas, and amongst individuals coming from lowers castes and socio-economic backgrounds, and who did not have access to education.

The second leading interpretation of the Qur'an in Pakistan reconciles *izzat* (honour consciousness) and religion (Islam) with Human Rights discourses, and the protection of women's Human Rights and agency, based on a systemic interpretation of the Holy book. Through a systemic interpretation of the Qur'an, the Holy book cannot view women as being inferior to man (Saleem, 2014). According to Saleem, Sura 4, verse 34 deals with the negotiation stages between husband and wife when marital conflicts arise. Sura 4, 34 is situated in the sections of the Qur'an dealing with family harmony, and the use of violence to "chastise" a "rebellious" wife would be contradictory to over-arching Islamic principles.

Esposito (1982) argues that before the advent of Islam, men generally subjugated their wives, treating them as property, since it was the prevalent cultural view of the time. He contends, moreover, that the Qur'an initiated an emancipatory movement in seventh century Arabia condemning discriminatory views of women, the killings of women as well as infanticide, and promoting women's agency and the protection of women's rights. As a result, women were granted the right of consent as a precondition to marriage, as well as being able to keep their dower for themselves. Previously, the dower was given to the bride's father instead (Esposito, 1982).

Yet another viewpoint sees honour consciousness being reconciled with a systemic interpretation of the Qur'an, and the Holy book's principles of honour and dignity. Through this perspective, in Sura 4, verse 34, views of womanhood and tradition are reconciled with women's fundamental rights, agency and female empowerment within the boundaries of tradition and religion. Such views are predominant in Pakistan's upper middle class, upper castes, and amongst individuals living in Pakistan's cosmopolitan city centres who have had access to education.

I argue that Pakistani Muslim women's lived experiences are shaped by honour consciousness and religious consciousness, navigating between these two leading (yet polarised) views on the role of women and women's rights in Islam. Honour consciousness and religious consciousness are two leading views of womanhood shaped within the boundaries of tradition and religion. These are hybridised and are affected by intra-cultural variation. Pakistani women's lived experiences of honour are impacted by intersectional multi-layered axes of inequality. Their lived experiences of honour consciousness and religious consciousness are shaped by their caste, class, socio-economic standing, and whether they live in rural or urban areas, as well as by their level of education.

2 The Effects of Class, Caste and Region in Lived Experiences of Honour Consciousness and Gender

Pakistan's diversity is pivotal in shaping Pakistani Muslim women's lived experiences of honour consciousness and religious consciousness, since the country is not homogenous in its demographic composition. The huge divides between Pakistan's living standards in the urban and rural areas is a key variable, shaping lived experiences of honour. Honour consciousness encounters intra-cultural variation depending on an individual's social class, caste, social standing as well as the geographic location in which they live. These variations are key in shaping gender power relations and women's lived experiences of gender.

For instance, personal power, and family social status, gives women access to education and better living conditions, and opportunities to pursue a career and even become a politician. In Pakistan, social cleavages and an individual's personal power and social ties are important variables leading to individual social ascension and access to positions of leadership (Gilani, 2001). Women from powerful upper-class families experience honour consciousness differently. On one hand they might internalise traditional views on womanhood and the role of women, but on the other they enjoy a high degree of agency, participate in the workforce in professional roles, and may be even involved in politics. Although there may be significant intra-cultural variation, depending on socio-economic status, and on the level of access to education and opportunities, honour consciousness internalises gendered norms which consolidate gender power relations in Pakistani society. Honour consciousness's gendered norms consolidate men's privileges and preferential treatment at all levels of society. Consequently, the first axis of inequality promoted by honour consciousness is the differential treatment of men and women based on their gender.

Honour consciousness reproduces traditional gendered roles, shaping the lived experience of boys and girls from the time of birth. Boys are seen as preferable in families than girls, and their elevated position within the family is reinforced by the mother and other women in the household (Gilani, 2001). In a typical Pakistani family, the father plays a distant role physically and emotionally, being mostly absent from the domestic sphere (dominated by women), as his sphere is the public sphere.

Gilani (2001) contends that Pakistan gender roles are firmly defined and strictly followed, with large parts of society functioning via strict gender segregation. In Pakistan, the role of the "breadwinner" belongs to males, and long work journeys may force them to stay away from home most of the time. In recent years, some men have to travel across cities (and even overseas) to work. Nonetheless, even for those living in the same city as their families, men typically spend the day at work, joining their families only at mealtimes or in the evening. Thus, they are not involved in raising their children or any domestic chores. These are seen as female roles and responsibilities. Pakistani boys growing up with absent and distant fathers are deeply affected in their perceptions towards gender within the family and society. Pakistani boys inhabit a feminine world in their early childhood, and then in their adult life they need to transition to a masculine world. Girls do not need to shift dramatically between these two worlds while transitioning from infancy to adulthood. In other words, in Pakistan there is a clear distinction between the domestic sphere, seen as a feminine world, and the public sphere, seen as a masculine world. For boys growing up in this environment, their ideals of masculinity are detached from reality and mostly fantasised (Gilani, 2001). These societal factors are arguably embedded in honour consciousness, reproducing honour consciousness' strict gendered norms. These are manifested through gender power relations where women are seen as having lesser value than men, as well as consolidating societal norms designed by men for the benefit of men.

Honour consciousness' strict gender roles consolidates men's leadership and authority in Pakistani society, shaping masculinities from early ages. However, this does not come without challenges. Pakistani boys struggle to transition from the domestic world of infancy, associated with femininity, to the adult external world of men (Gilani, 2001). A societal manifestation of this schism between the female world from the domestic sphere, and the private world of men, occurs when adult men decide to marry. The proverbial tensions between mother and daughter-in-law are intensified by a husband who looks for his mother in his wife, a quest doomed to disappointment (Gilani, 2001). In an Oedipal way, the mother-in-law also resents the role of a "stranger" in her territory (the daughter-in-law) trespassing into her boy's domain of emotions and snatching her son away from her care. When dealing with lived experiences of honour and social reproduction of gender roles within the realm of domesticity, women and mothers are key in teaching boys and girls the gendered norms of what is honourable for girls and boys. Based on honour consciousness, women should be pure and chaste, and men should be good providers and control their women.

Pakistani society has changed in recent years, with increasing number of women becoming educated and joining the workforce. Ali et al. (2015) explain how parents are supporting their daughters to pursue higher education in Pakistan, although traditional views continue as a societal barrier for women to excel in their careers. Honour consciousness, in fact more than before, shapes gender norms. For Gilani (2001) traditional views continue to permeates gender norms, with a strict separation of domestic spaces, seen as feminine (and inferior), and public spaces, as seen as masculine (and superior). Honour consciousness in Pakistan is still an impediment to the equal treatment of femininities and masculinities in the broader society, with men and women being seen as of equal worth. As can be seen, gender is a variable impacting Pakistani women's lived experiences of honour consciousness. But other factors should be taken into consideration in order to understand the different layers impacting lived experiences of honour. These other variables shaping "other notions" of honour are caste, class and geography (i.e. whether a woman lives in the urban or rural areas).

Women's' caste, class and region are key in shaping "different" lived experiences of honour consciousness, religious consciousness, and gender. This lays out an intersectional experience of honour consciousness in Pakistan. There is considerable intra-cultural variation in honour consciousness based on the grounds of caste and class throughout Pakistani society, with individuals from lower castes and classes having access to less education and fewer opportunities. There is limited social mobility outside Pakistan's castes and tribes, and marriage outside the family's caste or class would bring family dishonour, violating the honour code. In Pakistan, individual hereditary categories such as castes and class (*zat*) continue to be relevant, although they are adapting and changing in cosmopolitan city environments (Fisher, 1991). Honour consciousness, and status differentiation based on caste and class predominantly affects the lives of individuals living in the countryside. Nonetheless, even in cosmopolitan centres such as Lahore a person's *zat* (class) continues to play a role when families look for suitable spouses for their children for arranged marriages (Fisher, 1991).

Marrying individuals who come from the same class consolidates honour consciousness, and views associated with familial prestige and honour. In the urban setting, where women have greater access to education, understanding of women's rights, and information, if they "rebel" against their family wishes they would be seen in a negative light within their social milieu – with an urban upper middle class family upholding predominantly "enlightened" views of honour. "Enlightened" views of honour can lead to a family's rejection of a marriage choice, but not will not lead to domestic violence (in the name of honour), or honour killings. In a rural setting, however, those women who "rebel" against their family wishes, due to the lack of education about the rights of women and a lack of opportunities for rural women to have a voice, are predominantly taking the risk of being victims of domestic violence or even honour killings. However, "extreme" notions of honour, leading to violence towards women, can also be found in Pakistan's major cosmopolitan centres, as well as in the rural areas.

In Pakistan, the urban and rural cultural divide impacts women's access to education and information. Honour consciousness, gender differentiation and women's agency and empowerment are hybridised and suffer from intra-cultural variation throughout Pakistani society. Pakistani women's lived experiences of honour consciousness, religious consciousness, and gender are deeply intertwined with the area where they have been born. Their lived experiences of honour, religion, and gender are significantly impacted if they live in the urban or rural areas, and if they had access to education or not. Since the 1980's, Pakistan has gone through significant changes, which have affected the lives of women living in both cosmopolitan city centres and the rural areas. Women living in the urban areas are the ones who have historically engaged in political activism, with their living conditions improving in recent years.

Nonetheless, Pakistan continues to be a highly patriarchal society, and notions of honour consciousness and religious consciousness are variables which prevent women in the rural areas from being physically and economically independent. Their lived experiences of honour consciousness and religion are "different" from lived experiences of urban women. As contended by Alavi (1991, p.127), in many instances women in Pakistan are treated as "chattels, given or acquired through arranged marriages, to spend their lives in the service of a male dominated system." This lived experience is associated predominantly with Pakistan's countryside, where honour consciousness together with views of religious consciousness supress women's agency, curtailing women's fundamental rights.

Predominantly in rural areas, honour consciousness and religious consciousness deprive women of basic human rights such as financial autonomy, equal treatment before the law, access to education and even equal access to food. For example, in rural areas of Pakistan, women allegedly eat after men, and have many children, leading to high levels of malnutrition (Alavi, 1991). Since they are given less food than men, their underfed bodies are more prone to catch diseases and they may die at a younger age than men. Repeated pregnancies also take a toll on their overall health. Urban women from the lower middle class also have their physical and psychological health impaired, by living confined within insanitary homes. They have little sun exposure and limited access to fresh air and no recreation, whereas men have freedom to come and go as they please and are not affected as much by poor living conditions in their homes (Alavi, 1991). Notions of honour consciousness, and religious consciousness predominant in rural areas thus consolidate gender power relations. In these areas, women as seen as being of lesser worth than men; they lack freedom of choice, and are deprived of their basic human rights. Although a problem throughout Pakistani society, there is a greater risk that women in the rural areas, who rebel against cultural notions of honour and religion, may become victims of domestic violence (in the name of honour) or honour killings.

Women's struggle against male oppression, however, is a problem experienced throughout Pakistani society, in big city centres as well as in rural areas and remote regions (Nawaz et al., 2021). But the lived experiences of honour consciousness of Pakistani women living in urban areas take into account their relatively high levels of agency. Although women still uphold honour consciousness, traditional values, and religion in urban areas these can at the same time be articulated with women's rights within religion (Islam), agency, financial independence, and political activism. When discussing social status and class, women in urban areas working in the modern sector and in professional jobs come from higher classes and socio-economic status (Sathar & Kazi, 2000). Literature shows women's education in urban areas as being a key variable in measuring contraceptive access, infant mortality prevention, and their offspring's education levels (Mahmood & Ringheim, 1993; Sathar & Casterline 1988), all of which are important indicators of women's autonomy and freedom of choice. There is also literature discussing the benefits of women's access to education in securing employment in modern sectors and white-collar positions (Sadaquat, 2011). Honour consciousness and religious consciousness intersect, affecting their lived experiences of honour in the rural and urban centres. Nonetheless, caste, class and education are key factors reconciling (or not) honour consciousness and religious consciousness with women's agency and women's rights.

Pakistani feminist waves have challenged honour consciousness, religious consciousness, and traditional gender roles to a certain extent. The first wave of women's rights in South Asia started within the anti-colonial movement in the region, with women playing a pivotal role during the independence movement and the creation of the state of Pakistan. During those years, the improvement in the condition of women was seen as central for secular-nationalist modernist views in the region. For example, Jinnah denounced traditional purdah practices in 1944. In his words:

It is a crime against humanity that our women are shut up within the four walls of the houses as prisoners. There is no sanction anywhere for the deplorable conditions in which our women have to live. You should have taken your women along with you as comrades in every sphere of life (Jinnah, cited by Mumtaz & Shaheed, 1987, p.38).

Modernising secularist leaders such as Jinnah played a pivotal role in women's political engagement throughout the independence process.

To grasp the role played by tradition (honour consciousness) and religion (religious consciousness) in Pakistani Muslim women's lives, and views within Pakistan's contemporary feminist movement, one ought to understand how political activism was never divorced from Pakistani women's views on tradition, family and religion. In the early days of the women's movement, and through the activism of groups such as Anjuman-e-Khawatin-e-Islam (Muslim Ladies Association), traditional women's roles were seen as empowering for South Asian Muslim women. In their view, women's agency should be constrained within the boundaries of tradition, and women's traditional gender roles as nurturers, mothers, sisters, daughters, and nurturers. Minualt (1982, p. 171) explains the pre-independence women's movement:

These Muslim women recognised the power that women's traditional roles in the family gave them and build on that foundation. They thus remained within the bounds of traditional feminine roles, while engaging in a limited form of political activity. Without storming the citadel of male supremacy, these women gained social acceptance for an expanded role in society, albeit their own, female society.

Women had a significant contribution to the creation of the Pakistani state through the All Pakistani Women's Association (APWA), actively engaging in street protests. The engagement of women such as Fatimah Jinnah (Muhammad Ali Jinnah's sister) and Begum Raana Liaquat Ali Khan (the wife of Pakistan's Prime Minister Liquate Ali Khan) have shaped the Pakistani political arena. Punjabi women also joined street demonstrations during the fight for independence, with the Indian Muslim League capitalising on women's demonstrations to gain the support of Muslims throughout the region (Yasmeen, 1991). Regrettably, soon after 1947 these women were pushed back into their homes, returning to their traditional roles as mother, sisters and daughters (Yasmeen, 1991). This was possible since traditional gender norms, and honour consciousness, had not been fundamentally challenged. There was a tacit agreement between women's activists and those men in leadership roles that men's "headship" and privileges should never be questioned. Traditional gendered norms embedded in honour consciousness and religious conscious-ness continued. The societal and political structures consolidating gender power relations have never been fundamentally challenged.

In the early years of the Pakistani state (1947–1977) there was state support towards women's movements. The first wave of Pakistani women's movements emerged with organisations such as The All Pakistani Women's Association (APWA), created in 1949 by then first Lady, Begum Raana Liaquat Ali Khan, to work towards better economic and educational conditions for Pakistan's disadvantaged women (Haq, 1996). APWA enjoyed government support throughout the country, with many government official's wives heading local chapters. This organisation was well known for lobbying for Muslim Family Laws reform and for greater female participation in politics and government agencies. In the Pakistani context, nonetheless, women's agency and political participation post-independence was a privilege enjoyed by upper-middle class women, and operated within the constraints of Pakistani tradition, and honour consciousness.

Early attempts towards female leadership roles in politics failed, due to con-solidated views towards honour consciousness, religious consciousness, and male headship. Liaquat Ali Khan, during his re-election bid, did not shy away from lobbying together with Muslim clergy to extract a *fatwa,* ruling Fatima Jinnah's (the sister of Jinnah) candidacy "un-Islamic" (Muntaz & Shaheed, 1987, p. 56). In Pakistan's early years most women involved in the political pro-cess participated as the wives, daughters and sisters of politicians, not by hav-ing a political platform in their own right.

Pakistan's Prime Minister Ayub Khan introduced reforms such as Muslim Family Laws Ordinance of 1961, thus increasing women's rights in marriage, divorce, maintenance and child custody. These laws came into being through the active lobbying of women's groups such as APWA and the United Front for Women's Rights (Muntaz & Shaheed, 1987). Pakistan's modernising agenda continued during Zulifkar Ali Bhutto's Pakistani People's Party (PPP) years, increasing women's political participation, and the protection of women's rights.

The first wave of Pakistani feminism emerged post-1977, during General Mohammad Ziaul Haq's dictatorship. This is a pivotal moment in Pakistan's history of women's rights, characterised by a period of political resistance and struggle. In his first speech General Ziaul declared:

> Pakistan, which was created in the name of Islam, will continue to sur-vive only if it stays with Islam. That is why I consider the introduction of

an Islamic system as an essential prerequisite for the country. (General
Ziaul cited by Zaidi, 2017, *Introduction*)

Islamising reforms during his administration were radical, with a key promise
of the regime being to widely implement Sharia (Islamic Laws) in the country.
Ziaul's Islamisation agenda had as its main goal the limitation of women's freedoms and political participation. During his administration, state led television
censorship required women to wear headscarves and decent clothing to go on
air, with the federal government mandating the use of chador for all women
employees (Muntaz & Shaheed, 1987). Ziaul's rule envisaged the consolidation
of traditional social norms, curbing women's agency in Pakistani society.

The most radical legal changes of the status of women, however, were with
the Hudood Ordinances of 1979, and the 1984 Law of Evidence and *qisas* and
diyat. The 1979 Ordinances encompasses crimes such as adultery (*zina*) and
rape (*zina-bil-jabir*). The maximum penalty for the crime of adultery was ston-
ing to death for married persons, and 100 lashes for unmarried individuals,
requiring four Muslim male eyewitnesses, completely excluding women's
witnesses from the legislation (Muntaz & Shaheed, 1987). In 1984 the Law of
qisas (retribution) and *diyat* (financial compensation for murder) was ratified.
According to this legislation, the *diyat* for women would be half of that given
to men, whereas women guilty of murder would have a punishment equal to
that assigned for men (Muntaz & Shaheed, 1987). But Ziaul's aggressive legislation led a group of professional women to create, in 1981, the Women's Action
Forum (WAF). Although with only a limited number of members, and with an
active base predominantly in the urban areas, this pressure group started a
national debate on the unfairness of the new legislations which undermined
women's status in Pakistan (Haq, 1996). WAF was instrumental in delaying the
implementation of new legislation against women's equal treatment before
the Law, as well as blocking other laws.

Pakistani women never became fully detached from values associated
with honour and religious consciousness, demonstrating significant agency
during Ziaul's legal reforms on the status of women, within a political context
of repression and increasing misogyny. However, Pakistani Muslim women's
agency continued operating within the constraints of honour consciousness.

Women supporting Pakistan's first feminist wave came from urban educated middle and upper classes. They viewed traditionalism, the fanaticism of
fundamentalist religious leaders, the patriarchal culture of the sub-continent,
as well as a widespread lack of education for women, as key variables affecting the lower status of women (Haq, 1996). These women strived for Pakistan's
modernisation and "enlightened" policies as a gateway to raise Pakistani

women's societal status and political influence. Another important feature of this movement was their insurrection against Ulama's (and fundamentalists) prerogative to interpret Islamic Law. Their activism was spiritually charged by Muslim feminist theologians such as Riffat Hassan (Haq, 1996). Although revolutionary for their time, one of the main critiques towards WAF was its narrow support base, representing educated professional women but unable to reach out to women from rural areas and under-privileged backgrounds. The end of Ziaul's regime, and the election of Benazir Bhutto as Prime Minister was seen as a redemption for WAF, and the feminist movement. Benazir Bhutto's administration (1988–1990 and 1993–1996) saw a new feminist wave emerge, with NGOs and women's activism empowered through governmental initiatives.

Pakistani feminism differs significantly from western feminism, and in many ways, their brand of feminism emerges as a counter-narrative to western feminism. These views have developed to consolidate their identities, and to distance themselves from western ways of thinking when dealing with Pakistani women's rights and Pakistani women's agency both in the region and worldwide. Part of Pakistan's feminist movement is not dissociated from religion, or from cultural traits such as notions of honour and honour consciousness. Pakistan's feminism has two predominant discourses. There is Islamic feminism and secular feminism. Modern Islamic feminist scholars include names such as Riffat Hassam, Amina Wadud and Asma Barlas, who articulate women's rights with female centric laws in Islam. But secular feminists such as Shanaz Rouse and Fouzia Saeed see feminism as an extension of human rights (Ovais, 2014). In a post-colonial country like Pakistan, secularist views on feminism can be seen sceptically as colonising hegemonic forces, and as holding back indigenous ways of knowing and thinking. Secularist views on feminism can be seen in Pakistan as western whitening efforts (Zia, 2009), and as being out of touch with Pakistani women's lived experiences of honour and religion.

As can be seen, Pakistani Muslim women's lived experiences of honour consciousness, religious consciousness, and agency cannot be seen as a single configuration of identity. Their personal experiences can shift and change, and can also be reconciled with female activism, agency, feminism, and the fight for women's participation in the political arena.

Although there is women's empowerment in Pakistan, as has been demonstrated through women's movements, honour consciousness and religious consciousness continue to reproduce gender power relations. And even within those movements, women still make compromises to institutional and social norms which privilege men. Gender power relations can be demonstrated through Pakistani women's "extreme" and "moderate" notions of honour consciousness and religious consciousness. In "extreme" notions women resist "less" to gendered power and male hegemony. However, in "moderate" notions women resist "more" to gendered power, having greater societal agency, and promoting social change.

A manifestation of "extreme" notions of honour consciousness and religious consciousness in Pakistani society is demonstrated by the high levels of violence towards women and honour killings, which are still experienced throughout Pakistani society. The motivation behind those crimes is embedded in honour consciousness and religious consciousness, with literal interpretations of the Qur'an and readings of Islam based in the cultural notion of *izzat*.

"Extreme" views of honour consciousness and religious consciousness, leading to honour killings, are predominant in Pakistan's underdeveloped areas, such as Western Pakistan's Merged Areas. According to a study conducted by the Khyber Pakhtunkhwa government, with the support of the UNDP's Merged Areas Governance Project (MAGP), there are massive gender disparities in these areas, with women having no access to healthcare, employment opportunities, education and ownership of assets (Shawar & Abda Khalid, 2021). This survey indicated that 86 per cent of women were traditional housewives, responsible for household chores, as well as having to perform extended hard labour, with 85 per cent of the women over the age of 15 responsible for fetching water for their families (Shawar & Abda Khalid, 2021). These factors contribute to "extreme" views of honour consciousness and religious consciousness in Pakistan's remote areas, since women are not given a chance to challenge *izzat's* cultural norms through direct access to education, workforce participation, and an understanding of women's fundamental rights.

Nonetheless, "extreme" notions of honour consciousness and religious consciousness, female oppression, and violence towards women and honour killings are not issues restricted only to Pakistan's underdeveloped regions. In 2018, The Thomson Reuters Foundation ranked Pakistan as the sixth most dangerous country in the world for women. Pakistan ranked fourth worst for economic empowerment and discrimination against women, and risks associated with cultural traditional practices including honour killings, ranking fifth to non-sexual violence, and domestic violence (Reuters, 2018).

And this is not a new phenomenon in Pakistan. Human rights advocates contend that violence towards women in the name of honour, and honour killings, have been on the rise in the past 20 years. Most victims are women whose families oppose their social interaction with other men, or who are in marriages that are made against their will. According to the Aurat Foundation, in 2008 8,548 incidents of HBV were reported in Pakistan's four provinces and in Islamabad. In 2013, approximately 869 women died in honour-related attacks. In 2014, approximately 1,000 women died in honour-related crimes. In 2015 the

Human Rights Commission of Pakistan reported 1,987 cases of honour killings: 1,096 females and 88 males, with at least 170 of these crimes against minors (UN Women, 2016). And these figures are only estimated numbers, since these crimes go vastly underreported. They are usually disguised as "accidents" or are covered up by family members (UN Women, 2016)

As stated by Brad Adams (2014), Executive Director of Human Rights Watch Asia Division:

> So-called honour killings have been a long-festering problem in Pakistan, and the recent escalating trend makes it clear they won't go away on their own"..."The government need to step up its prosecution of these horrific cases and send a message of zero tolerance. (Reuters News)

In 2004, as the result of many years of domestic and international lobby by Pakistani women's groups, Pakistani's Criminal Law Act was amended, criminalising violence against women in the name of honour (Khan, 2020). Nonetheless, Pakistan's right of "qisas" and "diya" (pardon by family members), continued to provide a legal loophole for honour killings against women and girls (Khan, 2020). Despite Pakistan's move to criminalise honour killings, it continued to be a matter of concern as cases continued to rise throughout the country (UN Women, 2016). In 2016, the United Nations urged the Pakistani government to take immediate action against "honour killings," to ensure perpetrators would be brought to justice.

In 2016 international pressure against honour killings in Pakistan reached new heights after Pakistani film maker Sharmeen Obaid Chinoy won an academy award for the "Girl by the River" documentary, depicting honour killings in Pakistan. This created political momentum to pass new legislation clamping down on honour killings in the country (Human Rights Watch, 2016). In a diplomatic intervention, Prime Minister Nawaz Sharif stated: "Honour killings, the theme of the film, afflict segments of the Pakistani society" giving assurance to the international community that he intended "to rid Pakistan of this evil by bringing in appropriate legislation" (Dawn, 2016).

Still in 2016, the assassination of Pakistani model and social media start Qandeel Balochi was another important turning point for new legislation tackling honour killings in the country (Dawn, 2016). Baloch was murdered by her brother for breaking traditional Pakistani gender norms and expectations of "female piety." Baloch is an interesting case study. She lived life on her own terms. As Nida Kirmani explains: "[She was] a woman who was living life on her own terms, she wasn't afraid ... she was fun, loud, bold, brash and beautiful – We would like to drown out those voices who think she deserved it because of the way she was behaving" (Chughtai, 2016). Baloch's social media presence and individual activism is a predominant feature in the new wave of feminism in Pakistan and for millennials' lived experiences of gender and agency. Most importantly, Balochi's case demonstrates that "extreme" notions of honour consciousness are not restricted to those women with no access to resources and information, who live in remote areas of the country. Her case led Pakistan's senate to pass an anti-honour killings bill eliminating family rights to "qisas" and "diya" (pardon) for the murder of women "in the name of honour" (Dawn, 2016). However, even with the new bill, Pakistani legislation has been traditionally lenient with regard to punishment for honour killings, and the new legislation did not alter Pakistan's Criminal Code interpretation which allowed family members to pardon the perpetrators of honour killings.

On the other hand, "moderate" notions of honour consciousness and religious consciousness are based on religious views embedded in a holistic interpretation of the Qur'an and Islam. These "moderate" notions support the protection of women's rights and agency. These women experience high levels of societal freedom within the constraints of religion and tradition. Pakistan's women's movements, however, never completely refuted honour consciousness and traditional views on gender, as well as religious consciousness (being a Muslim woman) from women's activism and agency.

"Moderate" notions of honour consciousness and religious consciousness are predominant among Pakistani Muslim women from the middle and upper-middle classes, those who have had access to education, and who live in Pakistan's cosmopolitan centres. These are manifested through the Pakistani women's movement, women's agency, Pakistani feminist waves, and their own views of tradition and gender roles.

The work of NGOs, such as the Aurat Foundation, are of great significance in the fight for Pakistani women's rights, giving Pakistani women's issues a voice both domestically and internationally. Founded in 1986, the Aurat Foundation is committed to creating a widespread awareness of women's endowed Universal Human Rights, fighting for equal treatment before the law and society, ensuring both men and women lead "their lives with dignity and respect" (Aurat Foundation, 2021). With a head office in Islamabad, and regional offices in the provincial capitals of Lahore, Karachi, Peshawar, Quetta and Gilgit, the Aurat Foundation is known worldwide for its commitment in the fight for Pakistani women's empowerment, engaging with all levels of society, and at the grass roots level (Aurat Foundation, 2021).

Since 2018 the Aurat Foundation has promoted an annual march to raise awareness of women's rights in Pakistan. In 2021, the Aurat March conducted demonstrations in Karachi addressing patriarchal violence, in Lahore raising awareness of the current health crisis since COVID-19, and in Islamabad focus-ing on crisis care. Two organisers from the Karachi march tackling patriarchal violence stated: "Our social media campaign, 'A-Z of Patriarchal Violence', highlights some specific tools that are used to perpetuate patriarchal violence, for example, acid attacks, enforced disappearances, discriminatory legislation against women and trans people, surveillance etc," the duo told." (Dawn, 2021). The foundation's front line approach has been fundamental in the fight for women's protection against all types of violence and honour killings.

Another manifestation of Pakistani Muslim women's "moderate" views of honour consciousness and religious consciousness can be seen in women's indi-vidual activism, a predominant feature within Pakistani millennial feminists (Shaheed, 2021). Pakistani actor Mira Sethi, for instance, is a vocal advocate of women's rights, and she is highly critical of Pakistani masculine formation, and views associated with women's modest dress code, where a woman wearing tight jeans is seen as pushing men "into sin." In her view, men should stop the constant policing of women. When attending a movie award in Pakistan she received media criticism over her dress code, but she responded swiftly by stat-ing (International The News, 2021): "Go home. I don't dress for you. I don't dress to anyone or anything other than my own sense of joy and play and expansion."

Pakistan's feminist movement has a "secular" and a "culturalist" strand. Cul-tural feminists, who stand up against western feminist ideals, support tradi-tional views on women and men, as well as religion, together with women's right to political engagement, and freedom from oppression and violence. Standing up against western paradigms is not a synonym for lack of agency and activism towards women's rights. Pakistan has a long history of female political participation, and a thriving feminist movement, developing a secular as well as a Muslim feminist perspective. This places women's voices at the fore of Pakistan's broader political debate. With parts of the movement enmeshing tradition and religion, Pakistani women's fight for rights, voices and agency cannot be easily categorised. Their lived experiences cannot be explained through western feminist lenses.

This is a perspective loathed by them as "imperialist" and as having "sold out" to western interests.[1] Pakistani feminism is defined on their own terms. In the next chapter I explore how Pakistani women's honour consciousness, religious consciousness, and gender power relations are transmitted to Australia.

---

1   Western feminist voices reflect the oppression of white Western women and are insufficient
    to explain the experiences of women in the Global South. However, the need of non-Western
    women to express how their lived experiences differ from the West increasingly led to the
    global fragmentation of the feminist movement.

Pakistani Women's Honour Consciousness and Lived Experiences of Gender in Australia

Muslim women migrating to the West are constantly having to adjust to their new environment, and to the host nation's cultural norms, traditions and Law (Yasmeen, 2020). For instance, in western nations, both men and women participate in the workforce; the need for a higher family income is a major factor contributing to Muslim women's workforce participation. Indeed, as argued by Bhavnani and Phoenix (1994; cited in Yasmeen, 2020), Muslim women in the West develop a hybrid identity: a "dual identity," one operating within the domestic arena (domesticity), and the other operating in the public arena (workspace).

Muslim women's struggle to adjust to the Western lifestyle and their need to reconcile their hybrid identities (domestic and public roles) have been exacerbated since the terrorist attacks on the Twin Towers in the United States on 11 September 2001, and the increasing "othering" of Muslims and Islamophobia.

Muslim migration to Australia is not a recent phenomenon: it can be traced back to Macassan fishermen from Indonesia, and their trade relationship with Australia's first peoples, a century before European settlement (Ganter, 2008). In the 19th century, Afghan cameleers, originally from regions in Balochistan and Punjab, farmers, hawkers, and Malays working in the pearl industry settled in the country, with Albanians working in agriculture also settling in the 1920's (Jones, 1993; cited in Yasmeen, 2020). With the end of the Immigration Restriction Act in the late 1960s, also known as the White Australia Policy (Goodall & Ghosh, 2015), the number of Muslim residents in Australia sharply increased from 2,704 in 1947 to 22,311 in 1971. And as outlined by Rane et al. (2020), the Australian Muslim population has been steadily increasing, and between the 1970s and mid-1990s exceeding 200,000 people.

Since 2011, numbers continued to grow. According to the 2016 Australian census, there are approximately 604,200 Muslims in Australia, with Islam being the second largest religion in Australia, trailing only after Christianity (Australian census, 2016). Muslims in Australia constitute 2.6 per cent of the total Australian population, an increase of 18 per cent if compared with the 2011 Australian census (Australian census, 2016).

Since the 2000's, Pakistan's regional instability, increased Islamic militancy, and negative views towards Muslims in the United States have all contributed

© FLAVIA BELLIENI ZIMMERMANN, 2025 | DOI:10.1163/9789004711242_006

to growing numbers of Pakistanis making Australia home. Muslims in the US and globally have been impacted by the War on Terror and perceptions of Muslim as a national security threat, leading to high levels of Islamophobia. As highlighted by Yasmeen (2010), during the 2006–2016 period we can see a sharp rise in the number of Pakistanis migrating to Australia. According to the 2016 census there are 61,913 Pakistanis living in Australia.

Yasmeen goes on to argue, however, that after the War on Terror, perceptions of Muslims and Islam in Australia have also changed. They have been reproduced by the media in simplistic and stereotypical terms. This has led to societal exclusion of Muslims in Australia, and their "othering" from the wider Australian society. Arguably, Muslims in Australia blamed the Australian media for negative reporting and a sensationalist tone in covering issues dealing with Islam, and also blamed the Australian government for contributing to the relative exclusion ("othering") of Muslims. Perceptions of non-Muslims towards Muslims were influenced by their own views, as well as by media reporting, which encouraged to the "othering" and relative societal exclusion of Muslims in Australia. The exclusion of Muslims in Australia led to an insular movement negatively impacting Muslim identities, and their sense of belonging in Australia.

For the purposes of this chapter, I am including the Pakistani gender composition in Australia in the figure below:

According to the 2016 Australian census, there are approximately 37,720 Pakistani males and 24,195 Pakistani females living in the country, with 42.3

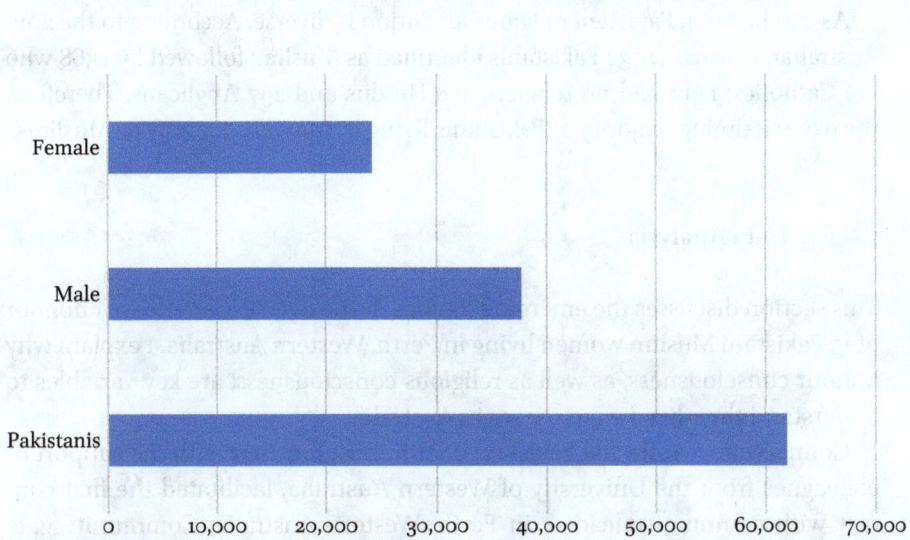

FIGURE 4.1   Pakistanis in Australia by gender
SOURCE: 2016 AUSTRALIAN CENSUS

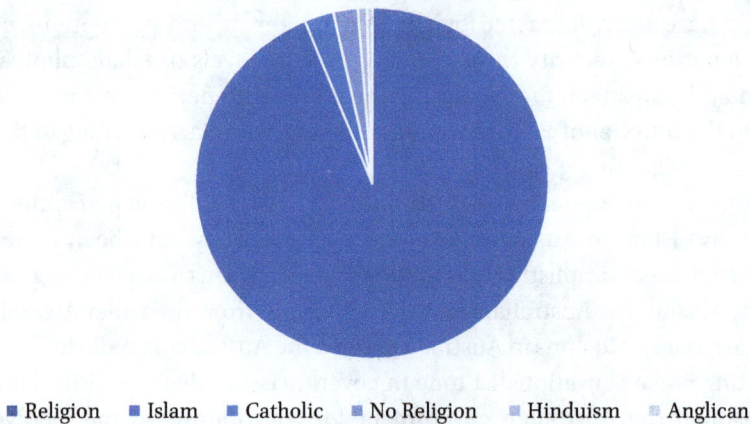

■ Religion   ■ Islam   ■ Catholic   ■ No Religion   ■ Hinduism   ■ Anglican

FIGURE 4.2   Pakistanis in Australia – religious affiliation
SOURCE: 2016 AUSTRALIAN CENSUS

per cent of total numbers being Australian citizens and 56.0 per cent not holding Australian citizenship.

Religion is another essential variable to understand Pakistani society, culture and Pakistani's identity. In the figure below estimated numbers for Pakistani's religious affiliation in Australian diaspora is shown:

As can be seen, Pakistani religious affiliation is diverse. According to the 2016 Australian census, 54,732 Pakistanis identified as Muslim; followed by 1,568 who are Catholics; 1,310 had no religion; 478 Hindus and 297 Anglicans. Therefore, the overwhelming majority of Pakistanis living in Australia identify as Muslims.

1   Data Analysis

This section discusses the emerging themes in the lived experiences of honour of 15 Pakistani Muslim women living in Perth, Western Australia. I explain why honour consciousness, as well as religious consciousness, are key variables to understand their lived experiences in Australia.

Connections within the Pakistani community, together with the support of colleagues from the University of Western Australia, facilitated the first contact with community leaders in Perth, Western Australia. Community gate keepers assisted with connections with members of the broader community. After meeting each member of the community, I applied the snow-balling method for participant recruitment, with samples reflecting a broad range of

TABLE 4.1   Pakistani participant number and culturally sensitive pseudonym

Participant number	Pseudonym
Participant 1	Fatima
Participant 2	Haniya
Participant 3	Inaya
Participant 4	Aalia
Participant 5	Madiha
Participant 6	Gul
Participant 7	Nazia
Participant 8	Abida
Participant 9	Kiran
Participant 10	Hiba
Participant 11	Jawaria
Participant 12	Shamaila
Participant 13	Naila
Participant 14	Zara
Participant 15	Uzma

views within the community in Perth. Spending time with community leaders and members ("deep hanging out"[1]) gave me insight into community dynamics and leading views towards honour, religion and gender.

Participants are referred to by numbers and have been de-identified in early stages of this research. In the table below I include participant's number with their culturally sensitive pseudonyms, which is followed by charts with participant's demographic composition:

Figures 4.3 and 4.4. displays Pakistani participant's age and registered marital status. This figure demonstrates a wide age range of collected samples, with the majority of participants being married. Figure 4.5 shows the sample's religious affiliation in Australia. This figure shows that the overwhelming majority of samples profess the Muslim faith.

---

1   "Deep hanging out" is an ethnographic technique where you spend time with participants before or after the interviews. I explained to each interviewee that our conversations before or after the interviews would be incorporated into my field notes. For Browne & McBride (2015) this is regarded as a useful method to access politically sensitive information, and to break down any power imbalances between interviewer and interviewee.

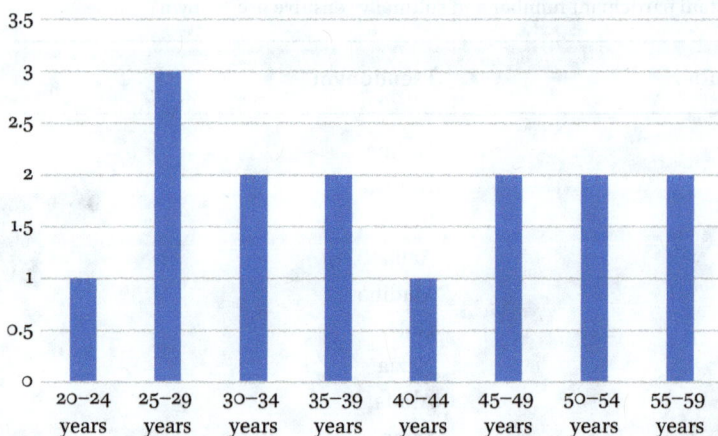

FIGURE 4.3   Participant's age

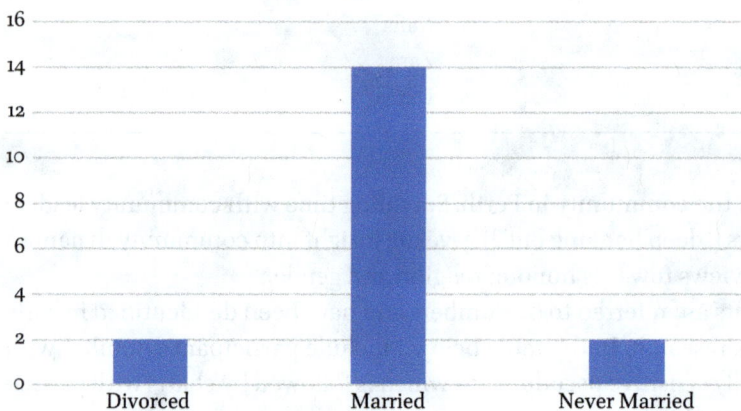

FIGURE 4.4   Participant's marital status

Figures 4.6, 4.7, 4.8 and 4.9 includes the sample's level of education, occupation, employment, years in Australia and migration status. These figures indicate that the majority of samples have university or tertiary education and are professional women, that they have high levels of part-time employment, and the majority have been in Australia for over 6 years and are Australian citizens. These figures demonstrate that samples reflect Pakistani migration waves (census, 2016), which predominantly are from upper middle classes, and have

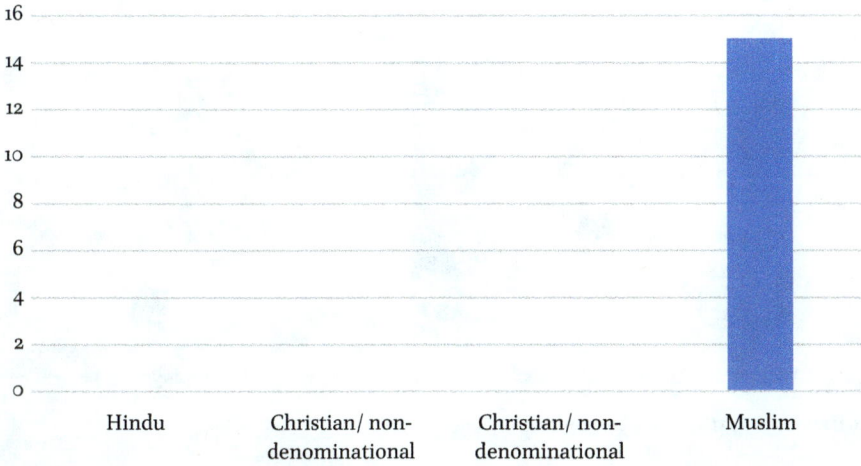

FIGURE 4.5   Participant's religious affiliation

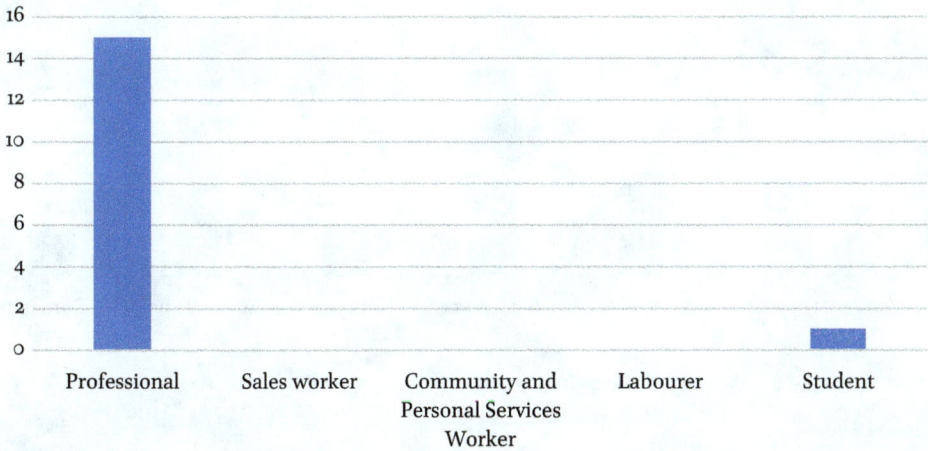

FIGURE 4.6   Participant's occupation

migrated within the family unit with the support of the Australian government, and are well established in Australia.

The wording used by the interviewees varied somewhat according to their generation and personal experiences. However, their lived experiences of honour and the meaning of honour are central to their sense of self, providing

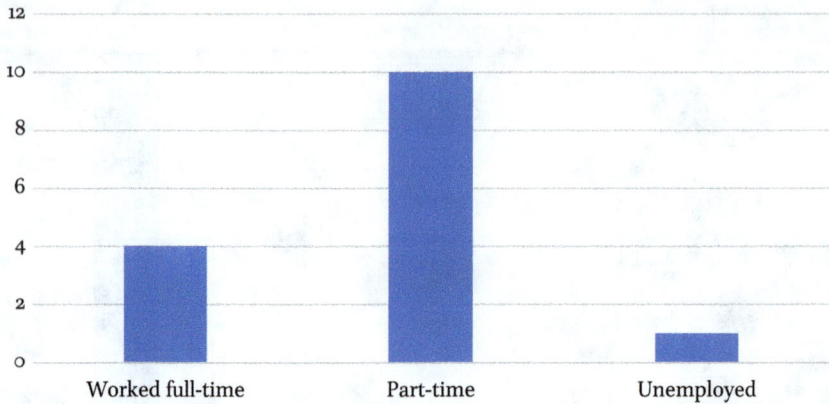

FIGURE 4.7   Participant's employment

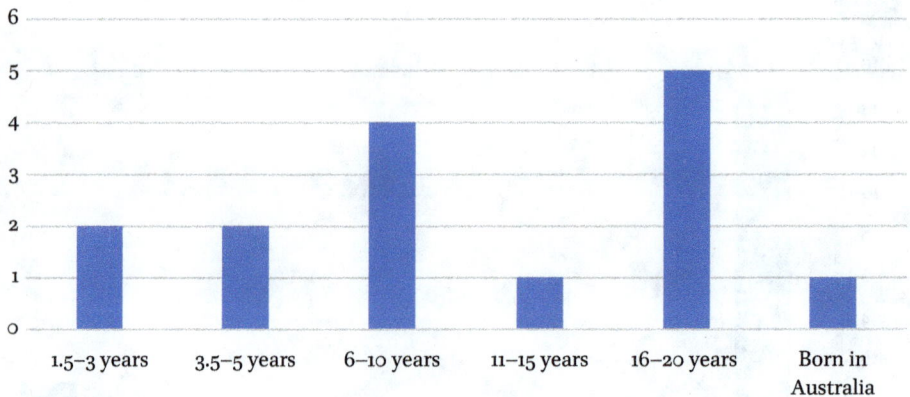

FIGURE 4.8   Participant's years in Australia

meaning to their interpersonal relations, familial relations and social relations in Australia. In all 15 interviews, Pakistani Muslim women described honour as an essential part of their values, their sense of "what is right and wrong," with honour defining the moral standards of respect and pride within families. I explain in this chapter how the theme of honour as a "value," or a "moral value" consolidating familial respect and pride, characterises Pakistani women's honour consciousness. This is a dominant theme in all the interviews, providing meaning to Pakistani Muslim women lived experiences of honour in Australia.

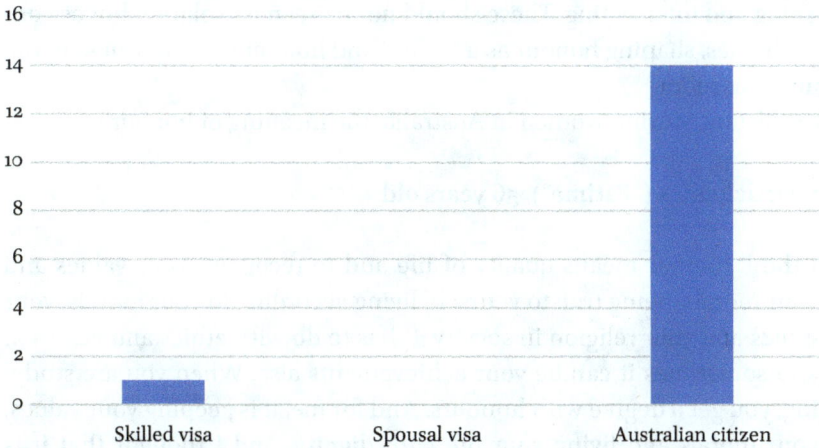

FIGURE 4.9   Participant's migration status

In some interviews, Pakistani Muslim women linked honour as a value and a moral compass, together with religious views (and morality) within Islam, which I define as their religious consciousness.

In this section I discuss the themes emerging from interviews. This chapter discusses, in depth, each participant's views of honour as "a value", empowering their voices, and giving greater clarity to the reader of Pakistani Muslim women's lived experiences of honour (and why it shapes honour consciousness). I lay out each participant's view of honour "as a value" since this is a key variable, bringing meaning to their lived experiences of honour consciousness. I decided to include participant's definition of honour, outlining how it shapes their perceptions of honour, and how honour consciousness continues to shape Pakistani Muslim women's lived experiences in Australia.

The underlying themes in participant's conceptualisation of honour (as honour consciousness), participants may fall into more than one group, as follows:

5)	Honour as a value and morality (Related or not to Islam)	Participants 1, 4, 5, 6, 9, 10, 12, 13, 14, 15
6)	Honour as respect for achievements, being respected in society	Participants 2, 3, 5, 8, 9, 11, 12
7)	Honour as respect and familial pride	Participants 7, 8, 9, 11

When providing a definition of honour, participants used the three sub-themes to explain the depth of honour in their lived experiences, with these enmeshing and intersecting. These should not be seen in isolation but as converging themes, shaping honour as a "value" and honour consciousness in the Australian diaspora.

For Pakistani Muslim women in Australia, the meaning of honour is:

For participant 1 ("Fatima"), 56 years old

> I think honour means quality of life and to recognise your values and your morals, being true to yourself, living according to your morals, your ethics and your religion in society. It has to do with ethics and values … and sometimes it can be your achievements also. When you are studying, you get a degree with honours. And for me, it is keeping your values, your morals and living your life with dignity. And I thought that it is the value set by your religion in your society, and that it means living by Islam. I am a Muslim, and personally feel that Islam gives a woman a lot of rights. It is actually a way of life. And if you know Islam, then you will know that it teaches you morality, good values, and how to be a good human being.

For participant 2 ("Haniya"), 45 years old

> Honour means, for example, an educational honour, on a roll kind of a thing, or achieving something which is honourable, in terms of whether it can be a work-related achievement, or educational achievement or even doing something for the society or the community. You don't need even to get awarded, just the honour of being on a specific roll, having the honour of serving the community, having the honour of being of value to anybody. All of these things, is what honour is for me. But everyone has a different definition or explanation.

For participant 3 ("Inaya"), 23 years old

> The definition of honour is very multifaceted. I mean, it could mean just to have honour. And to honour something is different, right? But if we are looking at honour at a societal level, I feel like to have honour is to be respected by your peers and to have moral values. I feel like to have honour is to know what's right, and what is wrong. I think that it is the basic level of what it means to have honour, and these are my values, those are your values, respect, and all that. I feel like, to me at least, at a basic level that is what it means. And then, I also feel like integrity is sort of involved,

to me as honour. I feel like if you really honour your word, or you need to have the integrity to be yourself, and also integrity to the society to have, like I said, moral values.

For participant 4 ("Aalia"), 55 years old

Whether it's in an honourable way or not ... is leaning towards, I suppose, the moral side, the moral code ... so the morality of things. How I conduct myself living within the boundaries of my religion. And of my own moral code, what is right and wrong. What I feel is right for me and what is wrong. Obviously, there's a background to where it comes from, but it is also about how I perceive that word (honour), which is really different to where I come from.

For participant 5 ("Madiha"), 33 years old

The word honour encompasses notions of respect, to being respectable, and also one's reputation in society. Like, for being honourable you would be considered to have a good reputation, or having good morals, or an inner reflection of morality.

For participant 6 ("Gul"), 52 years old

Honour to me means good character, people's good character, appropriate moral behaviour and sometimes related to cultural practices such as hospitality, reputation and social status. To me there are some boundaries, especially ladies, that they cannot trespass. Then they can be punished or in some extreme cases, and in some areas, they can get killed. And this is something personal. In our society men are more dominant, and they are also considered more powerful, they have the means to provide for the family, and they are considered to be responsible for keeping all these promises...Like, they are different. Maybe it is respect. Like if we are talking about the Islamic point of view, women have a very high priority. But in some countries like Pakistan, it is more a cultural, not an Islamic thing. People don't consider what is correct according to your own religion or God, but they just follow it, like our fathers and forefathers lived like this, so we will continue living this way. But because in Islam you cannot force anybody to do anything. Forced marriages in Islam! You cannot force anyone to marry a person. But in our culture, it is there. Women and men are forced into marriages.

For participant 7 ("Nazia"), 28 years old

Honour for me is like being proud of who you are and your family. But in Pakistan, people give the word honour different meanings. For me, honour is something that makes your family proud. But for others, it's like a girl having to get married or if they like some guy. Maybe it is a bit backwards. For me, honour is to be proud of something, that I will do to make my family, my mother proud. For me, honour is about those things which I will do in my life that makes my family proud. To say, yeah, my daughter is studying abroad. This is an honour for us.

For participant 8 ("Abida"), 54 years old

Honour means basic respect and protection, which in Pakistani culture people associate with honour, I don't think there is a word in English for that. But they use the word honour for that which is all right. But for me it's like protection and respect for everyone, not only for a woman, but every person. I was raised in a manner where I kept the honour for my family. I did not do anything against the values of my family. And it's not just because my family wanted that for me. I was raised in a manner that I believe those things. And I followed those things with my heart.... Maybe because the whole society was like that, and I was growing up around people who thought similarly. That makes it easy for everyone to follow these rules if you live in that society. It's hard over here. When you are living in a Western society and try to keep your own culture. But when you're living in a society where everyone is doing the same thing and is believing the same thing, it's easy to follow these rules. So I didn't do anything against my family's values or whatever I was taught.

For participant 9 ("Kiran"), 50 years old

For me, the word honour is integrity. Respect. I think it's more respect than anything else because it will be different in other instances. It's like, honouring someone. So, for example, when my grandfather was alive I would respect him, not esteem. If when we were growing up and even now when an older person comes into the room, you get up out of respect. For me, things like that means respect and honour. And another way of looking at it is when you give your word, like a promise you will fulfil. Again, it comes back to integrity. If you give your word to someone, you do it. Don't make false promises too... And I go to someone's house for dinner, I will say thank you, and respect them for the effort that they've put in. Honour for me in a religious context is very different because I think religion and culture gets very confusing. But I suppose, that achievement brings great honour. And then, the credit will go to the family, to the upbringing, to ethics and hard-work. So, I think keeping our family values, behaving appropriately in public, not dressing inappropriately.

For participant 10 ("Hiba"), 36 years old

It's like a concept, you know? So, with your own ethical values … ethical values which are very generalised. And ethical values that are appreciated and respected. Honestly, it's a respect that you earn for yourself, from wherever you live.

For participant 11 ("Jawaria"), 39 years old

For me, honour is about family and culture. And family in respect that, acting in a way that reflects on their families, so honour is about respecting them and living our lives in a way that doesn't bring shame on them. Living a life according to what your family thinks is right, or what your culture thinks is right. That is what honour is to me. Like reputation, social norms. It's a lot about honouring family and their beliefs, making sure that you are not behaving in a way which brings them shame or dishonours them.

For participant 12 ("Shamaila"), 52 years old

Like, it's a very deep word, I can't really explain it in one second. You know, for me, honour surrounds everything. Even if I am talking to you meaningfully, I am giving you honour. If you are talking to someone politely. That means that is honour. Like if you have a dignified personality, you should be respectable and honourable. That's my view about honour, like the highest, high regards. And, of course, it is very important for me.

For participant 13 ("Naila"), 34 years old

Honour is very personal. It has to do with how you conduct yourself, your beliefs and your values. It's related to your family being from town. Roles of males and females. And conforming to or not conforming to those roles, especially honour. Ethically sound, values, be a good human being,

I suppose. That would be an honourable thing for me. Ethics would basically be the same as everyone else. The ability to tell the difference between right and wrong, in any setting. Could be in ordinary life, everyday life, study, or in the workplace. As far as ethics is concerned, values are something that you have basically dictated from your family, your culture and your religion, and a mix of both, and how you've taken that in the area that you are living in and amalgamated all of that.

For participant 14 ("Zara"), 60 years old

Honour it's about everything. Honour is the most respected word for me. Because, you know, I told you, I am a Muslim. My Muslims concepts come from my religion. God gave us the right to be honoured. Like we should be physically respected, our emotions should be respected. Whatever belongs to us must be respected, like our family, our home, our friends, whoever we belong to must be respected. If no respect is not considered you are not fully human. Like what we were taught, that we should honour our elders, our teachers, and our authorities. Everyone who has authority, the laws and the rules that might belong to the family, or to the place where we live. So, we have to respect it and honour all those rules and regulations. For me it's such a big thing! I cannot even think of a thing that does not deserve honour. I think all should be honoured.

For participant 15 ("Uzma"), 43 years old

Well, honour means if you say you're going to do something, or if you commit to doing something, then you do it. If you give your word, you keep it. It means that you live your life without exploiting or hurting other people. It means that you're a honest and upright person and citizen. That's all that honour means because to be those, you must value hard work and integrity, you must value honesty, relationships and decency. So, it has to do with values, you should be a person with values. But that is because you have all these other values.

According to Pakistani Muslim women's views, honour as a "value," and a moral compass, shapes their honour consciousness, providing the cultural lenses through which they understand the social world. In some definitions of honour, Pakistani Muslim women explained that honour consciousness as well as religious consciousness are key elements in their value system. For these women, honour consciousness and religious consciousness are intertwined, and fundamental for an understanding of their lived experiences and their notions of womanhood. For the Pakistani participants, their lived experiences of honour consciousness are reconciled with traditional views of womanhood and religion, and with women's rights and female emancipation in the political sphere. According to their lived experiences, honour consciousness and religious consciousness are transmitted through their parent's values, views, and moral values, as well as through the values of their extended family – thus being a consciousness which is transmitted through the generations.

According to interviewees' lived experiences of honour consciousness and religion, the "othering" of "different" views of honour consciousness and religion provided greater meaning to their own lived experiences of honour, religion and gender. Consequently, based on their stories, lived experiences of honour consciousness and religion have a self-reflexive character. Through Pakistani women's perspective, honour consciousness and religion are positive experiences overall (although they reproduce gender politics in Australia), whereas "other notions" of honour consciousness and religion subjugate women, suppressing their voices, and can lead to violence in the name of honour and even to honour killings.

Family life plays a central role in the lived experiences of honour consciousness and religious consciousness for Pakistani Muslim women. Honour consciousness and religious consciousness as "a value" has been internalised in their ways of thinking through their family's upbringing ("the way I was raised") and has shaped their lives, based on their parent's values ("what I learned from my parents"). These themes were explored in depth by several participants.

Most participants agreed, and discussed at some point in their interviews, that honour consciousness and religious consciousness is not experienced in the same way by everyone in Pakistan. Participants agreed that there are "different" notions of honour, and that each person has their own notions of honour. Although there is a degree of subjectivity in individual notions of honour, some participants discussed in detail how honour consciousness and religious consciousness can be experienced in an "extreme way." Women taking part in this research explained that their own notions of honour were different from "extreme" notions of honour. I regard Pakistani Muslim women within the sample group to hold "moderate" notions of honour. "Moderate" notions of honour are manifested as follows: 1) Through reconciling traditional notions of womanhood and religion, 2) Support towards women's rights, 3) Women's political emancipation, 4) Women's empowerment in political leadership, 5) Women's right to work, and 6) Protection against domestic violence and inter-partner violence. Conversely, "extreme" notions of honour consciousness are manifested as follows: 1) Through women's subjection in religion 2) Suppression of women's rights, 3) Absence of women's political participation and having a voice in the political sphere, 4) Absence of women's political leadership, 5) Women's lack of rights in the workplace (control by their husbands), or no rights to pursuit paid work outside the home, and 6) Domestic violence in the name of honour and honour killings.

I will discuss women's stories, explaining the central role played by the family in shaping "different" notions of honour, and how the family's values are essential to the process of shaping honour consciousness and religious consciousness, including both "extreme" or "moderate" views of women's honour consciousness.

In Fatima's story, she explains how notions of honour consciousness and religious consciousness are values which are "learned." She explains how a mother's views on honour and religion are essential in shaping views of honour and religion. Through her story, she narrates the intergenerational transmission of ideas of honour, with women (as the primary care givers and the "queens of the domestic sphere") playing a critical role in the internalisation of values. The way she employs religion as a means of explanation demonstrates that her religious knowledge is limited, and that what she means by Islam and Muslim practices is more anecdotal than "studied." In Fatima's words:

> Actually, our problem is not that we are born Muslims, but rather we have learned only things from our communities, and our mothers, and grandmothers. We haven't actually studied Islam properly. It is sad, it's our whole way of life. It's not very easy to just learn from your mother or something, you have to actually learn it properly. And since it isn't in another language. The Qur'an is in Arabic, and we don't know Arabic, we just read it and we don't know the actual meaning of the words. So that is the problem. We didn't know what we are actually doing. They're doing what their mothers taught them, what they learned from them. We were very obedient, and we would do whatever we were told to without questioning. But not today's generation. They are very wise. They know how to ask questions, and they want answers, and then do the thing after knowing what they're being asked to do.

For Fatima honour is a value which was taught to her and her siblings by her parents and extended family, in the following terms:

> For me, I think my parents and my grandparents, they always taught us to do the right thing. I feel like that's got a lot to do with your honour. And, of course, if you do the right thing, that's the honourable thing to do. It

doesn't really matter if you benefit from it. And from a very young age that was instilled in us, like doesn't matter if you feel sad about it. Even if it's not what you want, you have to do the right thing.

Intergenerational transmission of honour consciousness is referred to by more than one participant. However, some are critical of the content of these ideas and their assumed links to religion.

Following this line of thought, most participants argued that honour is a "value," and a key variable shaping different "notions of honour."[2] Honour consciousness is something "taught" through family life and transmitted by their parent's values.

Another important theme emerging from honour as a "value" is that it is something which is taught or learned and is associated with your upbringing. Participants explained there are "other notions" of honour consciousness than their own. They distanced themselves, "othering" these notions of honour which are different from the ones they themselves hold. The "othering," and differences between their lived experiences of honour from "extreme" notions of honour was elaborated by most participants.[3] Pakistani Muslim women interviewed for this study regarded "extreme" notions of honour as "the other." In their stories, they associated the manifestation of "extreme" notions with less developed areas (remote rural areas) in Pakistan and to a lack of formal education. In their view, "extreme" notions of honour promote interpretations of Islam "not based on true Islam."

For instance, Hiba tells her story, of how she was brought up differently from "backwards" parts of Pakistan, areas lacking basic financial resources and where people are "ignorant." She explains that her lived experience of honour is different, "enlightened" when compared with "extreme" views of honour consciousness due to geography, that is, the Pakistani region where you come from. In Hiba's story, she explains how living in Pakistan's remote areas and not being able to access education, and also not having access to the rule of law, shapes "extreme" notions of honour and religion. She explains how "extreme" notions of honour consciousness are manifested:

People who are struggling for the basic needs, they're overpowered by people with the resources, but still living in ignorance and the absence of law. When it comes to ignorance, I would say both religious ignorance, and political ignorance. They sometimes think that honour is something

---

2 See Appendix, figure 3.
3 See Appendix, figure 3.

that is, like if somebody would go against them, they have the right to reprimand them. And they think on the basis of gender, their social standing
or their popularity amongst the people. In this sense, they have power, and
the right to reprimand others and feel like they are above the law. And in
those cases, mostly, the victim is a woman. Considering that she is weaker
physically. In our society, of course, predominantly females would cover
themselves because it is Pakistan's old tradition, in the southern part of
Pakistan. And it's nothing to do with the religion. It was there for a long
time, before Islam was actually there, you know? It's the concept of Karo-
Kari and it's found in the very backward parts of Sindh. Where if a woman
or a man, especially woman, is accused of adultery or lack of chastity she
would be stoned to death. And the man would only get lashes. But I think,
from the start, it's completely insane, its highly inhumane. It's something
that shouldn't happen. And still it is there. Look how gender unequal it
is. The woman is victimized compared to the men... It's men and women,
when they are from a more 'enlightened' part of the society, or are more
educated, you will see the difference. Girls are so confident, the religion
gives them a sense of security and a sense of privilege. I'll give you the
simple example of a girl studying at the university. I'm not covering my
head, and a boy would come to me [he is probably my classmate] and
he argues with me for three or four seconds. But if you see a girl in class
wearing a hijab, not covering her face just her head, he will talk to her
in a very respectful way. It's not that he wouldn't stop being angry, but
he would be more friendly, more respectful. Again, I don't know if I am
the right candidate to explain it, because I come from a part of Pakistan
where we are considered a bit more enlightened.

Hiba explains how "extreme" notions of honour consciousness are manifested
via the suppression of women's rights, and the privileging of men, and how this
can lead to honour killings (Karo Kari). She is critical of these notions of honour, explaining that in other parts of society there are views which are more
"enlightened," promoting women's rights and the empowerment of women
and girls within the boundaries of tradition and religion. Tradition and religion are reconciled with women's agency in her story, as Pakistani girls wearing
the headscarf (*hijab*) are more "confident," and would be treated with greater
respect by their male peers.

   She goes on to distinguish her lived experience of honour as "appreciation"
to herself, hard work and achieving excellency, as set out by ethical values
(honour consciousness), from the manifestation of "extreme" lived experiences of honour consciousness in Pakistan. These are manifested via women's

suppression, and violence towards women. For Hiba, "extreme" notions of honour are nearly "fictitious" in her lived experience of honour and religious consciousness, since she attended higher education, and enjoyed high levels of agency and empowerment. For her, "extreme" notions of honour consciousness were not part of her reality, or that of her friends, but something she would hear about on TV reports or the news. She also reflects upon honour consciousness's effects on religion (Islam), and how her lived experience of honour reconciles religious views with women's agency and empowerment. In her words:

> For me, honour is that. Appreciation. It is appreciation that I would earn myself. It is not something that my parents are expecting from me. Excellence is something that I think everybody sets for themselves, not by force, or even enforced by ethical values. Yes, I come from a culture where people, girls especially, they are very suffocated at home, some things are expected out of them. And some of them would follow these rules, whereas others would just rebel. Choices, yes. Society does not accept them and parents they react differently. Yes, we were brought up with these views. You've seen that on TV, on the newspaper. But for us, it has always been something like fictitious, because we haven't seen those things very close in our lives to literally witness it. So yes, extreme cases like that I have read in the newspapers, seen on TV, in the movies or heard people talking about that. But never really experienced that. I mean for us, it was still a very alien phenomenon that how could parents do that or how could anybody do that. We are influenced from Indians and Persians, and these are ancient civilizations we are a part of this culture. But eventually, it has nothing to do with religion, because I don't know if it's part of your question but to me, I have realized that there's nothing giving as much freedom as Islam gives us as women, the empowerment. It's when I look at it or study it in detail.

Similarly, some participants explained how Pakistan's "extreme" views of honour are different from their own views, and how "other" notions of honour in Pakistan condone women's suppression, as well as acts of honour-based violence such as honour killings.[4] Haniya elucidates, in her words:

---

4   See Appendix, figure 3.

So, you can go to that extreme level of people killing the whole family, sometimes boys kill the whole family, even their parents if they are supporting their daughter. It is very sad. So, this is extreme. Other level is like I was telling my own story, how I wanted to get a divorce. And my parents were super supportive. My grandmother and immediate family were supportive. But the extended family [like my mom's cousins] were not supportive at all. And they created so many issues. They would spread rumours, and then they called the tribal council to say: "Oh, this is this person is doing this, so let's punish them socially, not invite my parents to any social functions, or cut off contact with them," because they were supporting me. And why? Because it was dishonourable for a girl to ask for a divorce when a man have all rights to file for a divorce? So that's how they were justifying other divorces in the family, which had happened. They said, it was a man who had filed, but a girl asking for a divorce was seen as a dishonourable thing.

Haniya narrates how "extreme" views of honour can be manifested, in contrast with her own notions of honour consciousness and that of her parents. Interestingly, within the same family it is possible to oscillate between what I call "moderate" notions of honour and religion, and "extreme" notions of honour and religion. In Haniya's story, she was supported by her parents when she divorced her husband, but she was reprimanded by her extended family, who deemed her action "dishonourable." Being rejected by her extended family, and the social ostracism following divorce were the main reasons why she migrated to Australia. Although things have changed more recently in Pakistani society, honour consciousness continues to place women in a disadvantaged position, consolidating Pakistani men social hegemony.

In Aalia's story, she elaborates how "extreme" notions of honour consciousness and religious consciousness are manifested in Pakistan through the control of women, standards of sexual purity ("she might be having an affair"), and the social perception of female purity ("and sometimes they are not having an affair," meaning they have been seen together). I regard her view of honour consciousness and religious consciousness as "moderate," since she criticizes the manifestation of honour through patriarchy, violence towards women and honour killings, as well as those religious views supporting women's suppression and gender politics in the country. Although, in recent years, the Pakistani government introduced legislation clamping down on honour killings in Pakistan, Aalia explained how this is not enough or just "too little too late." She shares her story:

Even though sometimes they're not having an affair, they just want it for property matters. They feel that they're men and they need to keep the parent's property or land in their name, and they don't want their sisters to have it. They either get their sisters married into the Qur'an [which is totally un-Islamic and illegal], or they defame them, saying she's having an affair, and then get them both killed. And maybe she's not having an affair. And even if she is, I think our religion gives girls the right to choose her partner. Recently, we had one girl who was making online videos, posting them and singing songs [they were sort of explicit, provocative]. And unfortunately, she was killed by her brother. That is the extreme side of how, in a patriarchal society, men use their power and resources to sort of implicate women, their sisters or even their wives to get them killed. Because you know it's against their honour that their sister is talking to a guy. It's against their honour that she's interested in a guy or wants to marry a guy without their involvement. So, there are lots of cases when you listen in the news.

According to Madiha, when discussing experiences of honour for men and women, she contends that for men it is much easier to "regain" honour, and that in "extreme" cases you can have honour killings – associating "other notions" of honour to gender inequity in Pakistan, as follows:

First of all, it's quite hard from my perspective…It's very hard for a man to really lose their honour, but if they were both lose their honour…both men and women they are complete outcasts from the community or the society. Your family, in extreme cases, will disown you if you've dishonoured them. And there's the whole concept of honour killings. For women it can be much harder to regain acceptance into their families and into let's say the community, in the workplace or in their friend's circles. I think it can be more difficult to re-establish or to re-build your honour but for the men, I don't think that it is as difficult!

In Gul's story, she establishes a distinction between her notions of honour as "good character" and good moral behaviours, "cultural practices such as hospitality," "reputation" and "social behaviour," and 'other' notions of honour (from "some areas") with "extreme" cases – where women can get killed. She acknowledges male dominance in Pakistan as an on-going issue. Gul explains in her words:

To me, it means good character. And people's good and appropriate
moral behaviour and sometimes it is useful cultural practices such as
hospitality, reputation and social status. And to me that there are some
boundaries and if anyone, especially ladies, they passed beyond these
boundaries, then they can be punished or in some like extreme cases
sometimes, in some areas, they can be killed.

In Abida's story, "extreme" notions of honour consciousness are manifested
through violence towards women and honour killings and can occur throughout the country. However, she observes that they are prevalent in "tribal areas"
(those do not exist anymore, and her statement is based on the memories of a
long-term migrant), as well as in remote areas of the country. In her story she
discusses that, based on "extreme" notions of honour consciousness and religious consciousness, if a girl elopes, this can result in the family taking matters
into their own hands. Consequently, in order to protect and preserve the family honour and reputation, family members can kill their sisters or daughters.
She remarks that unless a girl elopes, thus bringing shame to the family, all
families in Pakistan are "normal" and "honourable." This indicates that Abida's
views of honour consciousness and religion might be tilting slightly towards
"extreme" views of honour consciousness and religious consciousness. In her
view, girls should not go against their parent's values system (boundaries); in
other words, girls should abide by their parent's views of honour and religion
to avoid any reprimands ("triggering men"). In her words:

> In cities it is still happening, but not like in remote areas, where people
> hear of honour killings and people getting killed. Yeah, that kind of stuff
> happens in those tribal areas, in the remote areas, but in cities it's a bit
> better. It's not that bad, maybe once or twice, overall, it's different. It's
> those views on honour killings and very extreme views, for people in the
> city it's like those views are foreign to them. Usually, everyone is honour-
> able, every family and person. Unless something happened. Like, if a girl
> just elopes and runs away from the house, or do something against the
> family values, something like that, that would trigger men, the family and
> the society. If that doesn't happen, everyone is honourable. If all things
> are normal like a normal family, everyone is honourable.

She explains further that she was brought up in a remote area of Pakistan (in a
small village). Although her views of honour consciousness and religious consciousness (learned from her parent's values) differ from "extreme" notions of

honour consciousness and religious consciousness, in her formative years she lived in a region where "extreme" views are predominant. She mentions that although her family gave her the freedom to choose her husband, and that she was not subjected to a forced marriage, which is common in remote areas of Pakistan, she did actually have an arranged marriage. She believes women and girls have to follow their family's values ("they had limits"), such as, that good Muslim girls should dress modestly, and at certain times are not allowed to go out (as these restraints are imposed by the society and religion). She was allowed to go out and live but within those boundaries of tradition and religion. This was the same lived experience of honour consciousness and religious consciousness of her extended family members and her friends. In her words:

> I was from a middle-class family in Pakistan, living in a city, but I was born in a small village. And then my father moved to the city, and I grew up over there, and I was allowed to get an education and to get married with whoever I wanted. Which I did. I actually had an arranged marriage. But if I wanted to marry someone else that would be okay with my parents and my family. But there are other things, which I can associate with honour, like there are certain things we were not allowed. Certain dress code. Like we had to dress like a proper Muslim girl, certain times where we were not allowed to go out. These limits come from the religion and society, so we have to follow them. So, within those limits I was allowed to do somethings. And because that's how my family and in my friends' families lived. I don't know anyone who tried to do things against their family values. It was the rule. So, I don't know any friend or anyone who wanted to go against their family values and society.

When sitting down and talking to Pakistani Muslim women in Western Australia other key sub-themes emerged such as the relationship between honour consciousness and religious consciousness, and the central role played by family relations in enforcing the honour code. Interviewees discussed how this shapes individual behaviour, and how honour consciousness and religious consciousness impacts the lives of women in Pakistan, shaping gender politics in the country.

According to participant's stories, honour consciousness and religious consciousness are consolidated through family life, as the family plays a central role when examining lived experiences of honour consciousness, and how it shapes notions of womanhood. The women interviewed hold "moderate" views of honour consciousness. In some participant's reflections they discussed not having experienced differential treatment, or having fewer opportunities to achieve higher education, from their brothers, although at the same time acknowledging that there were still more social constraints related to the behaviour of girls and women when compared to the behaviour (and freedoms) of boys and men. Most participants agreed that women's behaviour was under far more scrutiny than that of men. For example, girls have stricter curfews than boys.

Naila shares her story:

> I had tighter curfews as opposed to my brothers who were boys. You know, they had more leniency curfews, the right time to be at home. So, it was easier for boys. It was honourable for women to be at home at a certain time.

Family and honour are important themes consolidating honour consciousness and Pakistani's constructed gender roles. Even for Pakistani Muslim women holding "moderate" views of honour consciousness and religious consciousness, if they dishonour their families, they could be cut off from family ties, losing family support and their networks, as well as the parental rights for seeing their children.

Madiha explains women who lose their honour are cut off from their families, but this doesn't happen to men:

> For women it is much harder to regain acceptance into their families and into let's say the community, in the workplace or in their friend's circles. I think it can be more difficult to re-establish your honour but for a men, I don't think that it is as difficult!

Another consequence for women who challenge the honour code, for instance by filing for a divorce, is social ostracism and stigmatisation. The fact that they are divorced makes the community "talk" bad things about them, suspecting their standards of piety and purity, all of which contributes to them being seen as dishonoured. Not having a man by your side makes you dishonoured, since family unity is central to consolidate honour consciousness. Being divorced increases a woman's likelihood of suffering sexual harassment.

Haniya shared her story, and how divorce has affected her "status," as in Pakistan men felt entitled to "make advances" to a single, unmarried, woman. In her words:

I've quit jobs because of those kinds of things, I even stopped going to a doctor. Like they ask you: Are you married? And you say no, and then the doctor starts talking about stupid things. And you really don't know even to who you tell, like where you can go, instead of being crying to your father all the time.

A divorced woman is dishonoured for not having a man to protect her, and their father or a son would then need to protect her from harassment. Through the cultural lenses of honour consciousness, women play a vital role in the family as nurturers and home makers, and single women, particularly divorced women, are seen as dishonoured because they are not fulfilling their primary social duty: to look after a husband and family.

During interviews Pakistani Muslim women explained that losing honour can have dramatic consequences for families upholding "extreme" notions of honour consciousness, as women can become victims of an honour killing. However, they reflected that "nothing" happens to men (if they lose honour) as "they can do whatever they like." Although notions of honour suffer intra-cultural variation, with views oscillating between "moderate" and "extreme" notions of honour, honour consciousness and family relations promote male hegemony in Pakistan. Thus, honour consciousness and family still consolidate male privilege and gender politics throughout the country.

Pakistani Muslim women explained that honour impacts individual behaviour and also has a broader conceptualisation that applies to both men and women. Nevertheless, as mentioned in the previous section dealing with honour consciousness and family, there are also gender-specific guidelines applicable to women only.

Pakistani Muslim women discussed that to tell the truth, to fulfil your promises keeping your word, respect your parents and your elder, as well as work hard, put the best effort in what you do and strive for excellency are all behaviours which bring an individual honour. These behaviours are gender neutral, since both women and men should aim to have a "good name" and uphold the family name.[5]

When reflecting upon the meaning of honour and how it affects her lived experience and the behaviour upholding honour consciousness, Shamaila shares her story:

---

5   See Appendix, figure 3.

If I'm putting something especial for you, it means I am honouring you. Even if it relates to my home, my workplace. When you say that it's an honour, it means that if customers are coming to my shop it should be presentable, I need to give them honour, treat them nicely, politely. And at home, elders need to look after and be affectionate to young girls and they should be respectful to their elders, and love and peace should be evident, I can go on and on. So, honour for me is basically something to do with the organization of society. Sometimes you don't feel like doing it. But you do it. That's again is an honour.

In her story, Shamaila tells us how important it is to make your best effort in the way you do your work, the way you organise your shop, and the way you serve your customers. Doing things "the right way" and striving to do your best is a behaviour that confers honour. Through the cultural lenses of honour consciousness, the intergenerational relationship (and respect) paid to the elder and to your parents is very important. There is a hierarchy of greater respect which should be shown to senior members of the community (elder), older members of the family and your parents. These are behaviours increasing individual and family honour, as individual honour reflects on the honour and the "good reputation" and "good name" of the family (Christianson & Erikson, 2021; Cooney, 2019; Nisbett & Cohen, 1996).

Hiba elaborates further, in her words:

> Work, just striving for excellence, you know? So it is something that you've earned for yourself, or respect that you earned for yourself. And the people who are around you know, they're proud of you, they compliment you, they love you and respect you. So this is an honour. Whatever role I may have in life, I will do it with dignity and with respect.

In her lived experience of honour, Hiba explained that to excel in what you do, to be the best at what you do, increases individual honour and family prestige. Professional jobs such as doctors, lawyers etc. are seen as bringing greater honour to an individual and their families. Other participants contended, however, that in Pakistan some girls go to university in order to secure a good "honourable" marriage. After finishing their degree and getting married, they quit their jobs to look after their husbands and children, even if they have house servants. To be the nurturer and to look after their husbands, their children and their home is seen as women's primary role in Pakistan.

According to Pakistani Muslim women's lived experiences of honour, honour consciousness and religious consciousness shaped the way they should behave socially so that they are seen as "a good girl." For a woman to be honoured, there are several "boxes" they should tick, whereas for men they can do "whatever they like" and it is "impossible for them to lose honour."

Interviewees shared that for a Pakistani woman to be honoured she should dress modestly, showing no "cleavage" or "your legs." All participants agreed that to dress modestly and not to show "flesh" is a behaviour which brings honour. The full head covering was not essential, and some women would use a headscarf because "they wanted to," but "have never been forced" to dress this way. Thus, Pakistani Muslim women in this study perceive the head covering as a personal choice whereas dressing modestly is non-negotiable. Kiran explains:

> Look, again, every person is different. Everyone reads it differently [regarding the hijab]. I think that if you look at Pakistani culture, and it's different in other countries, but dressing conservatively, and that is something that we grew up with. Like in Pakistan, most women will not show their cleavage. It's just one of those things because it draws attention. You know, so it's like we wear jeans and Western clothes when we're going to work. For example, we wear jeans trousers or whatever. But you won't wear a pair of shorts or a skirt. You will wear a long skirt, but you wouldn't wear a knee-length skirt when you're going out. You just don't show your legs.

According to Pakistani Muslim women's views, not dressing modestly would bring shame to their families, as people are quick to judge, and people start gossiping. As illustrated by Kiran: "have you looked at her, how she is dressing?"

In Pakistani society, once a woman loses her honour it might be impossible to regain it. The social expectation is that women should dress and behave in a way that is honourable, and if their honour is tainted it might be impossible for them to regain it. However, Pakistani Muslim women explained that honour consciousness operates differently for men. In their view, men can "get away" with far more, they can even "commit a crime," but with time people forget and they can move on with their lives (as if nothing had happened). But with women the lived experience of honour is different: once tainted you will always be tainted.

Thus, in Pakistani Muslim women's lived experiences, honour consciousness is inherently gendered, with honour consciousness setting out high standards of behaviour for women. Only by following these guidelines can they be seen as honourable and bring honour to their families. Men can get away with any misdemeanour, but not women. Men are free to do as they please, even commit crimes, but eventually they are "forgiven" whereas women who defy the honour code are punished and never "forgiven."

These guidelines also mandate that women's bodies should be under constant surveillance and "controlled" to uphold individual and family honour, because women are the bearers of family honour.

In Madiha's lived experience of honour, it is harder for a man to lose his honour than a woman. She explains the impact of honour consciousness on women's social behaviour:

> I guess it's a lot harder for a man to lose his honour compared to a woman. For women to be accepted, to be honourable, that standard, or even the expectations are so high. You have to dress and talk in a particular way. You have to be educated and not have any relations with anyone considered slightly dishonourable. Whereas for men I think it's very hard for them to lose their honour, even if they commit like a crime. They can even temporarily lose their honour but then it is very easy for them to regain it. Whereas for a woman, I think what once you lose it, or what the community or society decides that is honourable, it's actually impossible to regain it. You're always somehow tainted.

Honour consciousness and religious consciousness is intrinsically gendered consolidating gender politics in Pakistan. Through Pakistani Muslim women's lived experiences of honour this chapter demonstrates how honour consciousness, as experienced by women taking part in interviews, demands far more from women than from men. For women to be regarded as honourable by their families they must obey strict curfews, obey their parents, and be married (be good daughters, wives and mothers), as family plays a central role in consolidating honour consciousness and gender relations. There are several "boxes" women have to tick, when considering their social behaviour: for example, they need to dress modestly, and behave in a way that is chaste and modest. If women "breach" the honour code, it will be impossible for them to regain it. Conversely, it is nearly "impossible" for a man to lose honour. Even if he commits murder, he will eventually be "forgiven" and be able to move on with his life (as if nothing had happened). All these factors promote male hegemony and privileges, consolidating gender politics in Pakistani society.

The table below shows honour consciousness's key ideas regarding behaviour and family relations, and the gap between women's and men's lived experiences of honour. The table also sets out the distinction between moderate and extreme manifestations of honour consciousness in the lives of men and women, as well as how women are disproportionally affected by the honour code.

TABLE 4.2   Honour consciousness's key ideas regarding behaviour and family relations, and the gap between women's and men's lived experiences of honour

Honour consciousness	Behaviour	Family Relations
Intrinsically gendered	**Women have more duties:** – they need to behave well – dress modestly – be pure – have curfews – they uphold the family honour	– to be married – be good wives – be good mothers – family must approve choice of spouse – house chores still predominantly their duty
	Men can do whatever they please: – no curfews – no need of purity – no restriction to dress code	– they are the breadwinners – they are the head of the household
What brings honour equally to men and women?	– education – professional career – ethical values – moral values – be hard-working	– respect of the parents – respect of elders – good family name
Moderate notions	– tradition coupled with women's rights – women's rights within religion (Islam) – fight for the protection of women's rights	– taught by the parents – values of the parents – where you came from – predominantly city centres
Extreme notions	– female suppression – female control – forced marriages – violence towards women – honour killings	– taught by the parents – values of the parents – where you came from – predominantly rural areas

This section will discuss Pakistani Muslim women's stories and how honour consciousness and religious consciousness continue shaping their lived experiences in Australia.

When discussing lived experiences of honour in Australia, Pakistani Muslim women's families and family life play a central role in their lived experiences of honour in Australia. Most Pakistanis migrated to Australia together with their families (Yasmeen, 2010), bringing with them their fidelity to the key role played by the family unit in transmitting their values and morals to the next generation, thus internalising honour consciousness in first generation Pakistanis in Australia.

Pakistani Muslim women interviewed in this study explained their lived experiences of honour in Australia, acknowledging that their parent's values, and upbringing, have been key in shaping their notions of honour (as well as the notions of honour of other members of the Pakistani community) in the diaspora. Thus, the family's values and notions of honour are transmitted via the parent's values, with the family being central to the process of internalising their notions of honour and religion. Accordingly, Pakistani honour consciousness and familial views of honour translate to Australia, with parents still having substantial influence in their offspring's lives. For instance, arranged marriages are not compulsory, but the views of the parents will still greatly influence their children's choice of spouse, with some setting up their children with eligible partners within their Pakistani Muslim networks.

Another important aspect of honour consciousness and family life in Australia are views regarded unmarried women, who are past their "marriage age," and divorced women. These women are ostracized by their families. For single women in their late 30's not yet married, the family, as well as the Pakistani community, would ask "what is wrong with you, why you are not married?" and "you should already have kids at this age." For divorced women, some members of the Pakistani community would interject: "why don't you find another husband" or "go back to your husband." These views are transferred to Australia due to the central role played by family life in the lives of women, since through honour consciousness cultural lenses, women's primary role is to be wives and mothers. For not being married, and not having a child by your late 30's, a Pakistani Muslim woman would be seen as breaching the honour code. In addition, a Pakistani Muslim woman who divorced their husband, and did not remarry, would be looked down upon, because she is "living for herself," instead of fulfilling her role as a pious and supportive wife.

Kiran tells her story and how there are arranged marriages in Australia. She explained that "perhaps, around 30 years ago" arranged marriages were very common within the Pakistani diaspora in Australia. Kiran migrated to Australia after an arranged marriage to her husband, whose family had migrated to Australia generations ago. She explained it was not a forced marriage "as she had the power to veto." In her story, however, honour consciousness and views regarding family life can clearly be transmitted through more than one generation, impacting first, second and third generations born in Australia from Pakistani parents. She explains:

> So my husband was here [in Australia]. His family's been here for quite a few generations. But having said that, I did have the power of veto. So, I was not forced into marriage and met him a few times. And then my dad said, they proposed. Would you like to marry him? And I am going, now it's too late, I am getting engaged tomorrow! But yeah, they asked my permission before I got married, whether I was happy with it.

The family plays a central role in internalising honour consciousness and religious consciousness in the lives of offspring, as well as consolidating the gender roles within family life. The "right choice" of partner for their children allows cultural transmission of the honour code to the next generation. According to participant's stories, a very "Western" or "Australian" partner is seen by the Pakistani community as "not bringing" honour, since they are not able to transmit honour consciousness to the next generation, jeopardising the transmission of respect to the parents, elders, and gendered roles within the family. In Madiha's view, the leading reason behind parents interfering in their children's choice of spouse is that of cultural transmission.

Another issue for Pakistani Muslim parents in Australia is that, both for themselves and in order to preserve their faith, their children should marry a Pakistani spouse. This requirement, however, is more flexible for men than women. According to Islam, men can marry women from Abrahamic faiths (Jews and Christians), but this does not apply to women. Participants explained how sons can marry Christian girls, but the reverse is not allowed. Madiha discussed how Pakistani views on marriage reproduce gender politics in the family and in Australia, as while men had freedom to choose their spouses, it was preferable that women should marry a Pakistani Muslim in Australia (or brought over from Pakistan), to bring honour to their family and to please their parents.

Thus, the parent's approval of their children's choice of spouse is an important variable in reproducing honour consciousness and religion in the Australian diaspora. Pakistani children are not forced to get married in Australia, but at the same time, going against their parent's wishes would make them "dishonourable" within their family, and before the Pakistani community. They would "lose face" before the community, as people would gossip about it.

Another interesting story of how parents continue influencing their children's lives in Australia, is Madiha's reflection upon parents setting up their children for marriages, as if parents were taking on the role of "tinder" (a dating app). In her words:

> There's definitely a lot of those parents. They set their children up. And, I guess, technically this isn't an arranged marriage, but not like what happens in certain rural communities where you might not even know the person that you are marrying. It's kind of like saying how we have all these dating apps now, you know? So instead of having tinder, this might be more useful. And maybe, some people probably wouldn't mind... I guess. Another reason that my parents would want us to hold onto Pakistani culture is because it is also considered an honourable thing in the community if you practice your culture.

Jawaria's story explains the depth of honour consciousness and religion within Pakistani families, and the broader Pakistani community in Australia. Jawaria is a Pakistani Muslim woman, first generation, born in Australia. As she approached her 40's, she discussed how much criticism and pressure she received from her family to get married and have a child. She reflected upon the pressure her mother had from the Pakistani community, constantly asking her why her daughter was still single and without children. Her mother saw the fact she was in her late 30's and single as an "embarrassment," compromising hers and her mother's reputation (did not look honourable) before the Pakistani community in Perth.

Honour consciousness's cultural lenses continue in Australia, and there are high demands from family members that women get married and have children, ideally with Pakistani Muslim men (either living in Australia or to be brought in from Pakistan). Through the lenses of honour, she and her mother face community criticism (even ostracism) since she is not complying with her primary role: to be a good wife and mother, as well as ensuring the cultural transmission of Pakistani values (honour and religious consciousness) to the next generation.

> So, I feel like not being married at my age, that's a big thing. But my mom once said to me, she was embarrassed because people keept asking her. So, for us like, it's not following the norms in our culture. It is like, if you

are a girl in your 20s you get married and have kids. And if you don't follow that you don't fall into the norm, and you get looked down upon.
Growing up here [in Australia] has been very difficult.

Regarding the social ostracism faced by Pakistani Muslim women who
divorced their husbands, few participants discussed the negative impact that
divorce had on the way they were perceived by the Pakistani community in
Australia.[6] In these three stories, they reflected upon the community's views on
a divorced woman, and how it made them, as well as their families, be seen as
"dishonourable" and not "respectable" in the eyes of the Pakistani community.
These women suffered community backlash for not complying with gender
roles consolidated through honour consciousness and religion. Through honour consciousness lenses, these women should be more submissive and should
have stayed with their husbands "for the sake of the family." Familial relations
play a key role in internalising honour consciousness (values and morals),
and gender politics within the home. The Pakistani community also attempts
to enforce honour norms in the diaspora, but individuals have the option to
avoid, or at least limit contact, with the Pakistani diaspora in Australia.

Fatima shares how honour consciousness impacted her life. Honour's
cultural lenses on family life, and the role of women, are reproduced in the
Pakistani community, consolidating gender politics within the family, and the
Pakistani community in Australia. She explained how being divorced and a
single mother, through the lenses of honour consciousness, made her "unre-
spectable." When she moved to Australia, she suffered harassment from a
female member of the Pakistani community, who called her on the phone,
encouraging her to return to her husband. She reminded her that she would
be respectable if she was a widow, but was not respectable as a divorcee. Honour consciousness consolidates familial views where women should be married, fulfilling their primary social role: being good mothers and good wives,
and looking after their husbands. These views consolidate gender politics and
social reproduction within the home, with women seen as the main care givers
and responsible for domestic tasks. A single divorced woman does not have a
husband to look after, thus subverting her social role.

Honour has shaped me a lot. Being a single woman in my country.
If a woman is divorced they are seen as not being respectable. In fact,
when I moved, a lady from the Pakistani community called me [I didn't

---

6   See Appendix, figure 3.

know her that well]. She just picked up the phone [took my number from someone else]. And called me and she said "Oh I've heard that you are divorced. And in our society [she was talking about Pakistani society] a woman who is a widow is respectable, but a divorced woman isn't respectable," so I should go back to my husband, who was not here but in another country.

Given that these are common views within Pakistanis in Australia, not all views are the same. Honour consciousness cannot be seen as a homogenous experience since it suffers intra cultural variation, depending on the way you were brought up by your parents (your parents' values), as well as on your class, caste and region. As previously discussed, views on honour and religion can be manifested in a "moderate form" through both tradition and religion being reconciled with women's rights, or, conversely, through "extreme" views leading to female suppression and violence towards women. Consequently, views within the Pakistani community are also not homogenous, with many people being supportive of women who divorced their husbands and are raising children single-handedly.

Fatima goes on sharing how some members of the Pakistani community in Australia accepted her, even though she was a divorcee:

It varies. Some people were very supportive. And they knew me as a person, not as a single woman or a divorced woman. So obviously, they respected me for the fact that I am raising these three children in a foreign country by myself. But there were exceptions. There were a few people who disrespected me and said things, but it didn't affect me much, because I had people around me who were very supportive.

Fatima's lived experience of honour consciousness and gender follows the literature exploring the role of family, family honour, women's submission to their parents and spouse as well as honour's standards of female purity (Cooney, 2014; Guerra et al., 2012; Johnson & Lipsett-Rivera, 1998; Nisbett & Cohen, 1996).

In Australia, honour consciousness is still a dominant framework for Pakistani Muslim women in the understanding of family, gender politics within their homes, and notions of womanhood in the broader Australian society. Hiba is married and has two children, but her husband works overseas, so in practical terms, she lives as a single mother raising two young children on her own. Hiba was a professional woman before having children and quit her job to look after the children and support her husband's offshore career. She reflected how she feels respected by Australian society, and by her neighbours, for raising children alone. Through the lenses of honour consciousness, she is "respected" and "honoured" by the community because she decided to be a stay-at-home mother to raise her kids, although she is university trained. This is seen as the primary role of women through the perception of honour, and she feels that it is an honour to receive the respect of Australian neighbours for her efforts in raising two children alone while her husband works.

Hiba reflects upon her experience:

> They are acknowledging your hard work. So, most norms are the same in Australia. [In Australia] they have the same criteria, they are with their children. I respect them, they respect me for being a mum, so for us this is an honour.

However, as explained by Aalia, in Australia domestic chores continue to be a women's duty: in her words:

> When I say yes [that things do not change in Australia] I am talking about men being given special priority over women. You know, them being given privileges over women. Whether it is at gatherings laying out the food, serving food or ironing their clothes. Things like that.

Aalia explained how honour consciousness continues along gendered lines in Australia. She acknowledges that women are still expected to serve men and "look after men" by ironing their clothes, for example. Although this is still somewhat of a problem in Australia, she understands that women have also been empowered in Australia. Most migrant women in Australia, as Aalia explains, are from privileged backgrounds. In her view, this fact has already had an impact on their degree of agency and empowerment. In the Australian experience, although the gender lines of honour continue, they shift, adjust and adapt to the Australian culture. For example, based on field notes, Abida was served a cup of tea by her husband before our WhatsApp video interview. In Australia, as was mentioned by some participants, there is no home help such as maids and nannies, so men need to "help." However, women are still the primary care givers of children, and they do most of the housework, while men remain the "breadwinners." In Abida's story, when her children were little, she would not work. Now that they are grown up, she works part-time.

After conversations with service providers and Pakistani Muslim women in Western Australia, field work results demonstrate that domestic violence occurs "in the name of honour" within the Pakistani community in Australia, and a service provider disclosed high levels of domestic violence towards Pakistani women in the Australian diaspora. However, women taking part in this study did not report any occurrence of domestic violence in their homes or within the Pakistani community. Only one participant (Aalia) acknowledged that there is violence in the Pakistani community in Perth and in Australia. Consequently, I argue that there are "extreme" notions of honour consciousness within the Pakistani community in Australia, and in Perth. According to interview results, individuals who "spend more time" within the Pakistani community "change less" after migrating to Australia. Thus, Pakistani views on honour consciousness are predominantly reconstructed within the Pakistani community in the Australian diaspora, enforcing Pakistani views on family honour, the role of men and women and the family. Cultural transmission within migrant families is an issue extensively addressed in migration studies (Kim, Knudson-Martin & Tuttle, 2018). The role of families in cultural transmission in Australia plays an important part in the intergenerational transmission of honour consciousness social reproduction (masculine privilege in Pakistani homes) in Australia.

Participants did not report the occurrence of violence in the Pakistani community, since they predominantly hold "moderate" views of honour consciousness and religion, thus diminishing the likelihood of their inner circle of friends being exposed to female oppression and violence. When dealing with the honour-violence nexus, there is extensive literature discussing women's role to "secure" male and family honour, and breaches in the honour code leading to violence in the name of honour (Tomsen & Gadd, 2019; Gill, 2010). The Australian Human Rights Commission follows the United Nations Declaration on the Elimination of Violence Against Women (1993, section 2) definition of violence against women, in the following terms: "Any act of gender-based violence that results in, or is likely to result in, physical, sexual or psychological harm or suffering to women, including threats of such acts, coercion or arbitrary deprivation of liberty, whether occurring in public or private life."

Pakistani women's perception of violence against women could be framed differently. Thus, possible factors which may inhibit any reporting of violence against women in the Pakistani community in Australia include: 1) fear of judgment, 2) individual definitions of violence towards women differ from that of the Australian Human Rights Commission (AHRC) of violence against women, and 3) an individual might associate "extreme" notions and violence toward women with honour killings, although there are in fact other forms of violence towards women in the name of honour, such as domestic violence (DV). Extreme cases do not happen overnight, and usually are the result of many years of psychological and financial abuse.

A service provider of Pakistani background, contacted during field work in Perth, explained, however, that there are also very high levels of domestic violence within other Culturally and Linguistically Diverse (CALD) communities, as well as within Australian families. Aalia, for instance, was reflecting upon violence towards women in the Pakistani diaspora, and high levels of violence towards women, and the killings of women, in Australia. Through the lenses of honour consciousness, she sees the high levels of killings of women in Australia as a form of honour killings. Nonetheless, literature shows that honour consciousness reproduces social behaviour dependent on family ties, on good family reputation, and on a system of patronage. In other words, the honour system is reproduced primarily via the family (parent's values and morals), and is intrinsically collective, as families depend on their good name and good ties of relationship to achieve positions of power and prestige. In Australian society, gender relations and notions of womanhood are accessed at the level of the individual, and hyper masculinity, male dominance and control, as well as Australia's "blokey culture," can be seen as key drivers behind domestic violence towards women, which may manifest in "extreme" forms such as the killing of women. Australia's "blockey culture" can be classified as Connell's (2005) "hypermasculinity." Existing literature discusses the impact of Australia's blokey culture in various ways, including sexual harassment in the workplace (Palmer & North, 2012; Saunders & AM, 2013), lived experiences of women in the film industry (French, 2014), the lived experiences of men in Australia's mining industry (Carrington, et al., 2012), and in the surf industry (Warren, 2016).

Through the cultural lenses of honour consciousness, Aalia understands that the high levels of killings of women in Australia can be a "sort of an honour killing," in her words:

> Domestic violence exists and it is rampant in Australia. Obviously, it is a problem across all cultures. We women are not treated well sometimes [in Australia]. Even though there are laws protecting women, still women are dying. You know, if compared it is sort of honour killings. Because men are killing their partners, they are blaming that they are having an affair, although they're not. I see a lot of women in prison that say, oh you know when he was drunk or when he was high on meth, he would say that I was having an affair, but I wasn't actually having an affair. It may be

about honour as well, but it's also about men feeling insecure about their
role as a provider, as a sexual partner, or as a father.

In Australia honour consciousness and religious consciousness continue to
affect views on family life, with women's role still being seen primarily as car-
ing for children, and of elders, and looking after their husbands and homes.
Pakistani women usually work part-time or do not work (as there is no domestic help), in order to look after the children and to manage domestic life, allowing husbands to substantially progress in their careers. Women's primary role
is still concerned with family duties (for example, minding the children, and
making sure dinner is ready for husband and children). They can work only
if they can successfully manage their family duties with out of home paid
employment, which is the leading reason behind them either working predominantly part-time (when they do have paid work), or simply abdicating
from their careers to look after their husbands, the home and the children.
There is a continuum with regard to honour consciousness and familial views,
regarding Pakistani family life, when these are carried over to the diaspora.
In Australia, Pakistani women's primary role is still that of being good mothers, wives and caregivers, continuing social reproduction in Australia, although
also shifting and changing to Australian culture.

Also, honour consciousness and religious consciousness views on womanhood and the family translate to Australia. Thus, women who are unmarried, or
who are divorced, are seen as "unworthy" or dishonoured by the Pakistani community in Western Australia. They are not fulfilling their primary role through
the lenses of honour consciousness and family life, that is, to be mothers, nurturers and good wives. Pakistani Muslim women who are single or divorced
might be seen, therefore, as bad mothers or wives, and are ostracised by some
members of the Pakistani community in Australia – although some are more
accepting than others due to "other" notions of honour.

Honour consciousness and religious consciousness can be manifested via
"moderate" or "extreme" views, and these are internalised in the way they see
the world – the "cultural lenses of honour." This continues impacting Pakistani
Muslim women's lived experiences and notions of womanhood in Australia. In
my view, honour consciousness and religious consciousness might desensitise
Pakistani Muslim women regarding their "home duties" and notions of womanhood and the family, allowing social reproducing processes in the home
which may well impact their financial independence and the advancement of
their careers, whereas their husband's privileges as "breadwinners" consolidate
Pakistani Muslim privilege in Australian society.

1.1   Summary

Honour consciousness	Social reproduction	Family Relations
Intrinsically gendered	– Women still seen as primary care givers of children, the elder, of their husbands and homes – Men can help minding the children, but this is not seen as their primary responsibility – Men's work is prioritised – Women sacrifice their careers after having children (work part-time or don't work at all)	– If women work (which is common in Australia) they still prioritise their children, husband and home duties – Unmarried women or divorcees seen as "unworthy" – Men need only to be good breadwinners. This makes them honourable before the family and the community – A good woman - honourable and respectable – is a good daughter, wife and mother. – Boys continue having more privileges than girls in Australia (spousal choice, lesser curfews)

2   What Changes in Pakistani Muslim Women's Lived Experiences of Honour and Gender in Australia?

Honour consciousness and religious consciousness continues in Pakistani Muslim women's lived experiences in Australia, with values, morals, and principles of family respect translating to Australia. Consequently, "moderate" or "extreme" notions of honour also transfer to Australia, depending on an individual's upbringing and the values internalised from the parents, as well as on the region where they spent their formative years. In Pakistan's big cosmopolitan urban centres, individuals are exposed to more progressive and modern views, manifested through "moderate" notions of honour, whereas those in more remote, rural areas hold more conservative views, leading to "extreme" notions of honour.

Participant stories demonstrate how honour consciousness's cultural lenses continue to give meaning to Pakistani Muslim women's lived experiences in the diaspora. But their notions of honour shift and change, creating new meanings when interacting with the broader Australian society, as well as with other cultures, since Australia is a multi-cultural and multi-racial nation.

Most Pakistani Muslim women's views of honour and religious conscious-ness, although still providing their bedrock of "right and wrong," shift and adapt to the Australian context. In some stories, however, their perception is that their views of honour and religion have not changed in Australia.

For Kiran, who has lived in Australia for over 20 years, her perception is that her views of honour consciousness and religion have not changed. Her lived experience in Australia only makes her more appreciative of honour con-sciousness and her family values, and although she does not regard herself as "super conservative," she is still conservative, compared with the standards of the wider Australian society. Kiran explains how her lived experience of hon-our in Australia makes her value her Pakistani heritage even more – in her words:

> It has widened my appreciation to it in the sense that you can see both sides when you were growing up. You know…you are growing up in a con-servative country, and your family, even if not super conservative, is still conservative.

It was a common perception during interviews that some members of the Pakistani community in Australia "do not change" or just "continue the same." However, their views also morph into new versions of honour consciousness and religious consciousness in the diaspora, due to exposure to other cultures, Australian culture, and other ways of life. Participant's views of honour con-sciousness and religion could be more malleable, shifting, adapting and being negotiated with the host country. The lived experiences of Pakistani women in Perth, Western Australia, expands research findings from Stirling (2013), in her thesis discussing the shifting, negotiating and remaking of religious and cul-tural identities of Iranian and Turkish Muslim Women in Brisbane, Gold Coast.

According to interview results, individual responses to the host culture's impact on lived experiences of honour consciousness are not homogenous. Interactions with the host culture can either lead to more relaxed notions of womanhood, or, conversely, to stricter views on gender roles, family life and lived experiences of religion in Australia. For example, some interview-ees believe that "other" members of the Pakistani community with "other notions" of honour consciousness might become even more conservative in the Australian diaspora. These notions of honour consciousness lean towards "extreme" notions of honour consciousness and religion. Lived experiences of honour, and cultural negotiation, reflect on how migrants conceptualise "home" and the on-going negotiations between migrant's identities, culture and the host culture (Erdal, 2014). These negotiations between migrant's identities, culture and the host culture influence the ways in which gender politics are manifested in the Pakistani community in Perth, Australia.

In Haniya's story, she explains that some Pakistani public events in Perth are gender segregated, and mosque gatherings are gender segregated, which she found appalling. She observed that this makes it even harder for Pakistani children to find potential future partners within the community. She explained that in one Islamic public lecture the auditorium was set up segregating men from women.

Haniya shares her lived experience, in her words:

> For example, in an Islamic lecture. I left very offended, and some students who were with me, were also very offended. We walked through to the lecture. And the men standing in front of the entrance, and they said: Sisters at the back, ok? Sisters should move and sit at the back of the auditorium.

This is not an issue experienced only within Muslims in Western Australia. During field work observation, I noticed gender segregation in community events promoted by the Pakistani Association of Western Australia, with children sitting with their mother in the women's section of the event. These events are hosted and organised by men, with women sitting as passive observers. In one particular event, men had preferential seats to watch a Pakistani folk music concern from a balcony. Although there were no signs preventing women from entering that area, only men were sitting on that space. This demonstrates how Pakistani Muslim honour consciousness and religious consciousness views on the role of womanhood, male headship and privilege, are being reproduced in Australia.

Most Pakistani Muslim women perceived honour consciousness and religious consciousness as still being a part of their lived experiences in Australia, but they see the Australian experience recalibrates their views, with their experiences being predominantly positive.

When discussing different notions of honour, Fatima explains that she taught her children values associated with respect and dignity. In the Australian experience, due to exposure to different cultures, this brings greater acceptance of difference and understanding towards others, in the following terms:

> I have taught my children that honour is to be respected, to have dignity, and that is to live your life with meaning, respecting other cultures

and learning from them, being honest, doing your job with dignity and achieving respect and honour from others by achieving high grades in education. Back in Pakistan, I didn't know much about other cultures. And didn't know about other religions. But now I have taught my children, and sent them to private schools, and they used to have a religious class. So, it doesn't mean that if they're attending those classes, they will become Christians, or Bahais or they will become Buddhists. I taught them, that, if you go to your class, try to read Islam's good values in them. And I said to them to learn good values from the Australians too. And that has made them good human beings, that I am very proud of the fact that I have three children who have dignity, honour, freedom, rights, and the right morally. They have freedom to respect people, not just because the way they dress, or if they have money or because of their skin colour.

Zara argues that honour changes in Australia, since she has a closer relationship with her children in Australia – "more friendly," in her words:

It has changed, of course, from the way we were brought up. We had a lot of respect for our parents. But our children do not show that kind of respect, they think that we are closer, more friendly. I would never say things like that to my father! And they say oh because you are so formal. You shouldn't be friendly with your father! And they think it's friendliness, that they are more open to us, they can say things that we could never think about saying to our parents.

The honour code is internalised by the family, and family relations are central to the reproduction of honour consciousness, religious consciousness, and gender politics within the home (social reproduction), in the Pakistani community, and in the broader Australian society.

As discussed earlier, some parents even "set up" their children with their future spouses. Nevertheless, in Australia parents cannot "force" their children into marrying someone, as the new generation is exposed "to other ways of living," and if you "impose" things on them they "might just rebel." The majority of participants argued that to marry a Pakistani Muslim in Australia "would be preferable" and "would bring them honour," but they acknowledged that "it is hard to find someone here." Furthermore, most participants explained that to marry a Muslim in Australia is "good enough," but not marrying a Muslim "would make them very unhappy" and "not bring honour" to them.

Aalia discussed how she was "shocked" with women's dress code in Australia (sleeveless, and wearing shorts, is common). She explained during her interview how a modest dress code (and to not wear shorts) was something taught by her mother in Pakistan. For her daughter growing up in Australia, however, it is harder to enforce this strict dress code. In her story, her daughter's exposure to Australian Western culture makes her more open to questioning parental views. Although her daughter has more flexibility in the way she dresses than Aalia had growing up in Pakistan, she dresses predominantly "modestly." In her words:

> It was like, mom, I want to wear it! She said [her mom back in Pakistan, when she was growing up] no you can't wear it. Similarly, when my daughter was growing up [in Australia], I wouldn't let her wear shorts. So, she would say: Mom, my brother wears shorts when cycling, why I cannot wear shorts? I would say no [in Pakistan], there are security guards and drivers sitting outside the house. You are on the bike, and I don't want you wearing shorts. In Pakistan it would be a normal request but in Australia it was hard to convince her. Although there is more flexibility in the dress code [in Australia], now she doesn't ask anymore, and rarely wears sleeveless and wears mostly dresses. Although she also likes the Western dress code, she wears crop tops and trousers, but in general they are quite modest.

When dealing with intercultural marriages in Australia, participants argued that "there is more acceptance" and that people become "more flexible" and more "understanding." Nevertheless, the parents still have a say in their children's choice of spouses. For example, India and Pakistan historically have a strained relationship, and in Pakistan, it is not acceptable to marry an Indian.

When discussing her children's lives in Australia, Zara tells us her story:

> They made their own choices when it came to marriage, of course with our approval. They told us that we like this man and we want to get married. So, it has changed, somewhat is different. You never think of getting married to an Indian. But one of my son's in law is Indian, ok? So, my daughter knew that she has to get married to a Muslim man. But it's okay to get married into another culture or a person coming from different countries because we are here [in Australia], it's a multicultural society. Get back to Pakistan to get a husband for them?' I think it's an honour that my son in law is very compatible, even though he is Indian. He has a multicultural background, he is educated, respectful. These are more valuable things than just being from a certain family, or country or ethnic background. That's a symbol of honour.

In her story, Zara explains that she still needs to approve her children's spousal choices and that her son in law is compatible "even though he is Indian." Other participants argued that in Australia "you can marry outside your culture" and that here the children can "marry into other cultures." This follows literature discussing lived experiences of religion of Muslim migrant women in Australia, and how lived experiences translate to the host nation, though shifting, negotiating and remaking their lived experiences in Australia (Stirling et al., 2014). Thus, many second and third generation Pakistanis are marrying Australians, and even Catholics, and are still "accepted by the community." Participants explained that it is common to see, in the Pakistani community in Australia, Pakistani men marrying non-Muslim girls, Australian girls, or girls from other faiths, although, conversely, Pakistani girls usually marry Pakistani Muslim men in Australia. Families even liaise with acquaintances and extended families in Pakistan to arrange a marriage with Pakistani Muslim men for their daughters in Australia. This has to do with the fact that Islam allows men to marry women of the Abrahamic faith, but women should marry a Muslim man.

Uzma explains as follows:

> A lot of families will have issues if their daughter marries a non-Muslim or non-Pakistani. Whereas if it is their son, they will not stop them. So again, it's very difficult to get rid of ideology and to change your values. And whereas they may not be saying cover up to your daughter. They will have an issue if the daughter chooses someone who is white and non-Muslim, or Asian or anything else. I'm trying to think of people and the last several weddings I've attended. There have been Pakistani men marrying non-Pakistani non-Muslim women. But I cannot recall Pakistani woman, or a second-generation Pakistani getting married to a non-Pakistani non-Muslim in Perth, basically, I don't know a single one.

And Uzma continues explaining why parents think their daughters should marry Pakistani Muslim men in Australia, in her words:

> Oh yeah, not just preferable but it's the only route. I mean, then there'll be a family that the women managed to get their own way and do what they want, but it is, by and large, it is the way things are done.

Uzma argued that she sees many Pakistani women and even second-generation Pakistani women marrying Pakistani Muslims in Australia but that she has seen only Pakistani men or second-generation men marrying into other cultures, or to Australian non – Muslim girls. And according to Uzma's story, for Pakistani women in Australia to marry Pakistani Muslim men not only is preferable but the "only route" – so it is their only given option. Interestingly, some women managed to "get away" with their own preferences. Some participants explained that Islam allows non-Muslims to marry "people from the book" or people following Abrahamic faith religions such as Judaism and Christianity, but that this "flexibility" would apply mostly to men. In Australia, although there are negotiations with the host culture and Pakistanis do become more accepting and "adapt" to a new way of living, the discourse of honour continues, albeit with some concessions and adaptations.

Pakistani Muslim women's values, transmitted through honour consciousness, such as the respect shown to their parents and to the elders, continue in Australia. However, their perceptions of honour consciousness and religion adapt to Australian culture and society. For instance, to "obey the Australian Prime Minister," or a more common theme, to be "a law-abiding citizen" or "to respect Australian law" is perceived as bringing honour to them, as well as to the Pakistani community. In the mind set of Pakistani Muslim women, they continue to see the world through the lenses of honour, following their values (as taught by their parents) of being ethical, respecting the elders, and obeying the Prime Minister and Australian laws. Their perception of what brings honour shifts and adapts in the Australian environment, but their main goal is still to bring honour to their name, and to the reputation of their families and that of the Pakistani community. Religious consciousness also intersects with honour consciousness in their views of how to behave in Australian society, and how Australian society and the Pakistani community will judge their behaviour.

For example, Zara shares her views, and how honour consciousness impacts their behaviour in Australia, shifting to the local culture:

> And the Holy Prophet used to (speaks in Arabic), he would greet the youngest, even though, as a norm that the youngest should greet the elders. But he would greet the younger ones. So that to teach them good morals, good manners. Okay. So, and then obey the laws of the country, authorities, teachers, police officials, your authorities, your Prime Minister. You have to respect them, you not allowed to just swear and say bad things all the time that you can discuss it. A person with authority you have to respect them. But for me you should also respect family values, the environment and the animals.

Although Pakistani Muslim women's honour consciousness and religious consciousness is transferred to Australia, they clearly shift and change in order to adapt to the Australian environment. This follows literature discussing lived experiences of migrants in the diaspora and cultural transmission, and the ambivalent ways of living within the Muslim South Asian diasporas in the West. For instance, Pnina Werbner (2004) explains the hybridity of South Asian Muslims lived experiences in the UK, with their different perceptions in the public sphere through South Asian media representations. And Nicole Stirling et al. (2014) explores how Muslim migrant women's lived experiences of religion, shift and negotiate with Australia culture "remaking" their identities in the diaspora.

In Uzma's story, she explains how moving to Australia makes people "more open-minded" and that for her, living in Australia exposed her to different views and ways of thinking, giving her access to information and greater freedom to discuss Islam with other women and their views of the role of women in Australia. She sees that her views of honour consciousness and religion have been softened by access to information, via social media channels such as Facebook. Her perception is that social media increases access to information and that being part of Facebook groups provides a non – judgmental platform for book suggestions and group discussion.

In her words:

> I don't know if it is because if I moved to Australia or it's because I was growing up and reading more. Perhaps, a mixture of both. But I think I am aware of other people and different ways of living and different books. I'm part of groups on Facebook, and if there is a book which is recommended, I want to go out and read it, something discussing Islam and women that I developed interest. So, my reading has increased. It started and continued here [in Australia], obviously here I have more access. And the world has become so much smaller through digital platforms and social media. Even to find out about what other people think and how they're doing things made me more open.

Kiran explained how migration had a positive impact on her identity, softening honour consciousness and religious consciousness with regard to notions of womanhood, and male privilege within her family in Pakistan, as well as the social privileges given to men in broader Pakistani society. For her, migrating to Australia helped her to grow as a person, and exposure to different ways of living and Australian culture helped her confidence, and her ability to question Pakistani culture and religion, and societal views promoting male hegemony.

"Kiran" shares her views:

> So, after migrating here. I have grown in my own personality and have become more confident in questioning certain beliefs and taking it from there.

The relationship between parents and children can be less hierarchical. Australia's principles of fair go and that there should be a level playing field (Bolton, 2003) might have an impact on Australian family life, with parents and children interacting in ways that are less hierarchical than other countries in the world. For Pakistani families, Australian culture can be seen, at times, as being too permissive, with children not respecting parents and elders as they should. But a more "relaxed" Australian approach to family life also provides benefits to Pakistani families in Australia, easing honour consciousness' strict requirements for family members, and the subjection of children to their parent's will, as well as strict gender norms within family life. Australian culture also "relaxes" Pakistani views on the privileges enjoyed by sons, as well as the strict control over their daughter's bodies to protect female purity before society.

As explained by Zara, things change in Australia, in her words:

> It has changed of course, from the way were brought up, we had a lot of respect for our parents. But our children they do not show that kind of respect, but they think that we are closer to you, more friendly. I will never say things like that to my father! And they say oh because you are so formal you are not friendly with your father! And they think it's friendliness, that they are more open to us, they can say things that we could never think about saying to our parents. They made their own choices when it came to marriage, of course with our approval. They told us that we like this man and we want to get married. So, it has changed, somewhat is different.

In Shamaila's story, she discussed the impact of Australia's wealth and digital technology on her children's upbringing in Australia, observing that in her childhood she did not have access to technology, as well as having far fewer toys. She discussed how her relationship with her children is more "relaxed," and less hierarchical, consequently making her closer to her children. Pakistani children born and raised in Australia feel free to share personal stories with their parents, developing a "mateship" of sorts with their parents. Shamaila observed that her children are far less compliant with parental orders than she was as a child in Pakistan. Children raised in Australia are more inclined to question parental orders – something she would not dare to do to her parents back in Pakistan.

Shamaila shares her story:

> Things are changing now. We didn't have that much technology and didn't have many toys. We didn't have all that. We were used to go out and play. It's not happening here [in Australia] as much. So, this is the biggest change which I experienced. That if I say to my mom says no you can't do it, I would say okay. Bu if tell my son that you can't do, or with my daughter that no you can't do it, they will ask why. The first thing they will say: What's wrong in it? So I said just, because I said it. Isn't this is good enough? Do I need to give a reason? My mother wasn't that close to me. I am very close to my children, and they come home, and they tell me everything. And sometimes they are telling what's happened with all details. And then I think, they shouldn't tell me all this!

Nazia, 28 years old, married but with no children and who has recently arrived in Australia, reflects upon social reproduction in Pakistan and how things change in Australia. She discussed her brother's and her father's role as breadwinners within the Pakistani family context. In her perception, honour consciousness and familial life in Australia is fundamentally different. She explains that in Australia both women and men work, and both are earning money. In Pakistan, if your husband is earning money, you just sit back and relax at home. In Australia it is not like this, as both have to work. In her words:

> [In Australia] it's not like Pakistan that your brother will do this, and your father will do that. I think they are [couples] doing [their work] on an equal base. If the wife is earning money, then the husband is also earning money. But if the husband is earning money in Pakistan, you will just relax in your home. I don't' think this happens in Australia. Both have to work.

Most childless Pakistani Muslim women living in Australia work, due to Australia's cost of living. However, as migrant Pakistani families settle in Australia and then have children, this dynamic changes, with women dropping their work hours down to part-time and casual work, or leaving work altogether to look after their children and support their husbands. This gives a continuum to honour consciousness views of womanhood and family life, and social reproduction in the home.

According to field notes, Shamaila, for instance, used to be a stay home mum until her children finished primary school. She works part-time now. During our interview, her husband made her "a cup of tea", and they explained how men need to help around the house in Australia because there is no "home help." During her interview, Shamaila discussed how in Australia men can "sometimes" cook and do the vacuuming. However, she acknowledged that she still does most of the cooking and housework and did not work to look after the children when they were young.

In Australia, there are fewer curfews and children have more freedom. However, honour consciousness and religious consciousness continues shaping gender politics in Australia. Abida, for instance, explains how Western values influence the behaviour of her boys. But as a Pakistani Muslim, if she had a daughter, she would try to control her behaviour more. In Abida's words:

> Ah the kids... Yeah, [in Australia] they are very different I would say. My kids are very different from their cousins in Pakistan because they are in a society where they learn things differently. And my kids over here, they don't understand all that thing of honour because they are growing up here. So yeah, the kids are totally different, mostly, the Western values, Western things. They are very open about everything, the freedom, and all that kind of stuff. Yeah, the boys [her sons] they do whatever they want" [If she had a daughter]. But yeah, it would depend on what the girl would be like, accept what we are expecting from her [the different treatment from boys]. But yeah, definitely, being a Muslim family and Pakistani, we would try different things.

In the Australian experience, honour consciousness and religious consciousness continues shaping notions of womanhood, and gender politics within the home and the broader Pakistani society. This gives an advantage to boys and men, allowing them to mingle and interact freely with broader Australian society, as well as to advance their careers in adulthood. Thus, Pakistani Muslim women's lived experiences of honour in Australia, and that of the Pakistani community, continue social reproduction of gender politics in Australia, although with changes and adaptations to Australian culture. For instance, boys still have looser curfews than girls. But after girls are over 18 years old, they can go to college and drive a car, for instance, making it harder to impose curfews. But Pakistani boys still continue to have more freedom and less accountability than Pakistani girls in Australia. Both women and men cook and clean, as there are no maids (when they are in single couples with no children and both working), but after women have had children, their primary role becomes that of being a good mother, to look after the house and after the husband. Subsequently, they tend to cut back to part-time work with some leaving their jobs, and this has an impact on gender politics and social reproduction in Australia. Honour consciousness and religious consciousness continues to give men privileges, and they are still seen as the primary breadwinners in Australia.

In Pakistani Muslim women's stories of honour consciousness and religious consciousness there are changes in their lived experiences in Australia, and they are mostly positive:[7] 1) In lived experiences of honour and religion in Australia, there is more tolerance towards different views and different religions, 2) Children of Pakistani parents born in Australia have more flexibility to choose their spouses. Boys and girls have greater freedom to choose from a list presented by their parents, or someone their parents will approve. Girls should marry Pakistani Muslim men, and boys have greater freedom to choose a partner of their choice, 3) Girls still have stricter curfews than boys, but after they are 18 years old, can drive and are attending college, it is hard to impose strict curfews. Boys raised in Australia have the freedom to come and go as they please, 4) Pakistani Muslim women are exposed to different ways of living and literature, becoming more open minded when dealing with honour consciousness and religion, notions of womanhood and society, as well as views within Islam, and 5) Individuals developing ties of friendship within the Pakistani community tend to change less, and change less than others in the Australian diaspora.

The cultural lenses of honour consciousness adapt, shift and change but to a lesser degree than for Pakistanis who mingle with the Australian broader community. Participants described them as "the same" "they don't change," but exposure to different ways of living in Australia makes them adapt to

---

7 Participants discussed in their interviews how Australians are predominatly accepting and that Australian multiculturalism has a positive impact in their lives, with Pakistanis becoming more open to different cultures and ways of living. However, participant 7 ("Nazia") and participant 14 ("Zara") disclosed experiences of Islamophobia. Nazia explained how one day she was in Northbridge, in Perth, wearing a hijab and an indigenous individual (who was inebriated) shouted at her to "go home" – an allusion that Australia is not a place for Muslims. Since, Nazia stopped wearing the hijab. Zara wears a hijab, but discouraged her daughters from wearing it. She fears they will be singled out as Muslims, and that they could face discrimination. Nazia and Zara observed that Islamophobic views are supported only by a fraction of the Australian population. They stressed out that the majority of Australians are welcoming, and that incidents of Islamophobia are extremely rare in the country.

Australian culture. However, their views on gender and the role of women continue to be very similar to those you might experience in Pakistan and could tilt towards "extreme" views of honour, manifested via violence towards women and female suppression.

3 Aspects of Honour Consciousness, Religious Consciousness, and Gender "Changing Less" in Australia

However, Pakistani women discussed that, in some ways, honour consciousness and religious consciousness "continue the same" in their lived experiences in Australia: 1) Honour consciousness continues shaping family life and gender roles within the family, giving preferential treatment to males (they can marry whoever they wish and have looser curfews, as unlike with girls, no one minds whether a man is married or not and with children – the situation is very different for women), 2) Gender segregation in events promoted by the Pakistani community in Western Australia/ in some events men will have preferential seats, 3) Notions of womanhood and family, since unmarried women and divorcees continue to be stigmatised by some members of the Pakistani community, those regarded by participants as people "who do not change." The diasporic experience softens some views of the Pakistani community, through the process of adaptation to Australian culture. Daily exposure to other ways of living has an impact on individual's lived experiences of honour in Australia, but some members of the community change more than others.

Participant's views aligned with "moderate" views of honour and religion, which are transmitted to Australia. Although holding "moderate" notions of honour consciousness and religion, Pakistani women are still impacted by honour consciousness and religious consciousness views on notions of womanhood, shaping the role of women within family life, social reproduction, as well as societal views within the Pakistani community in Western Australia. Pakistani Muslim women critically reflected upon "other" views (tilting to "extreme" notions of honour) within the Pakistani community in Australia, which consolidate gender politics within family life, social reproduction and male privilege. In terms of the interviews, there was a sense of consciousness that each Pakistani participant brought with them. But their consciousness did not manifest in the context of violent relationships.[8] One participant

---

8 According to interviewees responses, "extreme notions" of honour consciousness are the "social other." This view is manifested through female suppression, violence towards women and honour killings. Pakistani women interviewed for this research did not experience

acknowledged that there were domestic violence cases within Pakistanis in Australia, but she distanced herself from situations connected with violence towards women in the community, and created the "social other." There was also limited information I could get from participants. There are cases of violence against Pakistani women reported to the Australian media. For example, Pakistani-Australian Sajida Tasneem was allegedly killed by her father in Pakistani in June 2022 (Riches, 2022). These views towards honour consciousness might translate to the Australian community, but my sample groups reflected "moderate" views of honour. Participants taking part in this survey did not disclose any conflictual relationships in their lives, extended family or acquaintances. They distanced themselves from cases of domestic violence and honour killings – the social "other," and regarded as "extreme" notions of honour. In such case, there is no indication that there are conflictual cases in my sample groups. This contrasts with data from Pakistanis living in the UK.

In the next chapter I will discuss a new epistemological framework when looking at migrant women's experiences in Australia.

---

violence, and labelled these experiences as "the other" – distancing themselves from such perceptions. The women interviewed predominantly held "moderate" notions of honour consciousness. However, given the hybridised nature of their lived experiences, some participants might hold some views which are more aligned with "extreme"rather than "moderate" notions of honour consciousness.

CHAPTER 5

A New Perspective to Hegel, Foucault, and Gender

Drawing from interview results, I explain in this chapter how migrant women's lived experiences of honour consciousness are consistent with Hegel's epistemological perspective of human consciousness, and its self-reflective character. The chapter also outlines how Foucault's theory is consistent with their experiences and gender power relations.

Hegel is regarded as one of the most influential philosophers in Western history, with the significance of his contribution comparable to that of Plato, Aristotle, or Emmanuel Kant. The influence of his ideas has been "profound and wide-ranging" (Houlgate, 2011, p. 1). His work influenced the development of several schools of thought, including Marxism, existentialism, American pragmatism, and the Frankfurt school of critical theory. His epistemological perspective on religion has had a considerable impact on theologians, and he continues to influence contemporary philosophers such as Judith Butler, John McDowell, and Robert Brandom.

Nevertheless, the epistemological contribution of Hegel has been predominantly underrepresented by feminists and queer theory.[1] Kane (2014) and Brace (2002) have used Hegelian epistemology of the family in the "Philosophy of Right" to explain the condition of women and gender relations. Other scholars, however, have been reluctant to use his theory due to Hegel's views on women (Kane, 2014). Judith Butler's reconstructs Hegel's paradigms of human consciousness to explain human desire (Butler, 1987/2012). I, however, draw upon Hegel's contribution to human consciousness in the "Phenomenology of the Spirit."

Hegelian views in the "Phenomenology of Spirit" have been paramount for philosophical discussions around human consciousness, influencing the scholarly work of philosophers such as Michel Foucault. In Hegel's "Phenomenology of Spirit," human knowledge originates from human consciousness. He explores the evolution of human consciousness throughout history, and

---

1 Hegel's personal views on women's role in society has been stigmatised in the use of Hegelian epistemology within feminist studies. Kane (2014) illuminates why Feminist philosophers are highly critical of Hegel's perspective of women's physiology. For him, this is a determinant factor leading women to occupy "subordinate" roles in "nature and society." I agree with Kane's perspective that Hegel's personal views on women should not exclude the use of his dialectic approach within Feminist scholarship.

© FLAVIA BELLIENI ZIMMERMANN, 2025 | DOI:10.1163/9789004711242_007

possible ways to track the effects of consciousness in the development of the human soul, shaping individual notions of "truth." In "Phenomenology," Hegel discusses (although only occasionally), how desire integrates human consciousness, contending that "self-consciousness in general is Desire" (Hegel, 1807/1977, p. 106). In his view, desire exemplifies the reflexivity of consciousness, the necessity of othering desire to create our own individual notions of desire and self (Butler, 1987/2012).

For the purposes of this chapter, however, I draw exclusively on Hegel's understanding of human consciousness and its self-reflexive character. Through this perspective, individual consciousness is shaped through the interaction with the social "other," and different views of consciousness, being reproduced throughout generations, shifting, changing and adapting to each historical context. In the "Phenomenology of the Spirit," Hegel describes his work as "the science of the experience of consciousness" (Hegel, cited by Houlgate 2011, p. 9). In "Phenomenology," Hegel explores "truth" and lived experiences of consciousness by distancing himself from the whole experiment, where he objectively examines how "truth" develops through human experience (Houlgate & Baur, 2011). Metaphorically, Hegel can be seen as a priest or an artist, where his main goal is to point out philosophical "truths" about human existence, establishing the relationship between human consciousness with individual self-consciousness, and collective "truths." (Houlgate & Baur, 2011).

Following Hegel's dialectic method of analysis (thesis, antithesis, and synthesis), consciousness cannot be understood in isolation but rather as resulting from the interactions of different "consciousnesses." In other words: individual consciousness (self-consciousness) only develops meaning when exposed to the social "other," revealing the overarching lived experiences of consciousness, as well as how these are manifested socially. According to Hegel: "Self-consciousness achieves its satisfaction only in another self-consciousness" (Hegel, quoted in Hamlyn, 1986, p. 317)." In sum: in Hegel's view, in order for the philosopher to grasp what is individual consciousness, what he calls "self-consciousness," consciousness ought to be understood as being self-reflexive.

As elucidated by Ferro (2013), for Hegel the recognition of different self-consciousnesses acknowledges that every individual's mode of self-recognition is grounded upon their interactions with "the other." The relationship between self-consciousness and "other consciousnesses" feeds into one another – what Hegel's calls self-consciousness circularity. Self-consciousness acquires its identity not within itself, but rather through the interaction with another self-consciousness.

Through this epistemological framework, Hegel's phenomenology is key in understanding how consciousness is formed, how it is manifested, as well as how it travels throughout history, although undergoing adaptations within each generation. The Hegelian perception of the world, and how it interacts with individual lived experiences (self-consciousness) is a complex enterprise. In his view, consciousness, the awareness, and experience of the "other" or "objects," requires the experience of self-consciousness. For Hegel, one ought to develop awareness of "I," to then relate with "We," thus experiencing the world around us (Hoy, 1991). For Hegel, consciousness is a historical process which results from the interaction of self-consciousness with "other" consciousnesses, as well as with the broader social world. Hegel points out that "the sequence of Shapes through which consciousness passes on this road is the detailed history of consciousness" (Hegel, 1807/1977, p. 417).

In Hegel's articulation, principles of consciousness are universal, where self-consciousness only achieves satisfaction in another self-consciousness, thus making the interaction between "myself" with the social "other" central in the shaping of identities. Hegel, through his dialectic's lenses (thesis, anti-thesis, and synthesis), demonstrates self-consciousness assimilating the "object" (the social "other"), with consciousness being the outcome (synthesis). Consequently, the Hegelian perspective of consciousness is the result of tension, within a contradictory process whereby individual self-consciousness must be exposed to "objects" (the social "other"), producing individual as well as societal views of consciousness. For Hegel, therefore, self-consciousness produces effects on general consciousness, and this relationship is self-reflexive. According to interview results, and migrant women's self-reflective appraisal of their lived experiences of honour consciousness (when they address extreme notions as the "social other"), Hegel's epistemological framework provides an explanation for their lived experiences.

In this section I apply Hegel's views of human consciousness and his phenomenological approach to explain Brazilian and Pakistani migrant women's lived experiences. These women's lived experiences are consistent with Hegel's human consciousness and his phenomenological perspective to human history – what is deemed these women's "honour consciousness." I argue that honour consciousness is a sub-section within the broader encompassing epistemological framework of Hegel's human consciousness. Hegelian views of human consciousness provide individuals with an understanding of the world around them at the level of human consciousness. By providing meaning at the level of human consciousness, regardless of geographical location, individuals carry with them, their perceptions of the social world and how they relate to the social "other." Hegel's (1807/1977) key epistemological perspectives of human consciousness and phenomenology, as applied to an understanding of women's honour consciousness are: a) human consciousness' self-consciousness,

b) its reflexive character, c) it gives meaning to the human experience, d) individual understanding of the social world is acquired through "the other," e) understanding of the social world at the level of human consciousness, f) phenomenology' dialectics (thesis, anti-thesis, synthesis), g) it travels through history, h) it transcends time and history but adjusts to societal demands.

Based on women's interview data results, their experiences of honour are key in shaping their notions of right and wrong, their moral values and their moral compass – what I classify as their notions of "truth." According to women's lived experiences, honour represents a core part of their identities, providing the lenses from which they distinguish between "right" and "wrong," and what is expected from them by their families and society. In their lived experiences of honour, honour consciousness is predominantly a positive experience, with women enjoying agency and the protection of human rights. I regard these notions of honour consciousness as "moderate." During interviews, the women explained the impact of honour in their lives, with honour consciousness manifested through traditional notions of womanhood within the family, reconciled with women's agency, political activism, and the fight against violence towards women. When telling their stories, participants created the social other when explaning how "other" women have "different notions" of honour.[2] They distanced themselves from "other notions" of honour which they labelled "extreme," and are manifested through female suppression and violence towards women.

However, in their stories, honour consciousness develops greater meaning by acknowledging "different notions" of honour (the social "other"), where notions of honour can lead to female suppression, lack of agency, victimisation and even to gender-based violence and honour killings. I regard the "social other" notions of honour consciousness as "extreme." Therefore, honour consciousness, similarly to Hegel's notions of self-consciousness and consciousness, is self-reflective, with the true meaning of individual consciousness developing only through the interaction with "other notions" of consciousness and the social "other".

During interviews, Brazilian and Pakistani migrant women explained that there are "different" notions of honour, with each person having their own. From their viewpoints, "different" notions of honour, and individual values and morals associated with the honour code, are shaped by the parental values

---

2   The women interviewed for this research explained how honour is something subjective – each person have their own notions, pointing out that there are notions which are different from their own ("different notions"), and how some of these notions can be "extreme," when looking at female control and victimization to violence.

and familial views on honour. Thus, for migrant women taking part in this study, their values (honour consciousness) have been transmitted through their parents and family. Similarly to Hegel's epistemological views on human consciousness, Brazilian and Pakistani women's lived experiences of honour consciousness are reproduced through generations, adapting to a set historical social contexts, as illustrated by Hegel's epistemological views on phenomenology (Hegel, 1807/1977).

A key variable of Brazilian and Pakistani women's lived experiences of honour is "other notions of honour," and how these interact with women's honour consciousness. This variable is consistent with Hegelian reflexivity (Hegel, 1807/1977). In the view of the participants, their lived experiences of honour acquired greater meaning by the "othering" of different notions of honour. By distancing themselves from "other" notions of honour, participant's lived experiences of honour are seen as "better," or "enlightened" if compared to "other notions" of honour, which can be "extreme" through subjugating women, silencing their voices, as well as leading to masculine control and violence. Through Hegel's reflexive perspective, Brazilian and Pakistani women's lived experiences of honour consciousness are seen, overall, as positive, in contrast to "other" notions of honour, which may be associated with a negative outcome, where women are suppressed, do not enjoy basic human rights, as well as being victims of violence inflicted in the name of honour.

1   Foucault's Episteme and Gender

In this section I explain how Foucault's episteme has been applied within the field of gender studies, and how my new epistemological proposition shifts scholarly boundaries. This book moves beyond the use of Foucault's episteme for "the body," "the self" and "docile bodies," by applying the power-knowledge episteme to explain "power" reproduction at the level of human consciousness.

When Foucault developed his epistemology in the 1960's, he was highly critical of general norms of society and social relations, developing a critique of societal language dealing with mental illness, the prison system and sexuality. In Foucault's view, these institutions are shaped to suit society's "productivity." In his first work, "Madness and Civilisation" he differentiates between mental illness and madness (1961), with the latter being a social construct, designed through subjective judgment, instead of through objective evaluation (Kallman & Dini, 2017). Foucault's most relevant text to this analysis, "regime of truth," is discussed in his 1976 interview "The Political Function of an Intellectual," where he argues: "truth isn't outside power, or deprived of power," but rather "is produced by virtue of multiple constraints and it induces regulated effects to power" (Foucault, 1977, p. 13). In this context, "truth" is produced and reproduced through structural systems of power, manifested throughout society, the state, the judiciary and social norms.

Foucault (1977) elucidates in "The Political Function of the Intellectual" his epistemological perspective of power, as follows:

> The important point here, I believe, is that truth isn't outside power, or deprived of power (contrary to the myth whose history and functions would repay further study, it isn't the reward of free spirits, the child of prolonged solitudes, or the privilege of those who have been able to liberate themselves). Truth is of the world: it is produced by virtue of multiple constraints. And it induces the regular effects of power. Each society has its regime of truth, its general politics of truth: that is, the types of discourse it harbors and causes to function as true; the mechanisms and instances which enable one to distinguish true from false statements, the way in which each is sanctioned; the techniques and procedures which are valorised for obtaining truth; the status of those who are charged with saying what counts as true. (p. 13)

In Foucault's view, "each society has its regime of truth," and each "regime of truth" is manifested through: "1) The types of discourse (society) harbors and cases to function as true, 2) the mechanisms and instances which enable one to distinguish true from false statements, 3) The way in which each is sanctioned, 4) the techniques and procedures which are valorised for obtaining truth, 5) the status of those who are charged with saying what counts as true." (Foucault, cited in Lorenzini, 2015, p. 66). Foucault understands "regime of truth" as "a system of ordered procedures for the production, regulation, distribution, circulation and functioning of statements," connected with a "circular relation to systems of power which produce it and sustain it, and to effects of power which it induces and which redirect it" (Foucault, cited in Lorenzini, 2015, p. 66). In Foucault's view, truth should be contextualised as a "regime of truth," and seen as the condition for the formation and development of the Western institutions, as well as consolidating structural power relations.

For Foucault (1980, p. 138), the greatest challenge of our generation is to deconstruct "regimes of truth," since they set out the "political, economic, institutional regime of production of truth," with "regimes of truth" consolidating society's power structures, and hegemonic systems of power. Foucault contends that to change "regimes of truth," the main aim is not to change individual consciousness (or what is in each individual's head), but the political, economic, and institutional regime of the production of truth (Foucault, 1980). Scholars contend that Foucault's epistemological contribution is deeply embedded in his power-knowledge episteme, where he establishes the relationship between power, discourse, and the "effects power" in collective and individual consciousness. In other words, "the marriage of power and knowledge that allows the powerful to classify and control people and things." (Kallman & Dini, 2017, p.11).

Arguably, Foucault's most influential works in gender studies and feminism are "Discipline and Punish" and the "History of Sexuality," particularly its first volume, where Foucault expands the applicability of his power-knowledge episteme to the "body" (docile bodies) and sexuality. For instance, Foucault's conceptualisation of "the body," challenges the reader to re-think the world around them through different lenses, since our views of the world make us inherently unfree (Heyes, 2007). Following this line of thought, Foucault contends that power systems, and the discourse reproducing power relations shape our experiences, our bodies – and individual and collective consciousness (Foucault, 1976). In his view, attempts to resist power create resistance practices which, enticed by imagery and discourse, entrench power discourses even more in our consciousness. The relationship between the free and the unfree, lead to power resistance – although this "resistance" is constrained by systems of power, therefore, limiting individual agency to break free from structural power relations.

Foucault's "Discipline and Punish" (1975/1995) theorisation is of great significance for the social sciences, political sciences, and gender studies. In this work, Foucault contends individuals are shaped by systems of power and knowledge, raising doubts regarding individual human agency, and how systems of power shape identity. In "Discipline and Punish" he examines how power and systems of power are applied to people's bodies, constantly shaping their consciousness. He argues that power is not something which emanates from the state, the sovereign (king) or from wealth, with power having the ultimate function to "discipline." Foucault takes the criminal system as a case study, demonstrating how since the seventeenth century societal systems of power and control have been reflected in prison's disciplinary systems. According to Foucault, the disciplinary codes within the prison are "historically contingent," as they grew organically through the Western historical context.

In this work, Foucault's theorisation goes beyond the socio-historic context of disciplinary action, discussing the techniques and mechanism and effects of power to implement discipline – expanding his epistemological views on power-knowledge from the physical body to the individual. He contends that social institutions are instruments for the exercise of power, and discipline, on the bodies and souls of their subjects through *le regard* (the gaze) (Kallman & Dini, 2017).

As argued by Foucault (1975/1995, p. 187) in "Discipline and Punish: The Birth of the Prison":

> Traditionally, power was what was seen, what was shown, and what was manifested... Disciplinary power, on the other hand, is exercised through its invisibility; at the same time, it imposes on those whom it subjects a principle of compulsory visibility. In discipline, it is the subjects who have to be seen. Their visibility assures the hold of the power that is exercised over them. It is this fact of being constantly seen, of being able always to be seen, that maintains the disciplined individual in his subjection. And the examination is the technique by which power, instead of emitting the signs of its potency, instead of imposing its mark on its subjects, holds them in a mechanism of objectification. In this space of domination, disciplinary power manifests its potency, essentially by arranging objects. The examination is, as it were, the ceremony of this objectification.

Foucault sees the effects of power on the body and the individual as "permanent," since "surveillance is permanent in its effects, even if it is discontinuous in its action"(Foucault, 1975/1995, p. 177). According to his perspective, the *Panopticon* is paradigmatic to understand mechanisms of power applied not only in the prison system but throughout our institutions (Kallman & Dini, 2017). In his view, good behaviour is conditioned by the constant awareness of systems of power-control. For Foucault this is manifested through the *Panopticon*, and the constant surveillance of individuals to comply with social norms imposed by society, by the state or by state institutions. The metaphor of Foucault's *Panopticon* can exemplify women's lived experiences, and the overbearing societal expectations towards standards of female beauty, leading to women's objectification.

In Foucault's epistemology, "the body" is a key variable for the implementation of systems of punishment and control. In his words:

> [T]he punishment-body relation is not the same as it was in the torture during public executions. The body now serves as an instrument or intermediary: if one intervenes upon it to imprison it, or to make it work, it is to deprive the individual of liberty that is regarded both as a right and as property. The body, according to this penalty, is caught up in a system of constraints and privations, obligations and prohibitions. Physical pain, the pain of the body itself, is no longer the constituent element of

the penalty. From being an art of unbearable sensations punishment has become an economy of suspended rights (Discipline and Punish: The Birth of the Prison, p. 11).

Another key variable in Foucault's epistemology is the creation of the individual self, in his view a by-product of societal disciplinary systems. His definition of "docile bodies" describes individual bodies who are under constant surveillance and psychological control, thus shaping the individual self and the ways in which individuals self-regulate. Foucault's *Panopticon* metaphor, and surveillance in the prison system, can exemplify women's lived experiences, and dominating societal expectations towards female beauty standards, as previously mentioned, which can lead to the objectification of women. For example: women are constantly judged on their appearance, fashion choices and weight, and they internalise these beauty standards. Therefore, Foucault's theorisation in the prison system, and the *Panopticon,* provide a suitable framework to understand "docile bodies." The *Panopticon* system explains the effects of constant surveillance on the individual. This framework is key to subsequent feminist articulations of women's bodies objectification, unrealistic beauty standards, and female body's oppression (and possession) by men in a male-dominated world (Bordo, 2002; Cummins, 2014; Deveaux, 1994; Green, 2003).

Although Foucault's episteme has been extensively applied to explain the condition of women, and the *Panopticon*'s surveillance system is a good analogy of societal expectations towards "docile bodies," feminists also critique the limitations of his episteme. Feminists' scholars view Foucault's diffuse views of power, post-modern and post-structuralist thought, as impeding feminist's transformative and emancipatory goals. Consequently, feminists suggest that Foucault's views on the effects of "power" on "the body" are reductionist, with power structures overpowering "passive bodies" ("docile bodies"). Foucault's post-modern and post-structuralist reductionism is seen as failing to provide a framework for individual agency and social change (McNay, 1992).

In the section below, I discuss Foucault's epistemological contribution to gender studies in his leading work "The History of Sexuality Volume 1," where he develops a relationship between power-knowledge, the body and sexuality.

In "The History of Sexuality Volume 1" (1976), Foucault explores sex, and the discourse of sex developed in Western societies throughout the eighteen and nineteen centuries, and the pivotal role played by the Victorian age in repressing it. His epistemological approach challenges the "repressive hypothesis," which in his view was crafted by elite groups, the bourgeois classes, and the Christian Church. Foucault argues that the "repressive hypothesis" and discourses around sexuality were designed to control the use of sex as being reserved for an exclusively reproductive function, while at the same time clinicalising female sexuality, and pathologizing any groups with "deviant" sexual practices, which in effect are any practices other than traditional heterosexual marital behaviours.

In Foucault's words:

> A policing of sex: that is, not the rigour of a taboo, but the necessity of regulating sex through useful and public discourses. A few examples will suffice. One of the great innovations in the techniques of power in the eighteenth century was the emergence of "population" as an economic and political problem: population as wealth, population as manpower or labour capacity, population balanced between its own growth and the resources it commanded. Governments perceived that they were not dealing simply with subjects, or even with a "people," but with a "population," with its specific phenomena and its peculiar variables: birth and death rates, life expectancy, fertility, state of health, frequency of illnesses, patterns of diet and habitation" (Foucault, The History of Sexuality, Volume 1, p. 18).

And yet, the policing of sex, in his view, and attempts to suppress sex during the Victorian age, do not suppress desire (of alternative sexual practices). Foucault (1976) explains that state power through legislation has the power to dictate behaviours which are allowed or forbidden in society, thus shaping human consciousness and behaviour. The power of the state to regulate sexual practices creates an illusion about sex, legitimising exclusively heterosexual sexual relations within the bounds of marriage, and repressing all other forms of "illicit" sexual desire. For Foucault, alternative sexual expressions, although "illicit" in the eyes of the state, cannot suppress desire. The law can repress alternative sexual desires as "illicit," "against nature" or "sinful" (the repressive hypothesis), but not desire itself.

> [T]hus one should not think that desire is repressed, for the simple reason that the law is what constitutes both desire and the lack on which it is predicated. Where there is desire, the power relation is already present: an illusion, then, to denounce this relation for a repression exerted after the event (Foucault, The History of Sexuality, Volume 1, p. 81).

In Foucault's "repressive hypothesis" the sexual discourse promoted by the state silenced the pleasure of sex, with Western societies restricting sexual discourse to private domesticized spaces – the "controlled space" of married heterosexual couples. Following Foucault's premise, during the Victorian age the repression of sexual discourses led to the complete suppression of any public discussions regarding sex, the role of sex in people's lives, their identities, and any alternative expressions of sexuality. Foucault explains that the "repressive hypothesis" generated a discourse towards sexual activity, and sexuality, which was continuously "pathologizing" of any practices other than state sanctioned sexual practices within the heterosexual marriage bond.

In "The History of Sexuality" Foucault applies his power-knowledge epistemology to human sexuality, as he argues:

> We demand that sex speak the truth...and we demand that it tell us our truth, or rather, the deeply buried truth of that truth about ourselves which we think we possess in our immediate consciousness (Foucault, The History of Sexuality, Volume 1, p. 6).

In this body of work Foucault discusses power, knowledge, sex and the body, openly addressing the effects of the discourse of sex in gender identity and "legitimised" and "state sanctioned" sexual practices. His views on the relationship between power, knowledge, sex and the body contributed to a broader understanding of power, and how through institutional strategies of control it shapes discourses around sex, as well as sexual practises. This being so, the discourse of sex sets out the political agenda of what is "normal" and "acceptable," and the clinicalisation of sex, and it also describes "normal" versus "pathological" behavioural paradigms, with the latter being all those opposing the *status quo* (Foucault, 1982/2019).

Foucault's (1982/2019) epistemology breaks down societal impositions to gender, therefore, benefiting homosexual and heterosexual relationships alike. In his words:

> Rather than saying what we said at one time 'Let's try to re-introduce homosexuality into the general norm of social relations, let's say the reverse' – 'No! Let's escape as much as possible from the type of relations that society proposes for us and try to create in the empty space where we are new relational possibilities.' By proposing a new relational right, we will see that non-homosexual people can enrich their lives by changing their own schema of relations (Foucault, Ethics: Subjectivity and Truth, p. 160).

Foucault's ground-breaking contribution goes beyond his experience of gender (a homosexual male perspective), as a critique to traditional bourgeois sexuality, and the "legitimisation" of sex within husband and wife in a heterosexual family. His theory contributed to revolutionary epistemological discussions, paving the way for key scholarly discussions on gender, women and identity.

Feminist perspectives on Foucault have predominantly centred on his later work in "Discipline and Punish" and the first volume of "The History of Sexuality."

In Foucault's view, sexuality (and sexual preferences) were not inherently biological aspects of male or female bodies, and not determinant variables to gender identity and sexual experience (McNay, 1992). He regarded sexuality as a social construct supported through systems of power and exercised by a system of "control" and "repression." Arguably, Foucault developed his theory of power, knowledge, sexuality and "the body" in generic terms, discussing the effects of power and discourse in shaping the traditional family, and determining what could be considered either "normal" or "pathological" sexual behaviour, with women's experiences not developed extensively in his writings.

King (2004, p.30) elucidates the use of Foucault by feminists, when discussing the conceptual "appropriation" of Foucault's "Discipline and Punish" in the articulation of women's experiences (despite Foucault's gender-neutral approach):

> ...I shall explore how "woman" has been discursively constructed (condemned) as inferior yet also threatening to man, thus in perpetual need of containment and control and subjected (condemned) to particular disciplinary techniques. The body is an over-determined site of power for feminists as well as for Foucault: a surface inscribed with culturally and historically specific practices and subject to political and economic forces.

Despite Foucault's gender-neutral approach, King contends that his theorisation of power-knowledge, the production of subjectivity, and the body was highly influential for feminist scholarship. Foucault's theoretical legacy on how power produces subjectivity and shapes an individual understanding of the "body" (and suppression of desire) is indisputable. Although Foucault's work has been interpreted and applied to explain the condition of women, his episteme also suffers criticism by some feminist scholars for his omission with regard to the condition of women (Diamond & Quinby 1988; King, 2004), as well as issues of race and class (King, 2004).

It is argued by most post-modern thinkers that Foucault's theorisation and thought epitomise post-modern thought (Harstock, 1990; Hekman, 1990; Hoy,

1988). Thus, a leading critique to Foucault's views on gender and the use of his theory together with feminist theory is Foucault's lack of "action" or political response to systems of power and knowledge which are reproduced on women's bodies. Feminist scholarship elaborates on the congruence of Foucault's post-modern proposition in gender studies, and his deconstruction of gender, together with his attempts in negating universal claims to gender. However, feminists contend that through this epistemological perspective universal claims tend to "creep back" into their work. As contended by Nancy Hartsock (1990, p. 167):

> Thus, postmodernism, despite its stated efforts to avoid the problems of European modernism of the eighteenth and nineteenth centuries, at best manages to criticize these theories without putting anything in their place.

For authors such as McNay (1992), Foucault's episteme on sexuality is key in understanding the women's lived experiences. In her view, his insight into human sexuality as something not rigidly defined between male or female, provides a theoretical framework to women's repression as a pre-determinate cultural factor, shaped by a historical discourse of sexuality. She contends that Foucault's conceptualisation of "bodies," when applied to "women's bodies," reproduces systems of power, with the characterisation and use of the female body on cultural terms. McNay's perspective, is key in explaining the condition of women through feminist lenses.

Feminists might consider that Foucault's gender-neutral approach to the effects of power to "the body" provides a platform for adaptation and reflection. This perspective can bring greater meaning to those lived experiences seen as "abnormal," or for the contestation of traditional roles (masculinities and femininities) within the family – including women's domesticity, docility and submission. This being so, a generic theoretical approach gives voice to women and individuals from diverse gender orientations.

McNay elucidates, however, that a broader view on Foucault's work might provide greater insight on individual bodies resistance to power. In her view, Foucault's final work "The Use of Pleasure, the Care of the Self and various interviews and articles,"[3] provides greater clarity to the problematisation and effects of power, the creation of knowledge and the effects in the repressed body.

---

3   This is a rather obscure part of Foucault's work developed in the final years of his life.

Following McNay's perspective, in his final work, Foucault elaborates a conceptualisation of "self" in acknowledgement of the theoretical limitations in "The History of Sexuality" and his passive conceptualisation of "the individual body." This work brings to light a framework of analysis to resist mainstream discourses of power and sexuality. Through this perspective, McNay contends that Foucault's epistemological approach would not fit into post-modernism or post-structuralism thought, which is a label Foucault himself did not attribute to his work.

In "Crime and Punishment" and "The History of Sexuality," Foucault applies his power-knowledge episteme to the body and sexuality. In these two works, Foucault addresses the effects of the discourse of power on the repression of the body and sexuality, explaining the effects of power in shaping "docile bodies," as well as "legitimised' sexual practices" shaping gender identity.

Nonetheless, I propose a different perspective to Foucault's theory in order to explain Brazilian and Pakistani women's lived experiences of honour and gender. Through this perspective I draw exclusively from Foucault's power-knowledge conceptualisation of "regimes of truth" and "power." In this new episteme, Brazilian and Pakistani women's honour consciousness is manifested through gender power relations.

In Foucault's "regimes of truth," truth is not inscribed to reality, but rather is always produced in relations to a specific reality, with this production generating effects on the subject and power (Lorenzini, 2016). In "The Will to Know" Foucault elucidates about regimes of truth and its relationship with power: "...it is so deeply ingrained in us, that we no longer perceive it as the effect of a power that constrains us" (Foucault, 1978, cited in Lorenzini, 2016, p. 66) For Foucault (1980), regimes of truth and views of the social world are constantly negotiated with power, which holds hegemony over society. Moreover, when dealing with "power," Foucault explains 1) it is co-extensive with society, 2) relationships of power are inherently in the social fabric, 3) these power relations are not manifested only through prohibition or punishment, but take multiple forms, 4) that their interconnections establish conditions for domination, and this domination is organised into a more or less coherent strategy to maintain power, 5) that power relations utilise strategies. Concessions made by power is one of them, 6) there are no relations of power without resistance.

The effects of power, power structures and the way in which they create "regimes of truth" (consolidating power systems) are consistent with Brazilian and Pakistani women's lived experiences of gender. I argue that Foucault's "regimes of truth" and power relations, and the monopoly of the reproduction of truth, is consistent with Brazilian and Pakistani women's lived experiences of gender, and their struggle to break away from power systems. In this epistemological perspective, these are "gender" power systems repro-ducing "gender" power relations. They bring greater depth to the manifesta-tion of women's lived experiences of honour, and the reproduction of gender power relations (and masculine hegemony). Through this new epistemolog-ical approach, I understand "honour" (consciousness) manifested as Fou-cault's "regime of truth." This produces a continuum to power systems through "honour."

Foucault's (1980) views of "regimes of truth" and "power relations" provide individuals understanding of the world around them at the societal level. Fou-cault's key epistemological perspectives in his power-knowledge of "regimes of truth" and "power relations," provide understanding to women's lived experi-ences of gender, and what are clarified as: a) the subject reproduces "regimes of truth," b) regimes of truth are enforced through institutional power, c) insti-tutional and societal structures create "regimes of truth," d) there is resistance to power but power reorganises itself to exert dominion over subjects, e) power has hegemony over social structures, institutions, and subjects by designing "regimes of truth," consolidating power reproduction.

Given Foucault's epistemic limitations when dealing with "the individ-ual body," and the absence of discussions with human consciousness (and its reflexive character), I draw from Hegel's epistemological perspective on human consciousness to frame Brazilian and Pakistani migrant women's hon-our consciousness. This establishes a link between consciousness (and self-consciousness) and how these reproduce Foucault's "regimes of truth," and what is deemed "gender" power relations (gender politics) in Australia.

2 Hegel, Foucault, and Migrant Women

In the first part of this chapter, I classified honour consciousness through Hegel's framework of human consciousness. I contended that Hegel's epistemo-logical approach to consciousness is a suitable framework to explain Brazilian and Pakistani lived experiences of honour consciousness in Australia. Their lived experiences demonstrate a reflexive character when dealing with "other" notions of honour consciousness, as well as with the spectrum oscillating from "moderate" notions of honour consciousness to "extreme" notions of honour consciousness. Lived experiences of honour consciousness, moreover, follow Hegel's phenomenology, since they travel through history and are transmitted throughout generations.

As discussed earlier in this chapter, for Foucault "each society has its regime of truth." In Foucault's view, the greatest challenge of our generation is to deconstruct "regimes of truth." In his perspective, they set out the "political, economic, institutional regime of production of truth," with "regimes of truth" consolidating society's power structures, and hegemonic systems of power. Foucault contends that the individual self is shaped by structural reproductions of power, which are then internalised.

According to Foucault's power-knowledge episteme, "regimes of truth" are essential for the reproduction of truth. These consolidate structural systems of power and hegemonic power. Power sets its agenda ("regimes of truth") impacting the individual self at the societal level, and reproducing power structures at the institutional, governmental, and societal level. Although there is resistance to power, power re-organises itself since it holds hegemony over the production of "truth," what is deemed "regimes of truth." Power can make concessions to its subjects but continues to exert hegemonic influence and dominion over them. Power develops strategies to maintain control, consolidating power systems throughout society ("effects of power").

There are, however, limitations to Hegel's and Foucault's epistemological perspectives if seen in isolation. When dealing with Hegel's episteme of human consciousness and phenomenology, it is possible to understand Brazilian and Pakistani women's lived experiences of honour at the level of human consciousness. Conversely, when accessing Foucault's power-knowledge episteme, "regimes of truth" and "power relations," and the struggle of subjects to "break away" from hegemonic power, it explains Brazilian and Pakistani women's' "gender" power struggles at the societal, institutional, and governmental level. But these two frameworks, unless combined, would fall short in explaining their lived experiences in the diaspora.

Drawing from Hegel's and Foucault's episteme, I argue that honour consciousness through Hegel's phenomenology and views on human consciousness, is manifested through Foucault's epistemological views of "regimes of truth" as "power." In my analysis, migrant women's honour consciousness is conflated with Foucault's power-knowledge episteme ("regime of truth"), consolidating gender power relations, as well as honour consciousness, operating in a circular process. This chapter proposes a new epistemological framework to explain women's lived experiences of honour consciousness in Australia (through a Hegelian perspective), conflated with a new perspective on Foucault's epistemology within feminist studies. By applying exclusively Foucault's power-knowledge episteme of "regimes of truth" and "power," I bring an in-depth understanding to migrant women's lived experiences in Australia.

Through this new episteme, honour consciousness is manifested through gender power relations in Australia. This is demonstrated through women's "moderate" and "extreme" notions of honour consciousness, and women's challenges to break away from these gender power structures. Power makes "more" concessions to "moderate" notions of honour consciousness. In such case, there is "more" power resistance from women. These are manifested through women's rights, political engagement, and the fight against violence towards women. Conversely, in "extreme" notions of honour consciousness power makes "less" concessions and there is "less" power resistance from the women. This manifests through violence towards women, a lack of women's rights, and women's suppression. Honour consciousness consolidates gender power relations, with these enforcing honour consciousness' self-reflexive and circular character.

For example: The views shared by migrant Brazilian and Pakistani women during interviews (discussed in previous chapters), show lived experiences of honour consciousness as being predominantly "moderate". These support the rights of women, female political participation, female participation in the workforce, as well as the protection of women's human rights within their families, and freedom from oppression and violence from husbands or partners. Nonetheless, the 30 participants in this survey do not fully reject traditional female roles within the family, and social reproduction. Rather, they reconcile traditional views and honour consciousness with women's right to have a voice, to participate in the workforce and to be treated with respect (as an equal) by their family members, partners, and spouses. These traditional views give a continuum to social reproduction and masculine privileges in Australia. Consequently, honour consciousness continues to shape these women's lived experiences of gender. In such case, gender power relations are consistent with Foucault's "regimes of truth" and strategies of power, making concessions to "subjects" (Foucault, 1980). The lived experiences of "other" Brazilian and Pakistani women are regarded as "extreme." These migrant women have been labelled by participants as the social "other." These women's notions of honour consciousness are manifested through "extreme" notions, with "less" resistance from hegemonic power.

The table below highlights key epistemological perspectives from Hegel and Foucault applied to women's lived experiences in Australia. The summary highlights how Hegel's and Foucault's episteme are applied in isolation to migrant women's stories, and what parts of their episteme are conflated. This provides a holistic perspective to lived experiences of honour consciousness, and how it is manifested through gender power relations.

This chapter's framework goes beyond Foucault's proposition in countering "regimes of truth" by detaching the power of truth from forms of "hegemony, social, economic and cultural". I argue that honour consciousness conflated with Foucault's power-knowledge episteme is essential to understand gender

TABLE 5.1   Key epistemological perspectives from Hegel and Foucault applied to women's lived
experiences in Australia

Hegel's episteme	Human consciousness	Phenomenology
	– self-consciousness – reflexive character – circularity – a broad meaning to human experience – acquires meaning through the social "other" – understanding of the social world at the consciousness level	– dialectic (thesis, anti-thesis synthesis) shapes consciousness – travels through history – transcends time but adjusts to societal demands
	New episteme (Honour consciousness) – self-consciousness – reflexive character – circularity, reinforcing views of the social world – a sub-sect of human consciousness – "moderate" notions acquire meaning through interactions with "extreme notions" of honour consciousness – Understanding of the social world at the consciousness level	– Interaction between "moderate" and "extreme" notions of honour shapes honour consciousness – Taught by the family, transcending traveling through history – It is transmitted through the parents but adjusts to new societal settings

TABLE 5.1   Key epistemological perspectives from Hegel and Foucault (*cont.*)

Foucault's Power-Knowledge episteme	Regimes of Truth	Power Relations
	– The subject reproduces regimes of truth – regimes of truth are enforced through institutional power – systemic and institutional reproduction of power – understanding of the social world at the societal, governmental, and institutional level	– institutions and societal structures create "regimes of truth" – there is resistance to power, but power reorganises itself to exert dominion over subjects – power has hegemony over the social structures, institutions, and subjects by designing "regimes of truth"
Why combining Hegel's human consciousness and Foucault's Power-Knowledge to explain migrant women's experiences?	New episteme (honour consciousness conflated with regimes of truth) – the subject reproduces regimes of truth at societal level and at the level of human consciousness – honour consciousness operates in a circular way, reinforcing regimes of truth and views of the social world – regimes of truth are enforced (or not) through institutional power – regime of truth continues even if subject is removed from institutional power – regimes of truth shift and change to new institutional power/ new governments and societies	New episteme (gender power relations) – regimes of truth operate at the level of human consciousness reproducing gender power relations – there is resistance to power, but power reorganises itself at the level of human consciousness to exert dominion over subjects – power has hegemony over the social structures, institutions, as well as over subjects at the level of human consciousness reproducing "regimes of truth"

power reproduction in honour systems. Thus, "truth" exists in individual consciousness (self-consciousness) as well as in Foucault's "regimes of truth."
Consequently, the battle against gendered norms reproduced by honour consciousness should be fought at the level of individual consciousness as well as
Foucault's level of the structural, societal, and governmental level of reproduction of "regimes of truth."

This new epistemological framework expands Foucault's "regimes of truth,"
"the effects of power" and power structures beyond the societal level, incorpo-
rating power reproduction at the level of human consciousness. Through this
new perspective on Foucault and gender, I examine "regimes of truth" and its
effects in different societal, institutional, and governmental apparatus – and
how these "effects of power" (and power systems) are manifested in the migration setting. Foucault's perspective focused exclusively on the Western model
(Lorenzini, 2016). This epistemological approach applies his episteme to the
South American and South Asian Non-Western world, as well as to migrants in
the Western diaspora. Through this framework I demonstrate that the reproduction of power within gender systems is more difficult to break away from
than previously argued within feminist studies. This "gender" power struggle
makes no clear allusion to "the body," "female bodies" or even individual's "sexuality." The current perspective demonstrates how honour shapes women's
consciousness, constructing "self-regulation," and influencing their identities
in Australia, as well as providing a continuum to masculine privilege and dominance. In the next chapter I will compare data results from interviews with
Brazilians and Pakistanis, drawing from this theoretical perspective to provide
an explanation to their experiences in Australia.

A New Perspective to Hegel's and Foucault's Episteme and Migrant Women's Stories

As explained in chapter 2, Brazilian participants 1, 2, 3, 4, 9, 5, 10, 11, 13, 14 and 15 discussed during their interviews how honour is, for them, "a value" or "morality."

Participant 5 ("Alice," chapter 2), for instance, defined honour in the following terms:

> (The word honour means) for me ... its very linked to values, honour and respect. In my opinion. And for example, trying to have a life, trying to do things based precisely on these values ...

For other Brazilian women taking part in this study, this is also a key variable in understanding how honour consciousness shapes their moral compass. For these women, honour consciousness is a concept "inserted inside your head while you are growing up," as explained by participant 4 ("Maria Paula"). These concepts shape behaviour and has an impact upon gender power relations.

Likewise, in chapter 4, Pakistani participants 1, 4, 5, 6, 9, 10, 12, 13, 14 and 15 discussed their lived experiences in depth, speaking of honour as "a value" and "morality" (related or not to Islam). In their interviews, honour as a "a value" or "morality" is a key variable to understand other samples' views of honour and how honour consciousness comprises an inherent part of their moral compass, and their notions of right and wrong.

Nonetheless, Pakistani participants 1, 4, 6, 9, 13 and 14 explicitly conflated honour consciousness with religion (what I classify as "religious consciousness"). For example, participant 14 ("Zara," chapter 4), explicitly conflates honour consciousness with religion (Islam) in the following terms:

> (Honour) it's about everything. Honour is the most respected word for me. Because, you know, I told you, I am a Muslim. My Muslim concepts come from my religion. God gave us born rights to be honoured.

The lived experiences of honour consciousness for both migrant Brazilian Christian women and migrant Pakistani Muslim women was consistently

© FLAVIA BELLIENI ZIMMERMANN, 2025 | DOI:10.1163/9789004711242_008

described as "something deep" and as a "value." For example, Brazilian participant 6 ("Diolinda, chapter 2) explained: "...and what you have most precious is your honour. For me is a very strong thing." And Pakistani participant 12 ("Shamaila," chapter 4), reflected that honour is "... a very deep word... for me it surrounds everything."

Honour as "a value" is a key variable bringing meaning to their lived experiences of honour consciousness. Although there are other underlaying subthemes in their lived experiences of honour, "honour as value" is a crucial feature shaping their views of the world. Family plays a central role in consolidating lived experiences of honour, religion and gender, since honour is "something taught," and is then internalised in their ways of thinking through their upbringing in the family of origin. As explained by Brazilian participant 13 ("Poliana," chapter 2), honour is something learned ("I learned it from my mother"). Pakistani participant 8 ("Abida," chapter 4), elucidates that the family raises you to "keep honour" ("I was raised in a manner where I kept the honour of my family").

The women taking part in the interviews clarified that honour consciousness is not experienced in the same way by all women living in either Brazil or Pakistan. During their interviews, women from both sample groups explained how lived experiences of honour consciousness are multilayered. Honour consciousness, based on their stories, is shaped by "where you come from," from the values taught by your parents, from your level of education, from the region where you were raised (small country cities in Brazil or rural Pakistan, for instance), socio-economic background, as well as parental views on religion.

For example: Brazilian participant 2 ("Clara,"chapter 2) explained that "(notions of honour) depends on the context. Because for me it is very personal. I think it depends very much on where you come from, what were the values that were given to you. Then it will determine to whether it is an honour for me, or what it is not an honour for you".

Pakistani participant 10 ("Hiba," chapter 4) tells how social class, and "where you come from," shape your notions of honour consciousness. "Extreme notions" being prevalent for people who are "struggling" financially or are "ignorant," living in remote areas of Sindh province. In "Hiba's" words:

> People who are, who are struggling for the basic needs, they're overpowered by people with resources, but still living in ignorance and the absence of law ... It's the concept of Karo-Kari and it's found in the backward parts of Sindh [province].

Participants from both sample groups agreed that there are "different" notions of honour, and that each person has their own notion of honour. For example: Brazilian participant 3 ("Alana," chapter 2) discussed the subjectivity of "notions of honour," in her words: "For me (honour), it's not necessarily a cultural or religious thing. It's just a personal thing for me."

Pakistani participant 13 ("Naila," chapter 4) explains the "personal" character of honour consciousness, as follows: "Honour is very personal. It has to do with the way you conduct yourself, your beliefs, and your values. It is related to your family and the town you are from."

Most participants agreed that there is a degree of subjectivity in lived experiences of honour. In some interviews participants discussed in detail how honour consciousness can be manifested in a "negative way," or as "something which horrifies me," or in a "extreme way." These I classify as "extreme" notions of honour consciousness.

As explained by Brazilian participant 14 ("Laila," chapter 2), who comes from the Northeast region of Brazil, the region where you come from can influence "extreme" notions of honour consciousness. This is manifested through women's lack of agency (accepting all types of behaviour from men), paving the way for abusive relationships. In her words:

> [My notions of honour] have been influenced by accepting abusive relationships. So not being aware that that relationship was being abusive. It's a society that kind of raised women to accept any behaviour from a man, not just nay, not physical aggression, but going out without asking, and drinking, and hanging out with other women, and you will be the last one to know.

Now, living in Australia she distances herself from these "extreme" notions of honour consciousness.

Pakistani participant 2 ("Haniya," chapter 4) explained how Pakistan's "extreme" notions of honour are different from her own notions of honour ("moderate"), distancing herself from the "social other." These "extreme" notions of honour consciousness are manifested by violence towards women and honour killings. In Haniya's words:

> So, you can go to that extreme level of some people killing the whole family, sometimes boys kill the whole family, like parents, if they are supporting their daughter, those kinds of things. It is very sad. So, this is extreme.

Women from both cohorts explained, however, how their lived experiences of honour are predominantly "positive," or "something good." Brazilian Christian women[1] and Pakistani Muslim women distanced themselves from those "othering" notions of honour consciousness regarded as "extreme." Extreme notions of honour are manifested through female subjection, inter-partner oppression, lack of agency, violence towards women and honour killings. Women taking part in this study hold notions of honour consciousness which are predominantly "moderate," since they reconcile traditional notions of womanhood with women's agency, women's participation in the workforce and politics; they engage in political activism and in the fight against violence towards women.

Most migrant Brazilian Christian women discussed their lived experiences of honour consciousness in the light of traditional family values which were taught to them by their families, shaping their notions of womanhood. Although religion is not explicitly conflated, their views of honour consciousness as a "value" and an "inherent" part of their notions of "right from wrong," are an inherent part of what was taught "by their parents." Brazilian women's lived experiences of honour consciousness are deeply influenced by the Catholic values of the family and traditional notions of womanhood, transmitted through Brazil's "cultural Christianity."

On the other hand, Pakistani Muslim migrant women's lived experiences of honour consciousness are explicitly conflated with Islam (religious consciousness), which informs their "moral code" and "value system" and "understanding from right and wrong." Pakistani participants discussed extensively the role played by Islam in Pakistan, and "different" or "other" notions (regarded as "extreme") of honour consciousness. In their lived experiences of honour consciousness, they explicitly link it with Islam and religion (participants 1, 4, 6, 9, 13, 14, in chapter 4). Pakistani Muslim women taking part in this study also discussed how upbringing, the region where women come from, and levels of education influence religious consciousness, distancing themselves from "extreme views" which can lead to women's suppression, lack of women's rights, violence towards women and honour killings. In the views of survey participants, such perspectives are not supported by Islam. In Pakistani Muslim women's lived experiences, "there is nothing giving as much as freedom as

---

1 Not all Brazilian interviewees were practicing Christians. Within the interview cohort, there were practicing Christians and nominal Christians, with 2 participants (4 and 7) professing to be "Spiritualists." But in Brazil, all individuals are influenced by Christian Catholic values of the family and notions of womanhood. This is a result of what is referred to in this book as Brazil's "cultural Christianity."

Islam give us as a woman, the empowerment, it's when I look or study in detail" (participant 7, "Hiba", chapter 4).

In the light of the literature and the interview results, the key difference between their lived experiences of honour consciousness is the result of the interplay of historical, religious and cultural factors. As explained in chapter 1, honour consciousness in Brazil is the result of "whitening" colonial practices, which have played a part in the shaping of Brazilian women's lived experiences of gender. This chapter draws from Quijano's (2000) episteme of "coloniality of power," and Lugones (2008) perspective of "coloniality of power" and the ways in which class and race impact women's lived experiences in Brazil. In chapter 2 I also explained how "coloniality of power" and whitening colonial practices impact the lived experiences of honour consciousness of Afro-descendent women (Gonzalez, 1988). Additionally, Brazil's "coloniality of power" highlights honour consciousness' intersectional experience, and the effects of race and class on Brazilian women's lived experiences of gender.

As discussed in chapters 1 and 2, Brazil's "coloniality of power" and past whitening practices are key in consolidating those notions of womanhood embedded in traditional family values as taught by the Catholic church. From Brazil's colonial times until the end of the Empire, there was no separation between state and church, with Catholicism being the official religion of the state (Holanda, 2007). This shapes what has been termed as "cultural Christianity." This concept follows Demerath III (2000) epistemological framing of "cultural religion," where religion influences personal identity and a continuing attachment to religious values even after "participation in ritual or belief have lapsed." As explained in chapter 1, another key feature of "cultural religion" is that individuals influenced by these cultural values, who no longer attend religious rituals or see themselves as "believers" can be highly critical of church dogmas (for example, the Catholic views on sexuality, virginity, LGBTIQ+ rights, and homosexuality). However, in broader terms, the religious values of the Catholic church continue to shape individual paradigms, and individual meanings of right and wrong, and morality.

Consequently, Brazilian women, who may be practicing or non-practicing Christians, or even non-Christians, continue to be influenced by these notions of womanhood. Since they are so deeply embedded in Brazil's cultural fabric, these values are not explicitly linked to religion by participants (Catholicism or Christianity).

Notably, Pakistan's state formation is different from Brazil's, following a more secularist framework. I explained in chapter 4, how Pakistan's partition from India in 1947 was triggered by Indian Muslim aspirations or greater and fairer representation in India's political system (Jalal, 2014). The influence of

Indian Muslim identity in the creation of Pakistan's state is, however, hotly contested by the literature. Recent perspectives reveal a secularist view of Muslim nationalistic aspirations (Jalal, 1994). Consequently, Pakistan's secularist views of the state have shaped Pakistani Muslim women's lived experiences of honour consciousness and religious consciousness. According to interview results, Islam and Islamic values are highly influential at the level of the individual, and for those women professing to be Muslim and practicing Islam.

As explained in chapter 4, the South Asian notion of *izzat* is key in shaping Pakistani women's lived experience of honour. However, izzat is not confined simply to Muslims: it also affects the lives of Hindus and Sikhs alike (Gill & Brah, 2014). I point out how Pakistani Muslim women's lived experiences of honour are influenced by the sub-continent's cultural notions of *izzat* (honour consciousness) and readings of Islam (religious consciousness). These two variables can be manifested through "moderate" or "extreme" notions of honour consciousness and religion.

There are readings of Islam embedded in cultural notions of *izzat*, establishing a distinction between honour and dignity. Honour and dignity can be conflated as synonyms with Islamic texts, or it can be argued they have different meanings (Andisham, 2019). This is a contested issue amongst Muslim scholars, with several neglecting the distinction between honour and dignity in the Qur'an. This school of thought reconciles Islamic texts with modern views of human dignity though the framing of universal Human Rights (Andisham, 2019). Pakistani women taking part in this survey had predominantly "moderate" notions of honour consciousness and religious consciousness. Women living in big cosmopolitan centres have more access to information and education. This increases their likelihood of accessing those Islamic teachings which reconcile notions of *izzat* with the universal protection of human rights, women's rights of agency, and political representation.

1 Brazilian and Pakistani Women Honour Consciousness and Hegel

Significantly, both Brazilian Christian migrant women and Pakistani Muslim migrant women explained how honour consciousness has been transmitted to them through the way they were brought up by their parents, and by their parent's and family's "values" and "principles."

Their stories are consistent with Hegel's phenomenology episteme. In Hegel's perspective of human consciousness, it travels through history, determining possible ways to track the effects of consciousness in the development of the human soul shaping notions of "truth" (Hegel, 1807/1977). Since honour consciousness is "taught by the parents," these "values" travel through time and history, adjusting to societal values of the time.

My research findings on Brazilian and Pakistani women's honour consciousness are consistent with Hegel's understanding of human consciousness, which incorporates the development of meaning through the interaction with the social "other." Through Hegel's perspective, these different views of consciousness, being reproduced throughout generations, shifting and changing, adapt to each historical context (Hegel, 1807/1977). Another key feature of Hegel's epistemological perspective on human consciousness is its self-reflexive character. Brazilian and Pakistani lived experiences of honour consciousness are consistent with Hegel's dialectic method of analysis (thesis, antithesis, and synthesis), as well as his perspective on self-consciousness (reflective character of honour). Through this perspective, consciousness cannot be understood in isolation but rather as resulting from the interactions of different "consciousnesses" (Hegel, 1807/1977). In other words, individual consciousness (self-consciousness) only develops meaning when exposed to the social "other," revealing the overarching lived experiences of consciousness, as well as how these are manifested socially. According to Hegel: "Self-consciousness achieves its satisfaction only in another self-consciousness" (Hegel, quoted in Hamlyn, 1986, p. 317)."

Although Brazilian Christian women and Pakistani Muslim women's lived experiences of honour consciousness is manifested differently, both are consistent with Hegel's phenomenological perspective. Their lived experiences of honour consciousness travels through history, and through generations. In Brazilian women's stories, their lived experiences of honour consciousness are deeply influenced by the traditional Catholic values of the family, and by "cultural Christianity." Together with "coloniality of power" and whitening colonial practices (Gonzalez, 1988; Lugones, 2008; Quijano, 2000), the traditional values of the family and "cultural Christianity" (Cogell, 2001; Inserra, 2019) have been taught and transmitted for hundreds of years in Brazilian society. This gives a continuum to Brazilian lived experiences of honour consciousness for future generations. These also continue to shape "moderate" and "extreme" notions, with "extreme" notions predominantly manifested in small cities or in Brazil's Northeastern region. In Pakistani women's stories, honour consciousness and religious consciousness are taught by their parents and families and are deeply embedded in cultural notions of *izzat*. As a result, "moderate" or "extreme" notions of honour consciousness and religious consciousness have been reproduced within Pakistan's regions. Based on my research findings, in big city centres, for instance, "moderate" notions are predominant, whereas in rural and less developed regions "extreme" notions of honour consciousness and religion consciousness are more common. This is also consistent with Hegel's episteme, and his perspective on the transcendental character of human consciousness, and the way in which it travels through time and history.

2   Brazilian and Pakistani Women Honour Consciousness, Gender
        Politics and Foucault

This section discusses how migrant Brazilian Christian and migrant Pakistani Muslim women's lived experiences of honour consciousness shape gender politics in Australia. First, I discuss what "continues the same" in their lived experiences of honour consciousness, and gender power relations in Australia. Next, I discuss how honour consciousness and lived experiences of gender can "change," shift, adjust and adapt to Australian society and the exposure to Australian multiculturalism. Their lived experiences of honour consciousness, and gender power reproduction in Australian is consistent with Foucault's power-knowledge episteme.

Migrant Christian Brazilian and migrant Pakistani Muslim women lived experiences of honour consciousness is transmitted to Australia. The parents' "values" are still key in shaping "moderate" and "extreme" notions of honour consciousness after migration. During interviews, Brazilian and Pakistani women discussed how some members of the community "don't change." According to interview results, "not changing much" is the result of "how you live your life," how many friends you have within the community, and much time you spend within the community. All participants, however, explained how honour consciousness continues an inherent part of who they are, and their moral compass. It was reported by some participants that the parent's teachings vividly come back to their minds when they are faced with challenges to the honour code. Although their parents are not in Australia (some may have even passed away), participants have internalised notions of "right and wrong" as taught by their parents.

In their lived experiences, they continue to follow their family's "values." Women taking part in interviews explained how these "values" (honour consciousness) continue in Australia, changing depending on each person. Women's primary responsibility continues to be home duties, even if they hold full-time employment. Husbands are usually the "breadwinners," as women after becoming mothers tend to quit their jobs or work part-time in order to look after their children, their husbands and their homes.

For example, Brazilian participant 13 ("Poliana," chapter 2) discussed how the cost of childcare is an issue for young Brazilian mothers in Australia, with many quitting work altogether to look after their children, explaining "why to put a young child in Childcare? For her (the mother) to be waiting tables? Doesn't make sense, even financially." Pakistani participant 4, ("Aalia," chapter 4), explained: "(w)when I say yes (that things do not change in Australia) I am talking about men being given special priority over women. You know, them being given privileges over women whether it is at gatherings laying out the food, serving food or ironing their clothes." Brazilian and Pakistani women do not have maids or living in nannies in Australia. Consequently, they end up cutting back on paid work, or giving up their careers completely, in order to look after their children, their husbands, their families and their homes.

Brazilian Christian migrant women discussed how their lived experiences of honour consciousness and traditional views of the family (within religion) was shaped by their parents' values, and by traditional values of the family in their upbringing. Brazilian women predominantly migrate without their families, coming to Australia under skilled visas or as students (Rocha, 2013). Parental views on the dress code, with regard to dressing modestly, not wearing mini-shorts or showing cleavage are still seen as honourable and as showing "respect." Although their families are overseas and cannot enforce the honour code, honour consciousness continues to play a significant role in the shaping of Brazilian women's notions of womanhood in Australia.

In Australia, Brazilian women are free to choose their partners, but there is family involvement with these partners in Australia thorough WhatsApp and Skype calls, for instance. For example, Participant 14 ("Laila," field notes, chapter 4) explained how her mother contacted her Australian boyfriend asking him when he would propose (field notes, chapter 4). Unaffordable childcare was reported as an issue within the Brazilian community in Sydney. As there are no live in maids or nannies, Brazilian couples find it "more affordable" that women stay home looking after the children, since males' salaries are higher. Brazilian men are predominantly "the breadwinners", and couples will not pay the costs of childcare just for the wife to "be waiting tables." Brazilian community leaders and service providers in Sydney, New South Wales, as well as women taking part in this survey, reported incidents of "extreme" notions of honour consciousness where Brazilian women suffered inter-partner oppression, and violence in "the name of honour." Evangelical Christian preaching on female submission might also be leading to "extreme" notions of honour amongst Brazilians in Australia.

On the other hand, Pakistani Muslim migrant women discussed the role played by their parents and family life in shaping their lived experiences of honour consciousness and religious consciousness. The ways in which they were taught by their families have a major impact in their lived experiences

of gender and notions of womanhood in Australia. Pakistani women predominantly migrate to Australia within the family unit, and most participants taking part in this survey had their nuclear and extended families living in
Australia (Yasmeen, 2000). Consequently, family views regarding "marriage
age," segregation and ostracism of divorced women continue to influence attitudes and behaviour in Australia (participants 1, "Fatima" and participant 11,
"Jawaria," chapter 4). And as discussed by participant 2, ("Haniya," chapter 4),
gender segregation continues to be an issue in some events promoted by the
Pakistani community in Perth.

These gendered views are reproduced by children from Pakistani parents
born in Australia. During interviews, Pakistani women reported that arranged
marriages continue in the diaspora, as well as parental opining on their offspring's choice of partners. There is more freedom in Australia to refuse a marriage proposal, but parents operate like "tinder," introducing potential partners
to their children (participant 5, "Madiha," chapter 4). Although there is greater
flexibility regarding partner choice in Australia, Pakistani children would not
marry someone not approved by their parents. However, Pakistani women
predominantly do have less freedom to choose their partners than Pakistani
men, (who can marry whoever they want, even perhaps Australian Christian
women). For these Pakistani women there is more pressure from their families
and the community that they marry "Pakistani men", or at least "Muslim men",

There are several events organised by the Pakistani community in Perth,
Western Australia, where there is gender segregation. Pakistani community
leaders and service providers reported incidents of "extreme" notions of honour consciousness where Pakistani women have suffered from inter-partner
oppression and violence in "the name of honour" (field notes, chapter 4). During interviews, Pakistani women taking part in this survey did not report any
incidents of violence within their acquaintances or within the community.
Nonetheless, their views of "extreme" notions of honour and their interpretations of "violence towards women" are subjective, and not necessarily in
line with the Australian Human Rights Commission (AHRC) framing of violence towards women. As explained in chapter 4 the AHRC follows the United
Nations Declaration on the Elimination of Violence Against Women (1993)
classification of violence towards women.

The differences between Brazilian and Pakistani women's lived experiences of honour consciousness and gender are the result of the interplay of
historical, religious and cultural factors, as well as different migration cycles to
Australia. For example, arranged marriages are no longer an issue in Brazilian
society, whereas there are arranged marriages within Pakistanis in Australia.
Family issues are more "relaxed" for Brazilian women in Australia because they

predominantly migrate to Australia without their families (Rocha, 2013). However, there is still involvement from their families in Brazil with their partners here in Australia, via WhatsApp video calls. Brazilians' families do not pressure women to marry Christian or Brazilian men, since most are still living in Brazil. But families still try to influence their children's choice of spouse by getting involved with partners via regular video calls. Conversely, Pakistani women suffer pressure from their families, who usually live in Australia, with regard to whom they should marry, trying to set them up with a "Pakistani Muslim," or "Muslim" men.

3 Brazilian and Pakistani Women's Honour Consciousness and Gender Politics in Australia

Migrant Christian Brazilian and migrant Pakistani Muslim women's lived experiences of honour consciousness, religion and gender continue, but they shift, adapting and changing to Australian society and to Australian multiculturalism. "Moderate" and "extreme" notions of honour consciousness translate to Australia, as these are values which they have internalised. Brazilian and Pakistani migrant women, however, become "more relaxed," "more open minded" and enjoy greater freedom to be who they want to be in Australia.

For example, Brazilian participant 10 ("Noemia," chapter 2) explained how her notions of honour "have not changed" in Australia, "but the values change a little, they become more independent from the family." In Pakistani participant 14's ("Zara", chapter 4) story, she reflected how the relationship between parents and children "has changed, of course" with parents being "closer" and "friendlier" with their children. Australian multiculturalism makes them more accepting of different cultures, religions and ways of living. Australian culture and multiculturalism also make them question gender power relations (male hegemony) in Brazil and Pakistan.

Nonetheless, gender reproduction and traditional notions of womanhood continue in Australia, mostly unchallenged. Women are "helped" by their partners with childminding and home duties, which doesn't happen in their home countries. Brazilian participant 11 ("Viviana," chapter 2) explained how Brazilian husbands "participate" more and "help" in the upbringing of their children in Australia. And Pakistani participant 4 ("Aalia," chapter 4) discussed how, although things can change in Australia, domestic chores continue to be a woman's duty, and men continue enjoying privileges.

Overall, child minding, looking after the elders (Pakistani women), cooking, cleaning and domestic chores are seen predominantly as these women's main responsibility. If women work full-time, they have a "triple" workload. Families become more accepting and flexible during the process of adjusting to Australian culture, although, many times, they feel "shocked" by the Australian way of life. Participants explained how in Australia "there is too much freedom," men can earn less than women, men can "look after children," there is lack of respect for the family and parents, and there is a lack of modesty in the dress code.

Brazilian Christian migrant women reflected upon how lived experiences of honour consciousness and traditional views of the family (within religion) adapt to Australian culture. For instance, some Brazilian women taking part in this study lived with their boyfriends, something "unthinkable" in their hometowns in Brazil. However, although there is freedom to live with their boyfriends in Australia, there is huge pressure from their families back in Brazil for them to get married (participants 1 "Aurea," 12 "Fiorela," 14 "Laila" and 15 "Olivia," chapter 2). In their view, it brings more "respect." Brazilian women experience more freedom in Australia, but their families overseas make them "feel guilty" for living overseas and not spending time with them (participants 9 and 10, chapter 2).

It was discussed that Australian multiculturalism might challenge Brazilian Christian fundamentalism, depending on parental views of honour consciousness and gender (participant 3, "Alana" and participant 8 "Marielle," chapter 2). Brazilian women married to Australian and non-Brazilian men explain that these men "help more" than Brazilian men around the house and with looking after children. However, with honour consciousness they have internalised traditional notions of womanhood, and they still act as though women's primary role is to look after their children, their husbands, and their partners (if they are not married, they still see it as their role to "look after" their partners). For instance, participant 1 ("Aurea," chapter 2), explained how she irons her partner's work clothes at the expense of ironing her own. According to interview results, when Brazilian women work (full-time or part-time), they will still prioritise looking after their children, taking care of their husbands, and carrying out home duties.

Family life plays a central role in consolidating Pakistani Muslim migrant women's lived experiences of honour consciousness and religious consciousness in Australia. This differs from Brazilian lived experiences of honour consciousness, since they migrated to Australia predominantly with their families. Pakistani women explained during interviews, however, that the "values" taught by their families continue in Australia but that they do also shift and adapt to Australian culture. In Pakistani women's lived experiences of honour after migration, honour consciousness and religious consciousness continue to be the cultural lenses bringing meaning to their lived experiences of gender in Australia. As explained by participant 14 ("Zara," chapter 4), in Australia children respect their parents but have greater freedom to discuss issues with their families, which is "unthinkable" in Pakistani society. Arranged marriages still happen in Australia, but Pakistani women have greater freedom to reject marriage proposals. Participant 15 ("Uzma," chapter 4) explained that although there is great pressure for Pakistani Muslim women to marry Pakistani Muslim men in Australia, there are women "who manage to get their own way."

Regarding children's curfews, it is harder for families to control their whereabouts. As explained by participant 8 ("Abida," chapter 4), her sons are different from their Pakistani cousins and do "whatever they like." But if she had a daughter, she would try to enforce curfews and control her behaviour, because she is a "Pakistani Muslim." In Australia, parents still try to control their daughter's dress code, although girls do have greater freedom to dress "Western," "sleeveless" and "crop tops" (participant 4, "Aalia," chapter 4).

In Australia, parents have more "relaxed" gender norms within the home. And as explained by participant 7 ("Nazia," chapter 4) Australia is not similar to Pakistan, and couples do things on a more equal base. Participant 12 ("Shamaila," field notes, chapter 4), discusses how Pakistani men "help" around the house, making "cups of tea," as there are no live-in maids or nannies. However, childminding, cooking, cleaning, looking after the elders, and home duties are still seen as women's primary roles (participant 4, "Aalia," chapter 4). Participant 10 ("Hiba"), in chapter 4, for instance, was a professional woman until she had children. She quit her job to look after the children, the home, and to support her husband who works overseas. In Australia, due to the cost of living, most women hold part-time employment to help with the family finances. However, men continue to have higher salaries and are the "main breadwinner." The differences between Brazilian and Pakistani women's lived experiences of honour consciousness in Australia, and what "changes more" in the diaspora, reflects the historical, religious and cultural interplay in lived experiences of honour. For instance, Brazilian participant 2 ("Clara", chapter 2) said she was "shocked" to see Australian men looking after children, whereas Pakistani participant 4 ("Aalia," chapter 4) explained how she was "shocked" with women's dress code in Australia (sleeveless, wearing shorts is common).

Key variables shaping their experiences in the diaspora are different migration waves, and the fact that most Brazilian women's nuclear and extended families live overseas. With Brazilian women's nuclear and extended families still living in Brazil, they feel there is "freedom" in Australia for them to live the way they want (participants 1, 2, 4, 6, 9, 11, 12, 14 and 15, chapter 2). With Pakistani families migrating together to Australia, there is greater parental pressure to get married at a certain age and comply with parental expectations. However, Pakistani women in Australia have greater freedom to reject marriage proposals (participant 5, "Madiha," chapter 4), have less curfews, and can dress more freely if they choose to (participant 4, "Aalia"), compared to women in Pakistan. Children have more "relaxed" and "friendly" relations with their parents (participant 14, "Zara" chapter 4). However, there is still great social stigma in the community towards divorced women (participants 1 "Fatima," chapter 4) and towards women over 30 years old who are unmarried and without children (participant 11, "Jawaria," chapter 4).

Data results indicate that Brazilian and Pakistani women lived experiences of honour consciousness and gender are consistent with Foucault's power-knowledge episteme. Brazilian women and Pakistani women's notions of honour consciousness, which have been taught to them by their families in Brazil and Pakistan, translate to their lived experiences, shaping gender politics in Australia. According to interview results, honour consciousness is "something deep, operating at the level of consciousness, setting up values systems of "right and wrong." Honour as a "value" continues even if the nuclear and extended family lives overseas.

As discussed in chapters 2 and 4, Brazilians and Pakistanis who mingle only within the community "change" less, and gender power relations "change less" in Australia. But even for participants who do not spend time with their communities, and who live for years in Australia, honour consciousness continues to comprise an inherent part of who they are, "a moral compass" shaping notions of "right and wrong."

In Brazilian and Pakistani women's lived experiences of honour consciousness, they internalise "regimes of truth," which operate at the level of human consciousness. Honour consciousness is manifested through traditional views of the family and traditional notions of womanhood, reproducing "regimes of truth" institutionalising systems of power. This provides a continuum for male privilege and hegemony in the Australian diaspora. The gendered power structures affecting Brazilian and Pakistani women's lives are consistent with Foucault's power-knowledge episteme.

Structural gender norms continue to impact the lives of Brazilian and Pakistani women living in Australia, predominantly through social reproduction. According to interview results, women continue to be seen as the primary caregivers of children even if they hold out-of-home paid employment, and home duties continues to be seen as "their role." Men can "help," which they do occasionally because there are no maids or live in nannies in Australia. However, Brazilian and Pakistani men's "help" is not seen as a shared responsibility. Men continue to hold better employment than women (women tend to quit their jobs or work part-time after having children) and are predominantly seen as the households "breadwinners." These power systems are consistent with Foucault's "regimes of truth" and the institutional reproduction of power; they are institutionalised through family life, and are very difficult to break away from.

The lived experiences of women taking part in this survey are predominantly "moderate"; however, the honour code continues to enforce gendered lines of male hegemony, consolidating gender politics in Australia.

As explained by Brazilian and Pakistani women during interviews, honour consciousness and the "values" and "principles" learned from the parents continue in the diaspora, changing "more or less" depending on each person. In Australia, migrant women become "lighter," "more open" and have freedom to be "who they want to be." Nonetheless, gender power relations consolidated through honour consciousness continue mostly unchallenged in Australia. In the lived experiences of migrant women holding "moderate" notions of honour consciousness, traditional notions of womanhood continue to be reproduced, impacting social reproduction in the homes. This is consistent with Foucault's "regime of truth," and the inherent challenges to avoid the reproduction of power systems.

Brazilian and Pakistani lived experiences of gender are also consistent with Foucault's power-knowledge episteme, since honour consciousness is manifested through the continuum of gender power relations, consolidating male hegemony in Australia. Women holding "moderate" views of honour consciousness have a voice, have had access to education, they hold paid employment and are free to engage politically. Still, social reproduction continues in their homes.

In Foucault's perspective, these are women's "power resistance" to structural power systems transmitted to the Australian diaspora. Nonetheless, Foucault's "strategies of power" allows them to have agency, to access education, employment and political agency, without challenging the honour code (an essential part of their values system). Women holding "moderate" notions of honour are overburdened with childminding and domestic chores, even if they work full-time. Not fully challenging honour consciousness in Australia reproduces gender power relations, giving continuity to male hegemony in their households to the detriment of women's careers and employment opportunities.

Interview results show how "extreme" notions of honour consciousness also translate to Australia. According to women's interviews and field notes there are several reports of women's oppression, and violence incidence within both communities in Australia. As explained in chapters 2 and 4, some people "change more" than others, particularly if they mingle with other communities and with Australians.

The transmition of "extreme" notions of honour consciousness to Australia is consistent with Foucault's episteme of "regimes of truth." In Foucault's perspective, the greatest challenge of our generation is to deconstruct "regimes of truth," since they set out the "political, economic, institutional regime of production of truth" (Foucault, 1980, p.138). Although women are exposed to other ways of living and to Australian multiculturalism, some "don't change," and some members of these communities provide a continuum to "extreme" notions of honour in Australia.

Brazilian and Pakistani migrant women's lived experiences of honour consciousness is consistent with Foucault's power-knowledge episteme. In these communities, men continue being "the powerful" who "classify and control people and things." Although honour consciousness and lived experiences of gender shifts, adapts and adjusts to the Australian experience (men "help" in Australia), women continue to be disadvantaged.

Conclusion

This book as a whole is a substantial and original contribution to the existing knowledge of the subject with which it is concerned. I have analysed Hegel's and Foucault's episteme through a different angle, to see if they provide an explanation to migrant women's lived experiences of honour consciousness, and how these are manifested through gender power relations (gender politics). Through this perspective, this book has proposed a different approach to migration studies, moving from the institutional to the individual level of human consciousness. Next, I drew upon primary data from 30 qualitative interviews with migrant Brazilian Christian and migrant Pakistani Muslim women in Australia. The book discussed the interplay between honour consciousness and religion, and how these are externalised through gender power relations in both Brazil and in Pakistan, and how these are transmitted to Australia. In the last part of the book I compared these women's lived experiences of honour consciousness, and how its gendered dimensions are manifested amongst them, shaping gender politics. The book breaks down essentialising perspectives on women in the Global South, Global South "feminisms" as well as essentialising perspectives of honour, religion, and gender.

The book explored how Brazilian and Pakistani migrant women's lived experiences of honour operate at the consciousness level, which I have framed as "honour consciousness." By listening to women's lived experiences of honour, and understanding how it shapes their values system, I shift from previous paradigms focusing predominantly of how honour is manifested in women's lives. The book highlighted how Brazilian and Pakistani migrant notions of honour consciousness, and its interplay with religion, are constructed by parental values and familial upbringing, creating "different notions" of honour. I explained how these are manifested through gender power relations, demonstrated through "extreme" and "moderate" notions of honour consciousness and religion. In "extreme" notions, women resist "less" to gendered power, whereas in "moderate" notions women resist "more" to gendered power. "Extreme" and "moderate" notions are externalised on a spectrum, oscillating between 1) "Extreme" notions of honour consciousness, as manifested via female suppression, violence towards women and honour killings, and 2) "Moderate" notions, manifested via traditional notions of womanhood within the family, and reconciled with women's agency, political activism, and the fight against violence towards women. The book explained the hybridised and intersectional nature of women's lived experiences of honour and religion, and how "where you come from," "the way you were raised," "the views of your family," as well as

© FLAVIA BELLIENI ZIMMERMANN, 2025 | DOI:10.1163/9789004711242_009

the level of education, race (in the Brazilian case study), class (socio-economic background), caste (in the Pakistani case study), the region where you come from (small cities or rural areas, and also specific regions of the country), have all shaped lived experiences of honour and religion, and gender politics, in both Brazil and Pakistan. I have then examined how these views have been transmitted to their experiences in Australia.

When comparing Brazilian Christian and Pakistani Muslim women's lived experiences of honour, the book outlined the interplay between honour consciousness and religion. Parental upbringing, the views of the nuclear and extended family, the region where women were raised, and socio-economic factors are all important variables contributing to the shaping of "different" notions of honour. Their religious views (influenced by familial and societal factors) are an essential variable shaping women's lived experiences of honour and gender. The book goes on to point out that differing interpretations of Christianity and Islam can influence "moderate" or "extreme" lived experiences of honour, and how these impact gender politics. The book brings forth primary data showing that Brazilian women possess "honour consciousness," and how this interacts with traditional values of the family (within Catholicism), referred to as "Brazil's cultural Christianity." In Brazil, due to past whitening colonial practices, the values of Catholic Christianity and traditional notions of womanhood as taught by the Church have been implicitly incorporated in Brazilian cultural practices, and into Brazilian notions of womanhood. Brazilian women, even if they are not Christian, possess honour consciousness, and this is conflated with those traditional notions of the traditional family (and womanhood) taught by the Catholic Church. Conversely, when listening to Pakistani women's lived experiences of honour consciousness, they explicitly conflate honour consciousness with religious consciousness (Islam), with the moral values taught by their parents, and with what their upbringing has taught them.

Since Brazilian women hold "honour consciousness," I have pointed out, through epistemic disobedience lenses, how femicides against Brazilian women should be reframed as forms of honour killings, and honour-based violence. Thus, it brings a significant contribution to scholarship dealing with Brazilian studies, Brazilian women and society, and violence towards Latin American women.

The book also discusses how Brazilian and Pakistani lived experiences of honour consciousness and religion is transmitted to Australia, although shifting, changing, and adapting to Australian culture and multiculturalism. Nonetheless, although Brazilian and Pakistani lived experiences of honour consciousness and religion "become lighter," "more relaxed," and there is "more freedom" in Australia, they continue shaping gender power relations, consolidating male hegemony. Women taking part in the interviews hold predominantly "moderate" notions of honour consciousness. However, they are still impacted by traditional notions of womanhood, where women's primary role is to look after children, their husbands and their homes. Consequently, these beliefs continue to influence their lives, although adapting and changing through their encounters with Australian culture.

For instance, women usually work part-time (or quit their jobs) after having children in order to look after their families and their homes. Women's primary commitment is still seen as childminding, looking after their husbands, their families, and elders, even when they hold full-time employment. Men, on the contrary, need only to "have a job" or be "good providers." However, the Australian experience, leads men to be more involved in their children's upbringing, and, occasionally, they "help out" around the house. Their domestic agency is manifested when they make their wives "cups of tea," since there are no live in maids and nannies in Australia. The book also explains that "extreme" notions of honour consciousness and religion are transmitted to Australia, with reports of female inter-partner oppression, economic abuse, and domestic violence against women within both communities. This shows how honour consciousness and religion provide a continuum to gender power relations within the Brazilian and Pakistani communities in Australia, although it adapts and changes in response to Australian culture. Furthermore, some members of the community "change more" than others.

For this book, I conducted interviews with 15 migrant Brazilian Christian women in Sydney, New South Wales, and 15 migrant Pakistani Muslim women in Perth, Western Australia. There are limitations on the number of samples, and additional interviews could have provided more detail as well as more examples of how "moderate" and "extreme" lived experiences of honour are manifested in honour-based cultures. Another limitation of this study is that I have not interviewed men. Listening to men's perspectives on honour consciousness and religion and its gendered dimensions in Australia might provide a holistic view of the honour code and religion, and its impact on gender. Not all Brazilian women were practicing Christians or regarded themselves as Christian.[1] Nonetheless, the book cover a perspective which has been neglected by scholars in the field. It innovates by bringing to the fore of the global academic debate of how honour consciousness and Brazil's "cultural Christianity" continues to shape their lived experiences of gender in Australia.

---

1   Brazilian participants 4 and 7.

Another important point addressed in this book is how literature in the field of migration studies has not addressed migrant experiences in an integrated way and at the level of human consciousness. The book explains the hybridised experiences of migrant women and how these shape their views towards gender; in addition, it explores migrant women's lived experiences of honour consciousness and how they are manifested through gender power relations in Australia. I draw from Hegel's human consciousness episteme and Foucault's power-knowledge episteme to explain migrant women's lived experiences of honour consciousness and gender. Gender power relations can be demonstrated through Brazilian and Pakistani women's "moderate" or "extreme" notions of honour. In moderate notions of honour consciousness women resist "more" to gendered power, whereas in "extreme" notions of honour consciousness women resist "less" to gendered power.

The book brings significant contribution to comparative international studies, and works in the field, since it shifts the discussion dealing with honour, culture, and gender from the realm of its manifestations to the realm of its root causes, as well as explaining how lived experiences of honour are both hybridised and nuanced. I showed how lived experiences of honour consciousness can be conflated with religion (explicitly with Islam, or implicitly with Brazil's "cultural Christianity"), and how religion consolidates "moderate" or "extreme" notions of honour consciousness – a point which has not been addressed by previous literature. By comparing Brazilian Christian and Pakistani Muslim lived experiences in Australia, this book breaks down essentialising perspectives on honour cultures and honour-based violence as a Muslim or South Asian phenomenon.

The book illuminates how migrant Brazilian and Pakistani women hold "honour consciousness" as taught by their families overseas, and how it is trasmitted to their lived experiences of gender in Australia. Another key contribution that I bring to scholarship is to map out the ways in which lived experiences of honour consciousness are not homogenous and how they can be distinguished between "moderate" and "extreme." Literature on honour and culture focuses predominantly on honour and violence, or honour-based violence (HBV), a manifestation of "extreme" notions of honour consciousness. I contribute to the literature by exploring the nuances of honour consciousness,' and how "moderate" notions are manifested in Brazil, Pakistan, and I then explore how ("extreme" and "moderate") notions of honour continue to influence gender politics in Australia.

This book substantially contributes to scholarship in the field, by generating primary data on migrant Brazilian and Pakistani lived experiences in the Australian diaspora. In addition, the book explored their experiences of honour and religion, and its gendered layers, issues not discussed previously by the literature. Brazilian and Pakistani lived experiences are underrepresented in scholarship, as are the ways in which their views shift, change, and adapt when exposed to Australian culture. I provide an original contribution to the literature by writing about their experiences of honour, how their lives are affected by gender power reproduction, and how this is manifested in Australia.

The idea that honour develops at women's consciousness level is a breakthrough for those studies dealing not only with honour, but with gender studies more broadly, impacting new gender mainstreaming (and "side streaming") approaches. Brazilian women's honour consciousness has not been explored by the literature, and these interview results bring a new perspective to the fight against violence towards women, and more broadly against femicides in Brazil and Latin America. The book highlights the lack of understanding in Global North scholarship, as well as in the framing of international agendas, when concerned with Global South "feminisms." In this book I articulate Brazilian and Pakistani "feminisms," and new feminist discourses in the Global North's diaspora with Global South scholarship, bridging a significant void in the literature.

Moreover, by exploring in depth the lived experiences of honour of Brazilian and Pakistani women, the book outlined the nuances and cleavages, between honour consciousness, religion and how these are manifested. The book shows how the manifestation of honour consciousness is conflated with religion, as well as how cultural norms influence readings of religion and, additionally, how religion can influence social norms. An example of religion influencing cultural norms is that of Brazil's "cultural Christianity." In Pakistan, cultural notions of honour may lead to Islamic interpretation supporting the suppression of women. This thesis takes an innovative approach when considering women's lived experiences of honour, since scholarship dealing with honour culture has not considered its interplay with religion, addressing it solely as a "cultural norm."

In this work I explain the nuances between Brazilian and Pakistani women's empowerment, as well as the challenges for Brazilian and Pakistani women to break free from oppression, structural gendered relations, and male hegemony.

The book proposes a fresh perspective on the use of Foucault's episteme in the field of gender studies, where I have applied his power-knowledge episteme to migrant Brazilian and Pakistani lived experiences in Australia. With this new perspective on the use of Foucault within gender studies the question is: Can women from other cultures also have some form of "(gender) consciousness" which is taught by their families (religion, and societal cultural "values") and which reproduces gender power relations worldwide?

Consequently, Hegel's epistemological framework of human consciousness, conflated with Foucault's power-knowledge episteme, might provide a suitable epistemological framework to explain lived experiences of women from other cultures, including in the Western world. This fresh perspective of the use of Foucault's power-knowledge episteme within feminist studies can encourage women's movements (with what I call "strategies of resistance") to continue their progress, which in my view, have stagnated in many ways due to "strategies of power."

I also point out how the application of a new epistemological perspective to Foucault within gender studies paves the way for what I call "strategies of resistance." This new epistemological approach can potentially break down social reproduction in the home, and male structural privileges, as well as de-construct old paradigms in the fight against violence against women in the Global South, as well as in the Global North. This can be seen as different perspective to women's movements and feminism, and another strategic approach in the advancement of women's rights globally.

Racial miscegenation, indigenous cultures acculturation, and the enslavement of Africans are key to explaining Brazilians' lived experiences of honour consciousness as hybridised and multifaceted. In this light, and through a Latin American decolonial epistemological approach, the book discusses that to understand honour consciousness's hegemonic power in Brazilian society, one ought to consider Quijano's (2000) "coloniality of power" and the "coloniality of being," as well as Lugones (2008) viewpoint on the impact of Latin American colonialism in class, race, and gender relations. I draw from Lélia Gonzalez's (1988) perspective of "coloniality of power" to explain lived experiences of honour consciousness of Afro-descendant women in Brazil.

In the light of the data, the book recommends that the United Nations classification of honour-based crimes and honour-based violence includes Brazilian and Latin American communities. Brazil and other Latin American countries should re-consider the framing of femicides as a "crime of honour" and honour-based violence, since they are a type of "honour killings."

In this book I addressed honour at the level of human consciousness, opening the way to new emerging policy on gender mainstreaming, as it brings greater understanding of women's issues within migrant communities to the policy level, on behalf of women in the Global North and Global South alike. By framing honour consciousness as a layered and nuanced lived experience, influencing gender politics, this approach assists in the design of new strategic plans for women's empowerment in honour-based societies, as well as in the Global North and Global South. These findings also provide new evidence for a more effective framing with regard to violence prevention plans which are designed to meet the needs of women from honour-based cultures living in both the Global North and the Global South. I propose new policies which would fully subsidise childcare, both in Australia and in other countries, as a powerful mechanism with which to consolidate women's rights in honour-based societies, within migrant communities, as well as for women in Australia and worldwide.

The book pointed to the need to understand in greater depth women's lived experiences at the level of human consciousness, and how these impact gender power reproduction globally. Following on from the acknowledgement that Brazilian women hold "honour consciousness" there is a need for new emerging scholarship which can further investigate lived experiences of honour in Brazil, in other Latin American countries, and in other honour-based Mediterranean countries such as Portugal and Italy. New research, and data, is needed to clarify the impact of honour consciousness more broadly in these societies, and to understand in greater depth "extreme notions," and whether "moderate notions" can shift into "extreme notions," to expedite the development of violence prevention plans, thus improving the lives of women and men.

I acknowledge that there are limitations to this work. There are angles that have not been explored in this project due to time and budget constraints. But given the signicant research findings, it would be interesting to return to the field and interview a larger sample group, and conduct interviews with Brazilian and Pakistani men. Another limitation of this book is to not explore in depth Australian migration politics and anti-migrant sentiment, Australian gender politics, and Australian views towards migrants. Research findings should be expanded and new research built upon the book's data to investigate in-depth these issues.

Indeed, future research should apply the theoretical framework developed in this book to other family and honour-based societies globally, in Latin America, Middle East and South Asia, and in a migrant setting. There is a need for further research expanding this new epistemological proposition to the use of Hegel and Foucualt in gender studies. Further studies should explore if the framework presented in this book brings an explanation to the lived experiences of migrant women from other communities, and migrant women living in other countries apart from Australia. Future studies should explore in-depth the intersections between gender politics with these migrant communities and gender politics in the host country, particularly in the light of the global rise of far-right populism and anti-migrant sentiment. Current challenges faced by the feminist movement and on gender reform should consider data findings from this book and the epistemological perspectives used in this study for future gender policy reform. Studies building upon this book's epistemological proposition should investigate if this framework gives an explanation to gender norms and societal views in other societies globally. The book's new episteme to gender studies is a provocation against deeply seated gender norms, and how gendered structures should be challenged globally at the level of human consciousness.

Appendix

Qualitative Interviews Themes – Brazilian Interviewees

Themes	Participants
Honour consciousness as "a value" is internalised in their ways of thinking, ("the way I was raised" or "the way my mother raised me") and shapes their lives, based on their parent's values ("what my family taught me" or "what my parents passed unto me").	1, 2, 4, 5, 6, 8, 9 and 11.
The "othering," and the differences between their lived experiences "other" notions of honour.	1, 2, 4, 5, 6, 8, 10, 14 and 15
associated "extreme" notions of honour with a lack of formal education.	13 and 15
Discussed Brazil's culture and traditional views of The Catholic church.	1, 2, 4, 5, 6, 10, 11, 12, 14 and 15
Brazilian women explained that to uphold the law and be honest by not using Brazil's *jeitinho or the Brazilian way,* telling the truth, fulfilling your promises and keeping your word, respecting your parents, as well as working hard, putting the best effort in what you do, and striving for excellence, are all behaviours which bring honour to an individual.	1, 2, 6, 7, 9, 10, 12, 13 and 15.
To be hard-working, to study and to have a professional career is seen as something bringing honour, making you and your family proud.	1, 2, 3, 4, 6, 7, 13, 12, 14.
If a woman is to be honoured, she needs to behave and dress appropriately.	1, 2, 4, 5, 7, 8, 9, 11, 12, 14.
In Australia, Brazilian women continue to see housework as their responsibility	1, 3, 5, 6, 11, 12, 14, 15.
discussed how lived experiences of honour consciousness and traditional views of the family (within religion) are "more relaxed" and they "feel lighter" in Australia.	1, 2, 4, 6, 9, 11, 12, 14, 15
Participants have lived with their partners in Australia, without being married – something they regard as "unthinkable" back home.	1, 12 and 14.
co-habited with their partners before marriage, but felt strong pressure from their families for them to get married.	1, 12, 14 and 15
Brazilian women become less accepting of abusive relationships.	1 and 14.

© FLAVIA BELLIENI ZIMMERMANN, 2025 | DOI:10.1163/9789004711242_010

Qualitative Interviews Themes – Pakistani Interviewees

Themes	Participants
Honour consciousness and religious consciousness as "a value" has been internalised in their ways of thinking through their family's upbringing ("the way I was raised") and has shaped their lives, based on their parent's values ("what I learned from my parents").	1, 14, 15, 3 and 8.
Pakistani women argued that honour is a "value," and a key variable shaping different "notions of honour."	1, 10, 12, 14, 3, 6, 8, 9.
The "othering," and differences between their lived experiences of honour from "extreme" notions of honour.	1, 2, 4, 5, 6, 8,10, 14 and 15.
Discussed Pakistan's "extreme" views of honour are different from their own views, and how "other" notions of honour in Pakistan condone women's suppression, as well as acts of honour-based violence such as honour killings.	2, 4, 5, 6 and 8.
Discussed social ostracism faced by Pakistani Muslim women who divorced their husbands.	1, 2 and 5.
Discussed that both women and men should aim to have a "good name" and uphold the family name.	2, 9, 10, 12, 15.

Bibliography

Afzal, S., Raza, H. & Manzoor, A. (2021). Socio-Cultural Causes of Kala Kali (Honour Killing): A Case of Tehsil Jam Pur. *Global Regional Review,* VI (I), 17–22.

Agência IBGE *Notícias.* (2020, November 26). *Em 2019 expectativa de vida era 76,6 anos.* Retrieved August 21, 2022, from https://agenciadenoticias.ibge.gov.br/agencia -sala-de-imprensa/2013-agencia-de-noticias/releases/29502-em-2019-expectativa -de-vida-era-de-76-6-anos

Aghtaie, N., & Gangoli, G. (2014). Key issues: Researching gender-based violence. In N. Aghtaie & G. Gangoli (eds.), *Understanding gender-based violence: national and international contexts.* Routledge.

Ahmed, A. (2021, March 31). *Pakistan loses two spots on the Global Gender Gap Index, slides into the ranks of worst four countries.* Dawn. Retrieved August 25, 2022, from https://www.dawn.com/news/1615651.

Akpinar, A. (2003). The Honour/Shame Complex Revisited: Violence Against Women in the Migration Context. *Women's Studies International Forum, 26*(5), 425–442.

Alavi, H. (1991). Pakistani women in a changing society. In *Economy and Culture in Pakistan* (pp. 124–142). Palgrave Macmillan, London.

Alvarez, S. E. (2009). Beyond NGO-ization? Reflections from Latin America. *Development, 52*(2), 175–184.

Alvarez, S. E. (2000). Translating the global: Effects of transnational organizing on local feminist discourses and practices in Latin America. *Meridians, 1*(1), 29–67.

Alvarez, S. E. (1990). *Engendering democracy in Brazil: Women's movements in transition politics.* Princeton University Press.

Alvez, C. G. (2016). *Pedro Pinchas Geiger: Considerações Sobre a Divisão Geoeconomica no Brasil.* Grupo Geobrasil UERJ. Retrieved August 21, 2022, from http://www .grupogeobrasil.uerj.br/usuario/pedro_geiger/pedro_geiger_geobiografia_8 .pdf.

Ali, R., Jumani, N. B., & Ejaz, S. (2015). Higher Education of Women in Pakistan: Promises, Achievements and Barriers. *Pakistan Journal of Women's Studies: Alam-e-Niswan, 22*(2).

Alvi, M. H. (2018). *Difference in the Population Size between Rural and Urban Areas of Pakistan.* Munich Personal RePEC. Retrieved August 25, 2022, from https://mpra .ub.uni-muenchen.de/90054/1/MPRA_paper_90054.pdf

Amhad, Sadaf (2009). *Transforming Faith: The Story of Al-Huda and Islamic Revivalism among Urban Pakistan Women.* Oxford University Press.

Andishan, Hamid (2019). Honour and Dignity? An Oversimplification in Islamic Human Rights. *Human Rights Review, 20*, 461–475.

Assembly, U. G. (1993). Declaration on the Elimination of Violence against Women. UN General Assembly. Retrieved August 24, 2022, from https://www.un.org/en

/genocideprevention/documents/atrocity-crimes/Doc.21_declaration%20elimin
ation%20vaw.pdf

Assis, G. D. O. (2014, September). Gender and migration from invisibility to agency:
The routes of Brazilian women from transnational towns to the United States. In
Women's Studies International Forum (Vol. 46, pp. 33–44). Pergamon.

Assis, G. D. O. (1999). *Estar aqui ... , estar lá...: uma cartografia da emigração valadarense
para os EUA*. Cenas do Brasil migrante. São Paulo: Boitempo, 125–166.

Aujla, W., & Gill, A. K. (2014). Conceptualizing 'Honour' Killings in Canada: An Extreme
form of Domestic Violence? *International Journal of Criminal Justice Sciences, 9* (1),
153–166.

Aurat Foundation (2021). Aurat March 2021. Aurat Publication and Information Centre
Foundation. Retrieved September 02, 2022, from https://www.af.org.pk.

Australian Bureau of Statistics, Australian Census. (2016). Migration Australia, 2016–
2017. Retrieved August 26, 2022, from https://www.abs.gov.au/ausstats/abs@.nsf/
lookup/3412.0Media%20Release12016–17.

Australian Bureau of Statistics, Australian Census. (2011). Migration Australia, 2011–
2012. Retrieved August 26, 2022, from https://www.abs.gov.au/ausstats/abs@.nsf
/lookup/3412.0chapter12011–12%20and%202012-13.

Australian Bureau of Statistics, Australian Census. (2006). Migration Australia, 2006–
2007. Retrieved August 26, 2022, from https://www.abs.gov.au/AUSSTATS/abs@.nsf
/Lookup/3412.0Main+Features12006–07?OpenDocument=.

Australian Bureau of Statistics, Australian Census. (2010). Religion. Retrieved August
26, 2022, from https://www.abs.gov.au/AUSSTATS/abs@.nsf/mediareleasesby
ReleaseDate/7E65A144540551D7CA258148000E2B85.

Bagby, L. M. J. (2009). *Thomas Hobbes: Turning point for honor*. Lexington Books.

Baldassar, L. (1999). Marias and marriage: ethnicity, gender and sexuality among
Italo-Australian youth in Perth1. *Journal of Sociology, 35*(1), 1–22.

Baldwin, J. & DeSouza, E. (2001). Modelo de Maria and machismo: The social construction of gender in Brazil. *Revista Interamericana de Psicologia/Interamerican Journal
of Psychology, 35*(1), 9–29.

Baker, N. V., Gregware, P. R., & Cassidy, M. A. (1999). Family killing fields: Honor ratio-
nales in the murder of women. *Violence against women, 5*(2), 164–184.

Basilio, P. (2018, September 13). Grupo Mulheres com Bolsonaro Reúne mais the 440
mil Integrantes em Dois Dias. Época Negócios. Retrieved August 25, 2022, from
https://epocanegocios.globo.com/Brasil/noticia/2018/09/grupo-mulheres-com-
bolsonaro-reune-mais-de-440-mil-integrantes-em-dois-dias.html.

Bauböck, R. (2003). Towards a political theory of migrant transnationalism. *International migration review, 37*(3), 700–723. https://doi.org/10.1111/j.1747-7379.2003.
tb00155.x.

Baxi, P., Rai, S. M., & Ali, S. S. (2006). Legacies of Common Law: 'crimes of honour' in India and Pakistan. *Third World Quarterly, 27*(7), 1239–1253.

Brazilian Census (2010). Instituto Brasileiro de Geografia e E*statística* – IBGE. Retrieved August 26, 2022, from https://censo2010.ibge.gov.br

Begum, R. (2019). *A Resistance from Within: An Experience of Pakistani Migrant Women.* CUNY Academic Works.

Belsito Jr., W. J. (2016). *Lived Experience of Brazilian Immigrants in Connecticut and Crimmigration* [unpublished doctoral dissertation]. University of Connecticut. Bellieni Zimmermann, F. (2021, February 24). *How President Bolsonaro used* COVID-*19 to Erode Brazil's democracy.* Open Democracy. Retrieved August 24, 2022, from https://www.opendemocracy.net/en/democraciaabierta/project-authoritarian-bolsonaro-pandemic-erosion-democracy-brazil-en/

Bellieni Zimmermann, F. B. (2018, October 6). *Presidential Elections: Will Brazil be Condemned toRepeat its Authoritarian Past?* Brazzil Magazine. Retrieved September 1, 2022, from https://www.brazzil.com/presidential-elections-will-brazil-be-condemned -to-repeat-its-authoritarian-past/

Bickman, L., & Rog, D. J. (eds.). (2008). *The* SAGE *handbook of applied social research methods.* Sage publications.

Bolognani, M., & Erdal, M. B. (2017). Return imaginaries and political climate: Comparing thinking about return mobilities among Pakistani origin migrants and descendants in Norway and the UK. *Journal of International Migration and Integration, 18*(1), 353–367.

Bolton, T. (2003). Land of the fair go: an exploration of Australian identity. *AQ-Australian Quarterly, 75*(2), 16–22.

Bond, J. (2014). Honour as familial value. In *'Honour' Killing and Violence* (pp. 89–107). Palgrave Macmillan, London.

Bordo, S. (2002). Feminism, Foucault and the politics of the body. In *Up Against Foucault* (pp.189–212). Routledge.

Bourdieu, P. (1965). The sentiment of honour in Kabyle society. In J.G. Peristiany (ed.) *Honour and Shame: the values of Mediterranean society.* London: Weidenfeld and Nicolson.

Bourdieu, P. (2011). The forms of capital. In T.K. Imre Szeman (ed.), *Cultural theory: An anthology.* Oxford/ UK: Wiley.

Brace, L. (2002). The tragedy of the freelance hustler: Hegel, gender and civil society. *Contemporary Political Theory, 1*(3), 329–347.

Braude, A. (1997). Three. Women's History Is American Religious History. In *Retelling US religious history* (pp. 87–107). University of California Press.

Brettell, C. B., & Hollifield, J. F. (2014). Introduction: Migration theory: Talking across disciplines. In *Migration theory* (pp. 1–36). Routledge.

Brink, J., & Mencher, J. (2014). *Mixed blessings: Gender and religious fundamentalism cross culturally*. Routledge.

Browne, B. C., & McBride, R. S. (2015). Politically sensitive encounters: Ethnography, access, and the benefits of "hanging out." *Qualitative Sociology Review, 11*(1), 34–48.

Brownmiller, S. (1993). *Against our will: Men, women, and rape*. Ballantine Books.

Bryman, A. (2016). *Social research methods*. Oxford university press.

Butler, J. (2004). *Undoing gender*. Routledge.

Butler, J. (2012). *Subjects of desire: Hegelian reflections in twentieth-century France*. Columbia University Press.

Burazeri, G., Roshi, E., Jewkes, R., Jordan, S., Bjegovic, V., & Laaser, U. (2005). Factors associated with spousal physical violence in Albania: cross sectional study. *Ulrich British Medical Journal Publishing Group, 331*(7510), 197–201.

Burke, K. C. (2012). Women's agency in gender-traditional religions: A review of four approaches. *Sociology Compass, 6*(2), 122–133.

Burman, E., Smailes, S. L., & Chantler, K. (2004). 'Culture'as a barrier to service provision and delivery: domestic violence services for minoritized women. *Critical social policy, 24*(3), 332–357.

Carrington, K., Hogg, R., McIntosh, A., & Scott, J. (2012). Crime talk, FIFO workers and cultural conflict on the mining boom frontier. *Australian Humanities Review, 53*, 1–16.

Casamento Gay *não é lei mas é direito garantido pela justiça* (2018, November 5). Folha UOL.Retrieved August 21, 2022, from https://www1.folha.uol.com.br/cotidiano/2018/11/casamento-gay-nao-e-lei-mas-e-direito-garantido-pela-justica-entenda.shtml

Casimir, M. J., & Jung, S. (2009). "Honor and Dishonor": Connotations of a Socio-symbolic Category in Cross-Cultural Perspective. In *Emotions as bio-cultural processes* (pp. 229–280). Springer, New York, NY.

Catalano, S. M. (2006). *Intimate partner violence in the United States*. Washington, DC: US Department of Justice, Office of Justice programs, Bureau of Justice Statistics. Catecismo da Igreja Católica. Retrieved August 25, 2022, from https://www.vatican.va/archive/cathechism_po/index_new/prima-pagina-cic_po.html.

Caufield, S. (2000). *In Defense of Honour: Sexual Morality, Modernity, and Nation in Early Twentieth Century Brazil*. USA: Duke University Press.

Census of Population and Housing (2016). *Reflecting Australia – Stories from the Census*. Religion in Australia. Australian Bureau of Statistics. Retrieved August 25, from https://www.abs.gov.au/ausstats/abs@.nsf/Lookup/by%20Subject/2071.0~2016~Main%20Features~Religion%20Data%20Summary~70.

Chacham, A. S., Simão, A. B., & Caetano, A. J. (2016). Gender-based violence and sexual and reproductive health among low-income youth in three Brazilian cities. *Reproductive health matters*, *24*(47), 141–152.

Chalmers, A. F. (2013). *What is this thing called science?*. Hackett Publishing.

Charsley, K. (2005). Unhappy husbands: Masculinity and migration in transnational Pakistani marriages. *Journal of the Royal Anthropological Institute, 11* (1), 85–105.

Charsley, K. (2013). *Transnational Pakistani connections: marrying "back home."* Routledge.

Christianson, M., Teiler, A., & Eriksson, C. (2021). "A woman's honor tumbles down on all of us in the family, but a man's honor is only his": young women's experiences of patriarchal chastity norms. *International journal of qualitative studies on health and well-being*, *16*(1), 1862480.

Chughtai, A. (2016, July 17). Pakistan: Anger after honour killing of Qandeel Baloch. Aljazeera News. Retrieved September 02, 2022, from https://www.aljazeera.com /news/2016/7/17/pakistan-anger-after-honour-killing-of-qandeel-baloch

Clifford, J. (1999). *Travel and Transition in the Late Twentieth Century*. London: Harvard.

Clough, P. T. (1994). The hybrid criticism of patriarchy: Rereading Kate Millett's sexual politics. *Sociological quarterly*, *35*(3), 473–486.

Código Civil Brasileiro (Brazilian Civil Code) (1916). Lei 3.071 (1916, January 1). Retrieved August 21, 2022, from https://presrepublica.jusbrasil.com.br/legislacao/103251 /codigo-civil-de-1916-lei-3071–16.

Cogell, W. G. (2001). Cultural Christianity: The Puritan Heritage. *International Congregational Journal*, (2).

Cohen, S. P. (2004). *The idea of Pakistan*. Brookings Institution Press.

Cohen, R. (1997). Global Diasporas: An Introduction. London: UCLP.

Collins, P. H. (2015). Intersectionality's definitional dilemmas. *Annual review of sociology*, *41*(1), 1–20.

Collins, P. H. (2015). No guarantees: Symposium on Black American Feminist Thought. *Journal of Ethnic and Racial Studies*.

Collins, P. H. (2012). Social Inequality, Power, and Politics: Intersectionality and American Pragmatism Dialogue. *Journal of Speculative Philosophy, 26* (2).

Compendium on gender statistics of Pakistan (2019). Retrieved August 25, 2022, from https://www.pbs.gov.pk/sites/default/files//COMPENDIUM%20GENDER%20 2019%2018-06-2019%20%20printing.pdf.

Connell, R. (2005). *Masculinities*. University of California Press.

Constituição Federal (1988). Senado Legal Brasil. Retrieved August 25, 2022, from https://www2.senado.leg.br/bdsf/bitstream/handle/id/518231/CF88_Livro_EC91 _2016.pdf.

Coombe, R. J. (1990). Barren ground: re-conceiving honour and shame in the field of Mediterranean ethnography. *Anthropologica*, 221–238.

Cooney, M. (2019). *Execution by family: A theory of honor violence*. Routledge.

Cooney, M. (2014). Family Honour and Social Time. *The Sociological Review, 62* (2), 87–106.

Constituição Brasileira (Brazilian Constitution) (1891). Senado Federal, Secretaria Especial de Editoração e Publicações, Subsecretaria de Edições Técnicas. Retrieved August 21, 2022, from http://www2.senado.leg.br/bdsf/bitstream/handle/id/137570 /Constituicoes_Brasileiras _v2_1891.pdf.

Corbetta, P. (2003). *Social research: Theory, methods and techniques*. Sage.

Costa, A. A. A. (2005). O movimento feminista no Brasil: dinâmicas de uma inter-venção política. *Revista Gênero, 5*(2).

Costa, C. D. L., & Alvarez, S. E. (2009). Translocalidades: por uma política feminista da tradução. *Revista Estudos Feministas, 17*, 739–742.

Country meters. Pakistan population (2021). Retrieved August 25, 2022, from https:// countrymeters.info/en/Pakistan.

Coutinho, T. (2021). *Cai de boca no meu b# c3t@ o: O funk como potência do empodera-mento feminino*. Claraboia Editora.

Crenshaw, K. (1989). Race, Reform, and Retrenchment: Transformation and Legitima-tion in

Antidiscrimination Law. *Harvard Law Review, 101* (7).

Crown Prosecution Service (CPS) (2013). Violence Against Women and Girls: Crime Report. London: CPS. Retrieved September 04, 2022, from https://assets.publishing .service.gov.uk/government/uploads/system/uploads/attachment_data/file /339509/41097_HC_6_CPS_Print_Ready.pdf

Cummins, M. W. (2014). Reproductive Surveillance: The Making of Pregnant Docile Bodies. *Kaleidoscope: A Graduate Journal of Qualitative Communication Research, 13.*

Dabhoiwala, F. (1996). The Construction of Honour, Reputation and Status in Late Sev-enteenth – and Early Eighteenth Century England. *Transactions of the Royal Histor-ical Society, 6*, 201–213.

Da Cunha, E. (1984). *Os Sertões*. Biblioteca do Estudante. Retrieved August 21, 2022, from http://www.bibvirt.futuro.usp.br.

Data Folha (2016, December 28). 44% dos Evangélicos são ex-Catolicos. Retrieved August 25, 2022, from https://datafolha.folha.uol.com.br/opiniaopublica/2016 /12/1845231-44-dos-evangelicos-sao-ex-catolicos.shtml.

Datta, K., McIlwaine, C., Herbert, J., Evans, Y., May, J., & Wills, J. (2009). Men on the move: narratives of migration and work among low-paid migrant men in London. *Social & Cultural Geography, 10*(8), 853–873.

Dawn (2016, January 15). PM Nawaz vows to eradicate honour killings after the Oscars nod. Retrieved September 02, 2022, from https://www.dawn.com/news/1233168.

Da Silva *Gonçalves*, W. (2019). O ensino religioso nas escolas *públicas*: debate sobrea a *inclusão* das minorias e a representatividade de suas indentidades.

Retrieved September 02, 2022, from https://educacaopublica.cecierj.edu.br/artigos/19/28/o-ensino-religioso-nas-escolas-publicas-debate-sobre-a-inclusao-das-minorias-e-a-representatividade-de-suas-identidades.

DeBiaggi, S. D. D. (2002). *Changing gender roles: Brazilian immigrant families in the US.* LFB Scholarly Publishing LLC.

Deleuze, G. & Guattari, F. (1987). *A thousand plateaus: Capitalism and schizophrenia.* Minneapolis, MN: The University of Minnesota Press.

Demerath III, N. J. (2000). The rise of "cultural religion" in European Christianity: learning from Poland, Northern Ireland, and Sweden. *Social compass, 47*(1), 127–139.

Dengah, HJ Francois, William W. Dressler, and Ana Falcão. "The Domestication of Machismo in Brazil: Motivations, Reflexivity, and Consonance of Religious Male Gender Roles." *Behavioral Sciences* 14, no. 2 (2024): 132.

De Souza, S. D., & Oshiro, C. P. (2018). Mulheres Evangélicas e Violência Doméstica: O que o Poder *Público* e a Igreja tem a ver com isso?. *Revista Caminhos-Revista de Ciências da Religião, 16*(2), 203–219.

Deveaux, M. (1994). Feminism and empowerment: A critical reading of Foucault. *Feminist studies, 20*(2), 223–247.

Diamond, I., & Quinby, L. (1988). Foucault and feminism: Reflections on resistance. *Boston: Northeastern University.*

Dias, G., & Junior, A. M. (2018). The second Brazilian migration wave: The impact of Brazil's economic and social changes on current migration to the UK. *Século XXI, 8*(1), 112.

Dickson, P. (2014). Understanding victims of honour-based violence. *Community Practitioner, 87* (7), p.30.

Doğan, R. (2011). Is honor killing a "Muslim phenomenon"? Textual interpretations and cultural representations. *Journal of Muslim minority affairs, 31*(3), 423–440.

Doria, C. A. (1994). A tradição honrada: a honra como tema da cultura e na sociedade Ibero-americana. *Cadernos Pagu.* Campinas: Unicamp, 2, 47–111.

Dos Santos, N. A., Petrus, W., & Pugina, R. L. (2021). Sermões evangélicos e idealização do comportamento feminino. *Letras de hoje, 56*(3), 598–609.

Duarte, A. R. F. (2019). O Movimento Feminino pela Anistia na luta contra a ditadura no Brasil: entrevista com Therezinha Zerbini. *Revista Estudos Feministas, 27*(1).

Duarte, F. (2005). Living in 'the Betweens': Diaspora consciousness formation and identity among Brazilians in Australia. *Journal of intercultural studies, 26*(4), 315–335.

Dworkin, A. (1981). *Pornography: Men Possessing Women.* NY/New York: Penguin Group.

Dworkin, A. & MacKinnon, Catharine (1997). *In Harm's Way: The Pornography Civil Rights Hearings.* USA: Library of Congress Cataloging-in-Publication Data.

Eluf, L. N. (2021). *A paixão no banco dos réus.* Saraiva Educação SA.

Erdal, M. B. (2014). This is my home. *Comparative Migration Studies, 2*(3), 361–383.

Esposito, J. (1982). *Women in Muslim Family Law*. New York: Syracuse UP.

Evans, Y., Wills, J., Datta, K., Herbert, J., McIlwaine, C., May, J. & França, A. P. (2007). Brazilians in London: a report for the Strangers into Citizens Campaign. *Department of Geography, Queen Mary, University of London*.

Fanon, F. (2012). Black skin, white masks [1952]. *Contemporary Sociological Theory*, 417.

Fatima, H., Qadir, T. F., Hussain, S. A., & Menezes, R. G. (2017). Pakistan steps up to remove "honour" from honour killing. *The Lancet Global Health*, 5(2), e 145.

Faqir, F. (2001). Intrafamily femicide in defence of honour: the case of Jordan. *Third World Quarterly*, 22 (1), 65–82.

Feeley, M. M., & Simon, J. (1992). The new penology: Notes on the emerging strategy of corrections and its implications. *Criminology*, 30(4), 449–474.

Ferraro, J. Kathleen & Johnson, Michael P. (2000). Research on Domestic Violence in the 1990s: Making Distinctions. *Journal of Marriage and the Family*, 62, 948–963.

Ferro, B. (2013). The return from Otherness: Hegel's paradox of self-consciousness in the phenomenology of spirit. *Otherness: Essays and Studies*, 4(1), 1–21.

Fetterman, D. M. (2007). Ethnography. In Bickman, L., & Rog, D. J. (eds). *The SAGE handbook of applied social research methods*. Thousand Oaks, CA: SAGE Publications.

Fiddian-Qasmiyeh, E. (2014). *The ideal refugees: Gender, Islam, and the Sahrawi politics of survival*. Syracuse University Press.

Fijac, B.M. & Sonn, C. (2004). Pakistani-Muslim immigration women in Western Australia: Perceptions of identity and community. Edith Cowan University.

Firestone, S. (1970). *The Dialectic of Sex: The case for Feminist Revolution*. New York: Library Cataloguing Data.

Fisher, M. (1991). Marriage and Power: Tradition and Transition in an Urban Punjabi Community. In D. Hastings & P. Werbner (eds.). *Economy and Culture in Pakistan: Migrants and Cities in a Muslim Society*. St Martin's Press: New York.

Fórum de **Segurança Pública** (2019). *Práticas* de Enfrentamento a *Violência* Contra a Mulher. Retrieved August 25, 2022, from https://forumseguranca.org.br/?s=violencia +contra+mulher&post_type=publicacoes_posts.

Fórum de **Segurança Pública** (2021). Visivel and Invisivel: A Vitimizacao das Mulheres no Brasil. Retrieved August 21, 2022, from https://forumseguranca.org.br/wp -content/uploads/2021/06/relatorio-visivel-e-invisivel-3ed-2021-v3.pdf.

Foucault, M. (1980). *Power/Knowledge: Selected Interviews and Other Writings* (translated by Colin Gordon et al.). The Harvester Press.

Foucault, M. (1977). The Political Function of the Intellectual. *Radical Philosophy*, 7(13), pp.126–33.

Foucault, M. (1995). *Discipline and Punish: The Birth of the Prison*. Vintage books.

Foucault, M. (1976). *The History of Sexuality: The Will to Knowledge (Vol1.)*. Penguin Books.

Foucault, M. (2019). *Ethics: subjectivity and truth: essential works of Michel Foucault 1954–1984*. Penguin UK.

Foucault, M. (2019). *Power: the essential works of Michel Foucault 1954–1984*. Penguin UK.

Fox, R.L. (1987). *Pagans and Christians*. New York: Knopf.

Fraguas, L. (2014). Brazilians in Australia: A Snapshot of Brazilian Migration to Victoria. Retrieved August 26, 2022, from https://abrisa.org.au/wp/wp-content/uploads/2015/03/Brazilians_in_Australia_Book.pdf.

French, L. (2014). Gender then, gender now: surveying women's participation in Australian film and television industries. *Continuum*, 28(2), 188–200.

Freyre, G. (1956). *The Masters and the Slaves (Casa Grande and Senzala): A study in the Development of Brazilian Civilization* (translated by Samuel Putnam). Alfred A. Knoff.

Fuchs, M. M., & Fuchs, S. W. (2020). Religious minorities in Pakistan: Identities, citizenship and social belonging. *South Asia: Journal of South Asian Studies*, 43(1), 52–67.

Fundação *Getúlio*Vargas (2019). *Onde Estão os Ricos no Brasil?* Fundação Getulio Vargas.Retrieved August 21, 2022, from https://www.cps.fgv.br/cps/bd/docs/OndeEstaoOsRicos_Marcelo-Neri_FGV-Social.pdf.

Ganter, R. (2008). Muslim Australians: The deep histories of contact. *Journal of Australian Studies*, 32(4), 481–492.

Gifis, S. H. (2016). *Dictionary of Legal Terms: Definitions and Explanations for Non - Lawyers*. Barron's Educational Series.

Gilbert, P., Gilbert, J., & Sanghera, J. (2004). A focus group exploration of the impact of izzat, shame, subordination and entrapment on mental health and service use in South Asian women living in Derby. *Mental health, religion & culture*, 7(2), 109–130.

Gilani, S. F. (2001). Personal and Social Power in Pakistan. In A. M. Weiss & S. Z. Gilani (eds.) *Power and Civil Society in Pakistan*. Oxford University Press.

Gill, A. K. (2014). Introduction: 'Honour' and 'honour'-based violence: Challenging common assumptions. In *'Honour' Killing and Violence* (pp. 1–23). Palgrave Macmillan, London.

Gill, A. K. (2013). Feminist Reflections on Researching So-called 'Honour' Killings. *Springer online Science Business*, 241–261.

Gill, A. K. (2006). Patriarchal Violence in the Name of 'Honour'. *International Journal of Criminal Justice Sciences*, 1(1).

Gill, A. K. & Brah, Avtar (2014). Interrogating cultural narratives about 'honour' based violence. *European Journal of Women's Studies*, 21 (1), pp.72–86.

Gill, A. K., Strange, C., & Roberts, K. (2014). Honour killing and violence. *London: Palgrave Macmillan*.

Gilroy, P. (1997). Diaspora and the detours of identity. *Identity and difference, 3*. Global Americas Report (2022). Femicide and International Women's Rights. Retrieved

August 25, 2022, from https://theglobalamericans.org/reports/femicide-interna-tional-womens-rights/.

Global Gender Report Gap (2021). World Economic Forum. Retrieved August 25, 2022, from https://www3.weforum.org/docs/WEF_GGGR_2021.pdf.

Gonzalez, L. (1988). A importância da organização da mulher negra no processo de transformação social. *Raça e classe*, *5*(2).

Gonzales, L. (1984). Racismo e sexismo na cultura brasileira. *Revista Ciências Sociais Hoje*, *2*(1), 223–244.

Goodall, H., & Ghosh, D. (2015). Beyond the 'poison of prejudice': Indian and Austra-lian women talk about the White Australia policy. *History Australia*, *12*(1), 116–140.

Green, J. (2003). Foucault and the training of docile bodies in dance education. *Arts and Learning Research Journal*, *19*(1), 99–125.

Griffith, R. M. (1997). *God's Daughters: Evangelical Women and the Power of Submission.* Berkeley, CA: University of California Press.

Guerra, V. M., Giner-Sorolla, R., & Vasiljevic, M. (2012). The importance of honor con-cerns across eight countries. *Group Processes & Intergroup Relations* (*16*), 298–318.

Gukovas, R., Muller, Pereira, A.C., & Reimão, M.E. (2016). *A Snapshot of Gender in Brazil Today. Retrieved September 02, 2022, from* https://elibrary.worldbank.org/doi/abs/10.1596/25976.

Gunasinge, C. (2015). *Understanding how izzat impacts the lived experience of young Muslim Pakistani women in the UK. A Phenomenological approach* (Doctoral disser-tation, University of East London).

Habner, J. E. (2012). Honra e *distinção* das *famílias*. In C. B. Pinsky & J. M. Pedro (eds.), *História das Mulheres no Brasil*. Sao Paulo, Brasil: Editora Contexto.

Hagan, J., & Ebaugh, H. R. (2003). Calling upon the sacred: Migrants' use of religion in the migration process. *International migration review*, *37*(4), 1145–1162.

Hagemann-White, C., Katenbrink, J., & Rabe, H. (2006). Combating violence against women. *Stocktaking study on the measures and actions taken in Council of Europe member States. Strasbourg: Council of Europe.*

Hajjar, L. (2004). Religion, state power, and domestic violence in Muslim societies: A framework for comparative analysis. *Law & Social Inquiry*,*29*(1), 1–38.

Hammarquist, J., & Hajo Batti, V. (2017). Honour Culture: The thoughts and experi-ences of four young men, who have lived in a residential care home for unaccompa-nied children. Retrieved August 21, 2022, from https://www.diva-portal.org/smash/get/diva2:1090336/FULLTEXT01.pdf.

Hamlyn, D.W. (1986). Hegel on Self-Consciousness. *Proceedings of the British Acad-emy*,*72*, 317–338.

Hammersley, M. (2008). *Questioning qualitative inquiry: Critical essays*. Sage.

Hardesty L.J. (2009). A typology of domestic violence: intimate terrorism, violent resis-tance, and situational couple violence. *Journal Marriage and Family*, *71*, 802–804.

Harding, S (1991). Whose Science? Whose knowledge? New York: Cornell University Press.

Hartsock, N. (1990). Foucault on power: a theory for women? *Feminism/postmodernism*, *162*, 157–175.

Hassan, Sehar & Anila Amber Malik (2015). Factor for Intimate Partner Violence (IPV) in Urban Pakistani Families. *Pakistan Journal of Clinical Psychology 10* (1).

Haq, F. (1996). Women, Islam, and the State in Pakistan. *The Muslim World (Hartford)*, *86*(2), 158–175.

Heath, H., & Cowley, S. (2004). Developing a grounded theory approach: a comparison of Glaser and Strauss. *International journal of nursing studies*, *41*(2), 141–150.

Hegel, G.W.F. (1977). *Phenomenology of Spirit* (translated by A.V. Miller). Oxford University Press.

Hekman, S. (Ed.). (2010). *Feminist Interpretations of Michel Foucault*. Penn State Press.

Hermann, J. & Barsted, L. D. A. L. (1995). O Judiciário e a violência contra a mulher: a ordem legal e a (des) ordem familiar. In *O judiciário e a violência contra a mulher: a ordem legal e a (des) ordem familiar*, pp. 135–135.

Holanda, S. B. (2007). *Historia Geral da Civilisacao Brasileira*. Tomos 1–11. Editora Bertrand.

Houlgate, S. (2011). G. W. F. Hegel: An Introduction to His Life and Thought. In S. Houlgate& M. Baur (ed.), *A companion to Hegel*. Oxford: Wiley-Blackwell. https://doi.org/10.1002/9781444397161.ch.

Houlgate, S., & Baur, M. (eds.). (2011). *A companion to Hegel* (pp. 139–158). Oxford: Wiley-Blackwell.

House of Commons Home Affairs Committee (2008). *Domestic Violence, Forced Marriage and 'Honour' Based Violence*. London: The Stationary Office.

Hoy, D. C. (1991). A history of consciousness: From Kant and Hegel to Derrida and Foucault. *History of the Human Sciences*, *4*(2), 261–281.

Hoy, D. C. (1991). *Foucault: A Critical Reader*. Wiley.

Huda, S., & Kamal, A. (2020). Development and validation of attitude towards Honour Killing Scale. *Pakistan journal of psychological research*, 227–251.

Human Development Report (2020). The Next Frontier: Human Development in the Anthropocene. Brazil. Retrieved August 25, 2022, from https://hdr.undp.org/sites/default/files/Country-Profiles/BRA.pdf.

Human Rights Watch (2016, June 14). Pakistan: Prosecute Rampant "Honour Killings." Retrieved September 02, 2022, from https://www.hrw.org/news/2016/06/15/pakistan-prosecute-rampant-honor-killings.

Idriss, M. M. (2010). Honour, violence, women and Islam–An introduction. In *Honour, violence, women and Islam* (pp. 9–23). Routledge-Cavendish.

International The News. (2021, October 12). LSA 2021: Mira Sethi rebuffs criticism against female celebrities in a lengthy post. The International News. Retrieved

July 10, 2022, from https://www.thenews.com.pk/latest/899770-lsa-2021-mira-sethi
-rebuffs-criticism-against-female-celebrities-in-a-lengthy-post.

Inserra, D. (2019). *The unsaved Christian: Reaching cultural Christianity with the gospel.*
Moody Publishers.

Instituto Brasileiro de Geografia e Estatística (IBGE) (2013). *Distribuição* Racial no
Brazil. Retrieved August 21, 2022, from https://biblioteca.ibge.gov.br/index.php
/biblioteca-catalogo?view=detalhes&id=284235.

Instituto Brasileiro de Geografia e Estatística (IBGE) (2017). Divisão Regional do
Brasil. Retrieved August 21, 2022, from https://www.ibge.gov.br/geociencias
/organizacao-do-territorio/divisao-regional/15778-divisoes-regionais-do-brasil
.html?=&t=sobre.

Instituto de Pesquisa Datafolha (2016). Retrieved August 21, 2022, from https://
datafolha.folha.uol.com.br/opiniaopublica/2016/12/1845231-44-dos-evangelicos
-sao-ex-catolicos.shtml.

Jain, P., & Sharma, S. (2002). Honour, gender and the legend of Meera Bai.*Economic
and Political Weekly*, 4646–4650.

Jalal, A. (1994). Demand for *Pakistan*. Cambridge South Asian Studies.

Jalal, A. (2014). *The Struggle for Pakistan: A Muslim Homeland and Global Politics*. Harvard University Press.

Jalal, A. (2017). *The Creation of Pakistan*. Oxford University Press.

Johnson, M. P. (2006). Conflict and control: Gender symmetry and asymmetry in
domestic violence. *Violence against women*, *12*(11), 1003–1018.

Johnson, L. L., & Lipsett-Rivera, S. (1998). *The faces of honor: Sex, shame, and violence in
colonial Latin America*. UNM Press.

Jus Brasil (2021). Legítima defesa da honra é inconstitucional e viola o princípio da
proteção da dignidade da pessoa humana, bem como, proteção a vida e igualdade
de gênero. Retrieved August 21, 2022, from https://brcezar.jusbrasil.com.br/noti-
cias/1182697368/legitima-defesa-da-honra-e-inconstitucional-e-viola-o-principio
-da-dignidade-da-pessoa-humana-bem-como-protecao-a-vida-e-igualdade-de
-genero.

Kaiser, A. J. (2018, September 20). Celia Haddad murder: former Brazilian boyfriend
confessed to killing, court hears. *The Guardian*. https://www.theguardian.com
/australia-news/2018/sep/20/cecilia-haddad-former-brazilian-boyfriend-con
fessed-to-killing-court- hears?fbclid=IwAR0tohQmsyvgBsFD5vQ79MwDDCQocRj
AoqBwNv-pl7tw- rCN7OEJo4x8bC4

Kallman, M. & Dini, R. (2017). *An Analysis of Michel Foucault's Discipline and Punish*.
Macat Library.

Kandiyoti, D. (1988). Bargaining with Patriarchy. *Gender and Society* 2(3), 274–290.

Kane, L. W. (2015). On Hegel, Women, and the Foundation of Ethical Life: Why Gender Doesn't Belong in the Family. *CLIO: A Journal of Literature, History, and the Philosophy of History, 44*(1).

Karawejczyk, M. (2014). Os primórdios do movimento sufragista no Brasil: o feminismo "pátrio" de Leolinda Figueiredo Daltro. *Estudos Ibero-Americanos, 40*(1), 64–84.

Kardec, A. (2021) *The Spirit's Book*. Federação Espírita Brasileira (translated by Anna Blackwell).

Kelly, L. (1988). *Surviving Sexual Violence*. UK: Polity Press.

Khan, A. (2020). Honour Killings in Pakistan: Judicial and Legal Treatment of the Crime. A Feminist Perspective. *LUMS Law Journal, 7*, 74–104.

Khan, R., Saleem, S., & Lowe, M. (2018). "Honour"-based violence in a British South Asian community. *Safer Communities, 17*(1), 11–21.

Khuwaja, S. A., Selwyn, B. J., Mgbere, O., Khuwaja, A., Kapadia, A., McCurdy, S., & Hsu, C. E. (2013). Factors associated with the process of adaptation among Pakistani adolescent females living in United States. *Journal of Immigrant and Minority Health, 15*(2), 315–325.

Kim, L., Knudson-Martin, C. & Turtle, A. (2019). Transmission of intergenerational migration legacies in Korean American families: Parenting the third generation. *Contemporary Family Therapy, 41* (2), 180–190.

King, A. (2004). The prisoner of gender: Foucault and the disciplining of the female body. *Journal of International Women's Studies, 5*(2), 29–39.

King, M. L. (1991). *Women of the Renaissance*. Chicago: Chicago University Press.

Kulczycki, A., & Windle, S. 'Honor Killings in the Middle East and North Africa: A Systematic Review of the Literature' (2011) 17(11) *Violence against women* 1442.

Kushal, S., & Manickam, E. (2014). (Dis) honourable paradigms: a critical reading of Provoked, Shame and Daughters of Shame. *South Asian Diaspora, 6*(2), 225–238.

Laslett, B., & Brenner, J. (1989). Gender and social reproduction: Historical perspectives. *Annual review of sociology*, 381–404.

Lee-Koo, K. (2011). Gender Based Violence Against Civilian Women in Post-invasion-Iraq:(Re) Politicizing George W. Bush's Silent Legacy. *Violence Against Women 17*(12),1619–1634.

Lei do D*ivórcio* (Divorce Act) (1977). Retrieved August 21, 2022, from https://www2. camara.leg.br/legin/fed/lei/1970-1979/lei-6515-26-dezembro-1977-366540-publicacaooriginal-1-pl.html.

Leite, F.C. (2011). O laicismo e outros exageros sobre a Primeira Republica no Brasil. *Religião & Sociedade. 31*, 32–60.

Lindisfarne, N. (1998). Gender, shame, and culture: An anthropological perspective. *Shame:Interpersonal behavior, psychopathology, and culture*, 246–260.

Ljungqvist, F. C. (2012). Female Shame, Male Honor: The Chastity Code in Juan Luis Vive's De institutione feminae Christianae. *Journal of Family History 37*(2), 139–154.

Loizos, P. (1978). Violence and the family: Some Mediterranean examples, *in* J. P. (ed.) *Violence and the family*. New York: John Wiley & Sons.

Lorenzini, D. (2016). Foucault, Regimes of Truth and the Making of the Subject. *Foucault and the Making of Subjects*, 63–75.

Lowik, V. & Taylor, A. (2019, December 9) *Evangelical churches believe men should control women. That's why they breed domestic violence*. The Conversation. Retrieved August 26, 2022, from https://theconversation.com/evangelical-churches-believe-men-should-control-women-thats-why-they-breed-domestic-violence-127437

Lugones, M. (2008). The Coloniality of Gender. *Worlds & Knowledges Otherwise,1*(17).

Macro trends (2021). Pakistan Rural Population 1960–2021. Retrieved August 25, 2022, from https://www.macrotrends.net/countries/PAK/pakistan/rural-population.

Mahmood, N. & K. Ringheim (1993). Desired Fertility in Pakistan: What is the Influence of Husbands? Paper presented at the Population Association of America Conference, Cincinnati, Ohio.

Malik, M. (2009). *Religion, gender and identity construction amongst Pakistanis in Australia*. Minerva-access University of Melbourne.

Malik, S. (2014). Women and weapons: Redressing the gender gap: A Pakistani response. *Bulletin of the Atomic Scientists, 70*(5), 12–16.

Malik, S. (2018). Security Sector Reforms in Pakistan: Significance, Challenges and Impediments. *Strategic Studies, 38*(3), 1–21

Matos, M., & Simões, S. (2017). Emergence of intersectional activist feminism in Brazil: the interplay of local and global contexts. In *Global Currents in Gender and Feminisms*. Emerald Publishing Limited.

May, V. (2015). *Pursuing Intersectionality, Unsettling Dominant Imaginaries*. New York: Routledge.

May, V. (2012). Intersectionality. In C. M. Orr, A. Braithwaite, & D. M. Lichtenstein (eds.). *Rethinking women's and gender studies*. New York: Routledge.

Marcus, A. (2009). Brazilian Immigration to the United States and the Geographical Imagination. *Geographical Review, 99*(4), 481–498.

Martes, A.C.B. (2001). *Migration and religion a safe place for sociability: Brazilian immigrants and church affiliation in Massachusetts*. Migration World Magazine.

Martes, A.C.B. & Fazito, D. (2010). *Solidarity and social networks: Economic sociology of international migration and the Brazilian case*. Retrieved August 21, 2022, from https://www.econstor.eu/bitstream/10419/155951/1/vol11-n003-a6.pdf.

Martes, A.C.B. & Rodriguez, C.L. (2003). *Church membership, social capital, and entrepreneurship in Brazilian communities in the US*. Emerald Group Publishing Limited.

Martins, A. J. (2020). *Moving difference: Brazilians in London*. New York: Routledge.

Matos, M., & Simões, S. (2017). Emergence of intersectional activist feminism in Brazil: the interplay of local and global contexts. In *Global Currents in Gender and Feminisms*. Emerald Publishing Limited.

Mayblin, M. (2011). Death by marriage: power, pride, and morality in Northeast Brazil. *The Journal of the Royal Anthropological Institute*, *17*(1), 135–153. https://doi.org/10.1111/j.1467-9655.2010.01673.x.

Mazer, Dulce. (2019). "Rapper, musa, música, mulher:" Empoderamento feminino e imbricações do regionalismo gaúcho na cultura hip-hop. *De Vidas Artes*. DOI:10.21747/9789898969187/deva27.

McIlwaine, & Evans, Y. (2022). Navigating migrant infrastructure and gendered infrastructural violence: reflections from Brazilian women in London. *Gender, Place and Culture: a Journal of Feminist Geography*, *ahead-of-print*(ahead-of-print), 1–23. https://doi.org/10.1080/0966369X.2022.2073335.

McIlwaine, & Evans, Y. (2020). Urban Violence Against Women and Girls (VAWG) in transnational perspective: reflections from Brazilian women in London. *International development planning review*, *42*(1), 93–113.

McNay, L. (1999). Gender, Habitus and the Field: Pierre Bourdieu and the Limits of Reflexivity. *Theory, Culture & Society*, *16*(1), 95–117.

McNay, L. (1992). *Foucault and Feminism*. Polity Press.

Merriam-Webster. *Definition of Honour*. Retrieved April 10, 2022, from https://www.merriam-webster.com/dictionary/honor.

Mignolo, W. D. (2011). Epistemic disobedience and the decolonial option: A manifesto. *Transmodernity*, *1*(2), 3–23.

Millett, K. (1969). *Sexual Politics*.UK: Granada Publishing.

Miller, W.I. (1993). *Humiliation and Other Essays of Honour, Social Discomfort and Violence*. Ithaca. NY: Cornell University Press.

Minault, G. (1982). Purdah Politics: The Role of Muslim Women in Indian Nationalism, 1911–1924. In H. Papanek & G. Minault (eds.). *Separate Words: Studies of Purdah in South Asia*. Chanakya Publications: New Delhi.

Ministério das Relações Exteriores. *Brasileiros No Mundo*. Retrieved August 26, 2022, from http://www.brasileirosnomundo.itamaraty.gov.br/noticias/censo-ibge-estima-brasileiros-no-exterior-em-cerca-de-500-mil/.

Mucina, M. (2018). Exploring the role of "honour" in son preference and daughter deficit within the Punjabi diaspora in Canada. *Revue Canadienne D'études Du Développement*, *39*(3), 426–442.

Muntaz, K. & Shaheed, F. (1987). *Women of Pakistan: Two steps forward one step back?* Vanguard Books.

Nasrullah, M., Haqqi, S., & Cummings, K. J. (2009). The epidemiological patterns of honour killing of women in Pakistan. *European Journal of Public Health*, *19*(2), 193–197.

Nawaz, S., Shabbir, M. S., Bilal, K., Koser, M., & Latif, R. (2021). Does Literacy Rates Decrease the Sexual Harassment Cases in Pakistan?. *PalArch's Journal of Archaeology of Egypt/Egyptology*, *18*(18), 559–573.

Nisbett, R.E. & Cohen, D. (1996). *Culture of honor: The psychology of violence in the South*. Westview Press.

O'Doherty, S. (2018). Brazil: #elenão and the vibrant women's movement rallying against far – right candidate Jair Bolsonaro. The Conversation. Retrieved August 25, 2022, from https://theconversation.com/brazil-elenao-and-the-vibrant-womens-movement-rallying-against-far-right-candidate-jair-bolsonaro-104969.

Ohan, V. (2022, March 18). Bolsonaro Nunca Mais: Organisações Convocam Protesto para 9 de Abril. Carta Capital. Retrieved from https://www.cartacapital.com.br/politica/bolsonaro-nunca-mais-organizacoes-convocam-protesto-para-9-de-abril/.

Odeh, L. A. (2010). Honor Killings and the Construction of Gender in Arab Societies. *The American journal of comparative law, 58*(4) 911.

Ordenações Filipinas (1603). Under King Philip II. Retrieved August 25, 2022, from http://www1.ci.uc.pt/ihti/proj/filipinas/ordenacoes.htm.

Ortner, S. B. (1978). *The Virgin and the State. Feminist Studies, 4* (3), 19–35.

Ovais, M. (2014, September 23). Feminism in Pakistan: A brief history. Retrieved September 02, 2022, from https://tribune.com.pk/story/764036/feminism-in-pakistan-a-brief-history.

Pakistan Bureau of Statistics (2018–2019). *Key indicators of household integrated economic survey 2018–2019 (HIES)*. Government of Pakistan. Retrieved August 25, 2022, from https://www.pndajk.gov.pk/uploadfiles/downloads/hies_2018–19_writeup.pdf.

Pakistan Bureau of Statistics (2017). Population Census. Retrieved September 02, 2022, from https://www.pbs.gov.pk/content/final-results-census-2017.

Palmer, C., & North, L. (2012). *Blokey culture means sexism still rife in Australian newsrooms*. The conversation. Retrieved August 25, 2022, from https://theconversation.com/blokey-culture-means-sexism-still-rife-in-australian-newsrooms-10073

Papanek, H. & Minault, G. (1982). *Separate worlds : studies of purdah in South Asia* (1st ed.).Chanakya Publications.

Papanek, H. (1971). Purdah in Pakistan: seclusion and modern occupations for women. *Journal of Marriage and the Family*, 517–530.

Pastner, C. M. (1982). Gradations of Purdah and the Creation of Social Boundaries on a Baluchistan Oasis. *Separate worlds: Studies in purdah in South Asia. Delhi.*

Patel, S., & Gadit, A. M. (2008). Karo-Kari: a form of honour killing in Pakistan. *Transcultural psychiatry, 45*(4), 683–694.

Paul II, J. (1995). Encyclical Letter *Evangelium Vitae*. Retrieved August 26, 2022, from https://www.vatican.va/content/john-paul-ii/en/encyclicals/documents/hf_jp-ii_enc_25031995_evangelium-vitae.html.

Paul II, J. (1982). Encyclical Letter *Familiaris Consortio*. Retrieved August 26, 2022 from https://www.vatican.va/content/john-paul-ii/en/apost_exhortations/documents/hf_jp-ii_exh_19811122_familiaris-consortio.html.

Paul II, J. (1995). Encyclical Letter *Evangelium Vitae. Retrieved September 04, 2022, from* https://www.vatican.va/content/john-paul-ii/en/encyclicals/documents/hf_jp -ii_enc_25031995_evangelium-vitae.html

Paul VI, P. (1965). Encyclical Letter *Dignitatis Humanae.* Retrieved August 26, 2022, from https://www.vatican.va/archive/hist_councils/ii_vatican_council/documents /vat-ii_decl_19651207_dignitatis-humanae_en.html.

Peters, C. (2003). *Patterns of Piety: Women, Gender and Religion in Late Medieval and Reformation England.* Cambridge University Press.

Peristiany, J. G. (1965). *Honour and shame: The values of Mediterranean society.* University of Chicago Press.

Peristiany, J.G. & Pitt-Rivers, J.(eds.) (1992). *Honour and Grace in Anthropology.* Cambridge: Cambridge University Press.

Pew Research Centre (2011). Regional Distribution of Christians. Retrieved August 25, 2022, from https://www.pewresearch.org/religion/2011/12/19/global-christianity-re-gions/.

Pimentel, S., Pandjiarjian, V., & Belloque, J. (2006). " Legitima defesa de honra". Ilegítima impunidade de assassinos: um estudo crítico da legislação e jurisprudên-cia da América Latina. In *Vida em família: uma perspectiva comparativa sobre crimes de honra* (pp. 65–208).

Pitt-Rivers, J. (1965). Honour and social status. *In* Peristiany, J. (ed.). *Honour and shame: the values of Mediterranean society,* pp. 19–77. London: Weidenfeld and Nicolson

Pitt-Rivers, J. (1977). *The fate of Shechem.* Cambridge: Cambridge University Press.

Prado Jr., C. (1967). *The Colonial Background of Modern Brazil (Formacao do Brazil Con-temporaneo, Colonia)* (translated by Suzette Macedo). University of California Press.

Quijano, A. (2000). Colonialidad del Poder y Clasificacion Social. En Journal of World-Systems Research, Special Issue: Festchrift for Immanuel Wallerstein–Part I.*VI/2, (Summer/Fall 2000),* 342–386.

Quijano, A. (2000). Coloniality of Power, Eurocentricism, and Latin America." Tr. Michael Ennis. *Nepantla: Views from the South, 1,* 533–580.

Rago, M. (2001). Feminizar é preciso: por uma cultura filógina. *São Paulo em Perspec-tiva, 15*(3), 53–66.

Raj, A., & Silverman, J. (2002) Violence against immigrant women the roles of culture, context, and legal immigrant status on intimate partner violence. *Violence against women 8* (3), pp. 367–398.

Ramos, M. D. (2012). Reflexões sobre o processo histórico-discursivo do uso da legítima defesa da honra no Brasil e a construção das mulheres. *Revista Estudos Feministas, 20,* 53–73.

Rane, H., Duderija, A., Rahimullah, R. H., Mitchell, P., Mamone, J., & Satterley, S. (2020). Islam in Australia: A national survey of Muslim Australian citizens and permanent residents. *Religions, 11*(8), 419.

Raza, A. (2006). Mask of honor—causes behind honor killings in Pakistan. *Asian Journal of Women's Studies*, 12(2), 88–104.

Reed, E., Raj, A., Miller, E., & Silverman, J. G. (2010). Losing the "gender" in gender-based violence: The missteps of research on dating and intimate partner violence. *Violence against women*, 16(3), 348–354.

Rees, S. & Pease, B. (2007). Domestic Violence in Refugee Families in Australia. *Journal of Immigrant & Refugee Studies*, 5(2), pp. 1–19.

Rehman, S. (2021). Introduction. In S. Rehman (ed.). *Womansplaining: Navigating Activism, Politics, and Modernity in Pakistan*. Folio Books.

Recommendation, U. C. G. (1992). *On Violence against Women, UN GAOR, Doc. No.*A/47/38.

Reuters (2018, June 26). Factbox: Which are the world's 10 most dangerous countries for women? Thompson Reuters Foundation. Retrieved September 02, 2022, from https://www.reuters.com/article/us-women-dangerous-poll-factbox-idUSKB N1JM01Z

Reuters (2018, May 29). *Pakistan Prosecute Rampant "Honour Killings."* Thompson Reuters Foundation News. Retrieved September 02, 2022, from https://news.trust.org/item/20160623074010-r9pmo/.

Ribeiro, D. (1995). *The Brazilian people: The formation and meaning of Brazil*. University Press of Florida.

Riches, C. (2022, June 20). Australia's Pakistani community "in disbelief" after woman allegedly murdered by father-in-law. *SBS News*. https://www.sbs.com.au /news/article/australias-pakistani-community-in-disbelief-after-woman-allegedly -murdered-by-father-in-law/somn9lipn?fbclid=IwAR0ihJojjaeMRknrPUIoobSxY hKozEsapMRWZqJTIiuJ5MT em Rr--wuhBB4

Rocha, C. & Vasquez, M. (ed.) (2013). *Diaspora of Brazilian religions*. International Studies in Religion and Society.

Rocha, C. (2019). God is in control": middle-class Pentecostalism and international student migration. *Journal of Contemporary Religion*, 34(1), 21–37.

Rocha, C. (2014). Triangular circulation: Japanese Brazilians on the move between Japan, Australia and Brazil. *Journal of Intercultural Studies*, 35(5), 493–512.

Rocha, C. & Coronado, G. (2014). Imagining Latin America in Australia: migration, culture and multiculturalism. *Journal of Intercultural studies*, 35(5), 467–474.

Rocha, C. (2006). Two faces of God: religion and social class in the Brazilian diaspora in Sydney. In *Religious pluralism in the diaspora* (pp. 147–160). Brill.

Rodrigues, C., & Freitas, V. G. (2021). Ativismo Feminista Negro no Brasil: do movimento de mulheres negras ao feminismo interseccional. *Revista Brasileira de Ciênciam Política*.

Rodriguez, S. (2020, March 3). Conheça a história do feminismo no Brasil. Isto E. Retrieved September 1, 2022, from https://istoe.com.br/conheca-a-historia-do -feminismo-no-brasil/

Rodriguez Mosquera, P. M. (2016). On the importance of family, morality, masculine, and feminine honor for theory and research. *Social and Personality Psychology Compass*, *10*(8), 431–442.

Rodriguez Mosquera, P.M., Manstead, A. S., & Fischer, A. H. (2000). The role of honor-r related values in the elicitation, experience, and communication of pride, shame, and anger: Spain and the Netherlands compared. *Personality and Social Psychology Bulletin*, *26*(7), 833–844.

Rodriguez Mosquera, P.M., Manstead, A. S., & Fischer, A. H. (2002). The role of honour concerns in emotional reactions to offences. *Cognition & Emotion*, *16*(1), 143–163.

Sadaquat, M. B. (2011). Employment situation of women in Pakistan. *International journal of social economics*, *38*(2), 98–113.

Safari, F. (2013). A qualitative study of women's lived experience after deinfibulation in the UK. *Midwifery*, *29*(2), 154–158.

Saleem, S. (2014). *Islam and Women: Misconceptions and Misrepresentations*. Pakistan: Al-Mawrid – A Foundation for Islamic Research and Education.

Sanghera, G. &Thapar-Björkert, S. (2017). Transnationalism, social capital and gender – young Pakistani Muslim women in Bradford, UK. *Migration Letters*, *14*(1), 88–100.

Sanghera, J. (2009). *Daughters of shame*. Hachette UK.

Sardenberg, C. M. (2010). Family, households and women's empowerment in Bahia, Brazil, through the generations: Continuities or change? *IDS Bulletin*, *41*(2), 88–96.

Santos, M. (2011). *Cleasing Honour with Blood: Masculinity, Violence and Power in the Backlands of Northeast Brazil, 1845–1889*. Stanford University Press.

Sathar, Z. A. & Kazi, S. (2000). *Women's autonomy in the context of Pakistan. The Pakistan Development Review*, *39* (2), 89–100.

Sathar, Z. A. & Casterline, J. B. (1998). The onset of fertility transition in Pakistan. *Population and development review*, 773–796.

Saunders, S., & AM, P.E. (2013). The nature, pervasiveness and manifestations of sexual harassment in rural Australia: Does "masculinity" of workplace make a difference? *Women's Studies International Forum 40*, pp. 121–131.

Saunders, J. B., Fiddian-Qasmiyeh, E., & Snyder, S. (2016). *Intersections of religion and migration*. New York: Palgrave Macmillan.

Selby, J. A. (2018). Muslim Canadians. *Exploring Religion and Diversity in Canada: People, Practice and Possibility*, 207–235.

Shaheed, F. (2021). The Women's Movement in Pakistan: Anatomy of Resistance. In S. Rehman. *Womansplaining: Navigating Activism. Politics and Modernity in Pakistan*, Lahore: Folio Books.

Shawar, D. E., & Abda Khalid, B. N. (2021). Women in Politics: Critical Analysis of Government Policies for Gender Mainstreaming in Khyber Pakhtunkhwa (KP), Pakistan. *Linguistica Antverpiensia*, 5785–5825.*interaction*. Sage.

Shah, N. (2016). *Honour and violence: gender, power and law in southern Pakistan* (1st ed.,Vol. 39). Berghahn Books.

Schneider, J. (1971). Of vigilance and virgins. *Ethnology*, 9, 1–24.

Sheringham, O. (2013). Brazilian churches in London: transnationalism of the middle Brazilian. *In* C. Rocha & M. Vasquez (ed.) (2013). *Diaspora of Brazilian religions*. International Studies in Religion and Society.

Siddiqui, H. (2005). There is no 'honour' in domestic violence, only shame! Women's struggle against 'honour' crimes in the UK. In Welchman, Lynn and Hossain, Sara (eds.), '*Honour': crimes, paradigms, and violence against women*. UK: Oxford University Press.

Silverman, D. (2013). *Doing qualitative research: A practical handbook*. SAGE Publications Limited.

Silverman, D. (2006). *Interpreting qualitative data: Methods for analyzing talk, text and* Slany, K., Kontos, M., & Liapi, M. (2010). *Women in new migrations: Current debates in European societies*. Cracow: Jagiellonian University Press.

Soihet, R. (2000). A pedagogia da conquista do espaço público pelas mulheres e a militância feminista de Bertha Lutz. *Revista Brasileira de Educação*, (15), 97–117.

Soihet, R. (2012). A conquista do espaço público. *Nova história das mulheres. São Paulo: Contexto*, 218–237.

Sonbol, A. E. A. (1998). Ta 'a and modern legal reform: A rereading. *Islam and Christian-Muslim Relations*, 9(3), 285–294.

Souza Júnior, Z. S. D. (2015). Coronéis e compadres: família, poder e lealdade no sertão. Sapientia.pucsp.br. Retrieved August 25, 2022, from https://sapientia.pucsp.br /handle/handle/3659.

Sokoloff, N. J. & Dupont, I. (2005). Domestic violence at the intersections of race, class, and gender challenges and contributions to understanding violence against marginalized women in diverse communities. *Violence against women*, 11(1), 38–64.

Stanley, L. & Wise, S. (1983). *Breaking Out: Feminist Consciousness and Feminist Research*. UK/London: published by Routledge and Kegan Paul.

Statista (2021). *Pakistan: Urbanisation from 2010–2020*. Retrieved August 25, 2022, from https://www.statista.com/statistics/455907/urbanization-in-pakistan/.

Steigenga, T. J., & Smilde, D. A. (1999). The Strange Case of Conservative Christians and Gender Equality in Latin America. *Latin American religion in motion*, 168–181.

Stirling, N. A. (2013). *Sifting, Negotiating and Remaking Identities: The Religious, Cultural and Ethnic Identities and Practices of Diasporic Iranian and Turkish Muslim Women in Brisbane, Australia* [*Unpublished doctoral dissertation*]. The University of Queensland.

Stirling, N. A., Shaw, S., & Short, P. (2014). Sifting, negotiating and remaking religious identities: A redefining of lived religion among muslim migrant women. *International Journal of Humanities and Social Sciences*, 4(8 (1)), 17–29.

Talbot, I. (1998). *Pakistan: A Modern History.* New Delhi, India: Oxford University Press.

Tapper, R., & Tapper, N. (1992). Marriage, honour and responsibility: Islamic and local models in the Mediterranean and the Middle East. *Cambridge Anthropology*, 3–21.

Teofilo, S. (2021, January 3). Maioria da Bancada Feminina na Camara e Conservadora. Correio Brasiliense. Retrieved August 25, 2022 from https://www.em.com.br/app /noticia/politica/2021/01/03/interna_politica,1225503/maioria-da-bancada-femini-na-na-camara-e-conservadora-e-aliada-de-bolsonaro.shtml.

TGEU Report (2018). Protecting LGBTQI Rights in Europe. Retrieved September 1, 2022, from https://tgeu.org/coe-recommendation-2018/.

Thomas, D. Q., & Beasley, M. E. (1994). Domestic violence as a human rights issue. *Alb. L. Rev.*, *58*, 1119.

Thomson Reuters Foundation (2018). Factbox: Which are the world's 10 most danger-ous countries for women? Retrieved August 25, 2022, from https://www.reuters. com/article/us-women-dangerous-poll-factbox-idUSKBN1JM01Z

Tomas, A. B. (2016). *Honor Culture in Brazil: Assessing Intra-Cultural Variation* (Doc-toral dissertation, University of Nevada, Reno).

Tomsen, S., & Gadd, D. (2019). Beyond honour and achieved hegemony: Violence and the everyday masculinities of young men.*International Journal for Crime, Justice and Social Democracy*, 8(2), 17.

Tonsing, J. & Barn, R. (2017). Intimate partner violence in South Asian communities: Exploring the notion of "shame" to promote understandings of migrant women's experiences. *International Social Work*, 60(3), 628–639.

United Nations Women Convention on the Elimination of All Discrimination Against Women (1992). Recommendation 19. Retrieved September 02, 2022, from https:// www.un.org/womenwatch/daw/cedaw/recommendations/recomm.htm

United Nations Women (2016, February 23). Prime Minister: There is no honour in honour killing. Retrieved September 02, 2022, from https://www.unwomen.org/en /news/stories/2016/2/pakistan-prime-minister-there-is-no-honour-in-honour-kill-ing

United Nations Women (2016, June 20). The United Nations in Pakistan urges Govern-ment action to end "Honour Killings." Retrieved September 02, 2022, from https:// asiapacific.unwomen.org/en/news-and-events/stories/2016/06/the-united-na-tions-in-pakistan-urges-government-action-to-end-honour-killings.

United Nations Human Development Report (2020). *The Next Frontier: Human Devel-opmentand the Anthropocene.* Briefing note for countries on the 2020 Human Development Report. Pakistan. Retrieved August 25, 2022, from https://hdr.undp .org/sites/default/files/Country-Profiles/PAK.pdf.

Vandello, J.A.,& Cohen, D. (2003). Male honour and female fidelity:implicit cultural script that perpetuate domestic vilence. *Journal of personality and social psychology, 84*(5),

Vandello, J.A. (2000). Domestic violence in cultural context: Male honor, female fidelity and loyalty. University of Illinois at Urbana-Champaign.

Vandello, J. A., Cohen, D., & Ransom, S. (2008). US Southern and Northern differences in perceptions of norms about aggression: Mechanisms for the perpetuation of a culture of honor. *Journal of cross-cultural psychology, 39*(2), 162–177.

Vargas, N. S. A. (2015). Crime passional ou Legítima Defesa da honra? *Etic-encontro de iniciação científica.* 11 (11).

Verma, A. K. (2001). *Reassessing Pakistan.* New Delhi: Lancer Publications and Distributors.

Vertovec, Steven (2009). *Transnationalism.* Routledge.

Waiselfsiz, J. J. (2015). O Mapa da Violência Contra as Mulheres no Brasil. Retrieved August 24, 2022, from https://flacso.org.br/files/2015/11/MapaViolencia_2015_mulheres.pdf.

Walmsley, B. (2018). Deep hanging out in the arts: an anthropological approach to capturing cultural value. *International Journal of Cultural Policy, 24*(2), 272–291.

Warren, A. (2016). Crafting masculinities: gender, culture and emotion at work in the surfboard industry. *Gender, Place & Culture, 23*(1), 36–54.

Weedon, C. (1997). *Feminist Practice and Poststructuralist Theory.* UK/Oxford: Blackwell Publishing.

Weiss, A. M. (1985). Women's position in Pakistan: Sociocultural effects of Islamization. *Asian Survey, 25*(8), 863–880.

Welchman, L. & Hossain, S. (2005). *"Honour": crimes, paradigms, and violence against women.* Zed Books

Werbner, P. (2002). The place which is diaspora: citizenship, religion and gender in the making of chaordic transnationalism. *Journal of ethnic and migration studies, 28*(1), 119–133.

Werbner, P. (2004). Theorising complex diasporas: purity and hybridity in the South Asian public sphere in Britain. *Journal of ethnic and migration studies, 30*(5), 895–911.

Werbner, P. (2007). Veiled interventions in pure space: Honour, shame and embodied struggles among Muslims in Britain and France. *Theory, culture & society, 24*(2), 161–186.

Werner, L. (2006). "That Which is Different from Difference is Identity" – Hegel on Gender.

Nordic Journal of Women's Studies,14(3), 183–194. https://doi.org/10.1080/08038740 701195141.

Westphal, K. R. (2009). Hegel's phenomenological method and analysis of consciousness. *The Blackwell guide to Hegel's phenomenology of Spirit,* 1–36.

Willig, C. (2001). *Introducing Qualitative Research in Psychology: Adventures in theory and method*. New York: Open Press.

Wiper, C. (2012). Responding to violence against South Asian women in the British domestic violence movement. *Graduate Journal of Social Science, 9*(3), pp. 1572–3763.

World Atlas (2020). *Ethnic groups in Pakistan*. Retrieved August 25, 2022, from https://www.worldatlas.com/articles/ethnic-groups-in-pakistan.html.

World Bank. *Pakistan* (2020). Retrieved August 2025, 2022, from https://data.worldbank.org/country/Pakistan.

World Bank (2022). *Population Brazil*. Retrieved August 25, 2022, from https://data.worldbank.org/indicator/SP.POP.TOTL.

World Economic Forum. Global Gender Index Report (2020). Retrieved August 25, 2022, from https://www.weforum.org/reports/gender-gap-2020-report-100-years-pay-equality.

World Population Review (2021). *Pakistan population 2021*. Retrieved August 25, 2022, from https://worldpopulationreview.com/countries/pakistan-population.

Wulfhorst, C. (2011). Intimate multiculturalism: blurring the boundaries between Brazilians and Australians in Sydney.*PhD diss., Western Sydney University.*

Wyatt-Brown, B. (2007). *Southern honor: ethics and behavior in the old South* Oxford University Press.

Yamin, S., & Malik, S. (2014). *Mapping conflict trends in Pakistan*. Washington, DC: United States Institute of Peace.

Yasmeen, S. (2015). Muslim in Australia: Celebrating National Days. *Contemporary Review of The Middle East, 2*(2), 104–118.

Yasmeen, S. (2014). The Dynamics of Exclusion/ Inclusion: Australia as a Case Study', *in* Yasmeen, Samina and Markovic, Nina (ed.), *Muslim Citizens in the West: Spaces and Agents of Inclusion and Exclusion*. UK: British Library Cataloguing in Publication Data.

Yasmeen, S. (2010). *Muslims in Australia: The Dynamics of Exclusion and Inclusion*. Melbourne University Press/.

Yasmeen, S. (2008). *Understanding Muslim Identities: From perceived relative exclusion to exclusion*. Centre for Muslim States and Societies.

Yasmeen, S. (2007). Muslim Women as Citizens in Australia: Diverse Notions and Practices. *Australian Journal of Social Issues, Autumn, 42* (1), 41–54.

Yasmeen, S. (1991). Hearing the difference: Pakistani feminism, *Asian Studies Review. 15* (1),108–110.

Yasmeen, S. (2020). Politics for Jihadi Women: Lashker-e-Taiba and Jamaat ud Dawah as a case study. In *Routledge Handbook of Political Islam* (pp. 351–362). Routledge.

Yoshihama, M., Horrocks, J., & Kamano, S. (2009). The role of emotional abuse in intimate partner violence and health among women in Yokohama, Japan. *American journal of public health, 99*(4), 647–653.

Zaidi, A. S. (2017, October 17). Special Report: Darkness Descends 1977–1988. *Dawn*. Retrieved August 25, 2022, from https://www.dawn.com/news/1364410.

Zannettino, L. (2009). Getting Talking: Empowering Liberian Women to Address Issues of Domestic Violence and Promote Healthy Relationships. *South Australia: Central Domestic Violence Service*.

Zia, A. S. (2019). Can Rescue Narratives Save Lives? *Honor Killing in Pakistan. Signs: Journal of Women in Culture and Society, 44* (2), 355–378.

Zia, A. S. (2009). The reinvention of feminism in Pakistan. *Feminist Review. 91*, 29–46.

Index